GEOLOGICAL SURVEY OF OHIO.

PART I.

REPORT OF PROGRESS IN 1869,

BY J. S. NEWBERRY,

CHIEF GEOLOGIST.

PART II.

REPORT OF PROGRESS IN THE SECOND DISTRICT

BY E. B. ANDREWS,

ASSIST. GEOLOGIST.

PART III.

REPORT ON GEOLOGY OF MONTGOMERY COUNTY,

BY EDWARD ORTON,

ASSIST. GEOLOGIST.

COLUMBUS:
COLUMBUS PRINTING COMPANY, STATE PRINTERS.
1870.

COLUMBUS, O., March 25, 1870

To His Excellency RUTHERFORD B. HAYES, *Governor:*

In compliance with a resolution passed by the Senate, directing that certain portions of our geological report heretofore submitted should not await the engraving of the plates, but be published immediately, I have made the selection of the materials called for by the resolution, and transmit them herewith. They consist of—

I. A sketch of the progress of the Geological Survey, in 1869, by myself.

II. A Report on the Straitsville Coal Field, by Prof. E. B. Andrews.

III. A Report on the Geology of Montgomery County, by Prof. Edward Orton.

All of which are respectfully submitted.

Your obedient servant,

J. S. NEWBERRY,
Chief Geologist.

PART I.

REPORT ON THE PROGRESS OF THE GEOLOGICAL SURVEY OF OHIO IN 1869.

BY J. S. NEWBERRY.

CHIEF GEOLOGIST.

HISTORICAL SKETCH.

The first information obtained by the citizens of Ohio in regard to the geological structure and mineral resources of the State, was derived from the report of a committee appointed under a resolution of the Legislature, passed the 14th day of March, 1836, "To report to the next Legislature the best method of obtaining a complete geological survey of the State, and an estimate of the probable cost of the same." This committee consisted of Dr. S. P. Hildreth, chairman, Dr. John Locke, Prof. J. H. Riddell, and Mr. I. A. Lapham.

In the execution of the task assigned to this committee, geological reconnoisances were made during the succeeding summer, of the Coal Measures of South-Eastern Ohio, by Dr. Hildreth, and of the western and northern portions of the State, by Prof. Riddell and Mr. Lapham; while chemical analyses of various iron ores and limestones were made by Dr. Locke. The observations and conclusions of this committee were embodied in reports from all the members, which reports were submitted to the Legislature at their succeeding session, and were published by State authority. At this time the science of geology had nowhere attained anything like its present perfection; and very little was known by any one in regard to the structure of our own country. The geological survey of New York was then in progress, but the splendid results accomplished by it had not yet been announced. As a consequence, the gentlemen who formed this committee prosecuted their investigations, not only in an untried field, but with little that could serve to guide them in observations made elsewhere by other geologists. At that time almost nothing was known in this country of palæontology. No one had learned what are the characteristic fossils of our formations, and, consequently, the relative positions of the different strata met with were to be painfully worked out by a careful examination of the rare exposures of their lines of contact. It was not easy nor even possible, in all instances, to identify any of the formations by their lithological characters alone, for these are proverbially unreliable, and they are often found to change completely in going from county to county. It is now well understood, not only that fossils are safe and convenient guides in studying the relations and distribution of fossiliferous rocks, but that their assistance is indispensable, and that no conclusions can be regarded as accurate and trustworthy unless confirmed by their evidence. The well-read palæontologist finds in every characteristic fossil an infallible record of the age of the rock that contains it, so that, when he can read the language, the fossiliferous rocks are all ticketed to his hand. Nothing can better illustrate the truth of these statements than the laborious and painful efforts of our pioneer geologists to determine, without palæontological data, the age and relations of our formations. After spending a summer in the study of the group of limestones which underlie the western part of the State, Dr. Riddell, with considerable hesitation and diffidence, announces the opinion that the blue limestone of Cincinnati underlies and is older than the buff limestone of Columbus. Even, two years afterward, when the Geological Board, subsequently created, had devoted two seasons of field work to the study of our geology, the exact geological ages of these formations were still undecided.

Much valuable information was, however, contained in the reports of the special committee, especially in that of Dr. Hildreth, where the first glimpse is given to the public of the structure and richness of the southern iron district—lying between Marietta and Portsmouth—where the Coal Measure ores exhibit a development equalled in no other part of our country, and where the iron industry of Ohio has, till lately, been mainly centered.

In obedience to their instructions, the committee submitted a plan for a general geological survey of the State, with an estimate of the necessary expenditure. The Legislature of 1836–37 at once acted on the recommendation of the committee, and passed a bill on the 27th of March, 1837, providing for a geological survey, appointing a corps of geologists, and voting an appropriation of $12,000 for the prosecution of the work during one year.

The board then organized consisted of the following members:

W. W. Mather, State Geologist.
Dr. S. P. Hildreth,
Dr. John Locke,
Prof. J. P. Kirtland,
J. W. Foster,
Charles Whitlesey,
C. Briggs, Jr.
} Assistants.

These gentlemen entered upon their duties during the following spring, and the results of their summer's work were embodied in the "First Annual Report on the Geology of Ohio" (8vo. pp. 134), presented to the Legislature at the ensuing session, and immediately published.

This report includes records of geological reconnoisances by Prof. Mather, Dr. Hildreth and Mr. Briggs, and preliminary reports on zoology by Prof. Kirtland, and on topography by Col. Whittlesey. Prof. Locke, having spent the summer in Europe, took no part in the geological work of the corps during the first year, and made no report.

In the succeeding summer the work of the Geological Survey was continued under the same organization. The observations made during this season were presented, and published in a report of 286 8vo. pages, entitled "The Second Annual Report of the Geological Survey of the State of Ohio, Columbus, Ohio, 1837." This volume includes reports of W. W. Mather, pp. 30, Col. Whittlesey, pp. 32, Mr. Foster, pp. 36, Prof. Briggs, pp. 47, Prof. Kirtland, pp. 46, and Dr. Locke, pp. 86; and contains much valuable information in regard to the geological structure and mineral resources of the State.

In consequence of the financial panic of 1837, and the paralysis of business that followed, it was considered necessary to diminish in every possible way the public expenditure, and, accordingly, the Legislature of 1838–9 made no appropriation for the continuation of the Geological Survey, and it was at once suspended. However plausible the arguments in favor of such a step may have appeared, there are comparatively few of our citizens who do not now feel that it was dictated by a short-sighted policy. The benefit derived by the State from the geological reconnoisance—for it was little more—made by the State Board, conclusively demonstrated that the Geological Survey was a producer and not a consumer; that it added far more than it took from the public treasury, and therefore deserved special encouragement and support, as a wealth-producing agency, in our darkest financial hour.

By the arrest of the work of the Geological Corps, the development of our mineral resources was not entirely stopped, but it was greatly retarded and thrown from public into private hands. During the thirty years that elapsed before a new Geological Survey was organized, much was done by private parties in the investigation of the geology and economic value of certain tracts and districts of the State. Careful surveys of mining properties, elaborate analysis of coal, iron, &c., &c., were made at private cost, and there is very little doubt that for such investigations, in the long interval of time I have designated, more money was paid than would have sufficed to complete the public survey begun in 1837. All the information thus gained was, however, monopolized by those who paid for it, and instead of enlightening the landholder as to the abundance and value of the minerals his farm or tracts contained, it oftener served the purposes of the speculator only, guiding him in his purchases and placing the farmer quite at his mercy. There are many who think the development of the mineral resources of our State should be altogether left to time and private enterprise; but no one who has watched with any care the progress of events during the last twenty-five years, in this and other States, will have failed to notice that it very rarely happens that the owner of a farm containing coal, iron, clay, or any other useful mineral, will, of his own accord and at his own expense, have any or all of his subterranean treasures so far investigated as to learn with accuracy their value. To do this, he must invoke the aid of the geologist and chemist, personages with whom he is not only unacquainted—since they are probably residents of a distant city—but of whose professions he has in all probability only a dim and shadowy idea. He therefore holds his land at its agricultural value, and sells it at such valuation to the first speculator who suspects, tests, and then discovers its hidden wealth.

The publication of the reports of the First Geological Board did much to arrest the useless expenditures of money in the search for coal outside of the coal field, and in other mining enterprises equally fallacious, by which, through ignorance of the teachings of geology, parties are constantly led to squander their means. From the tendency which all mining schemes have to excite the imagination, it is scarcely less important to our people to know acurately what we have not, than what we have, among our mineral resources.

During the last twenty years, efforts have been made by members of the Legislature who appreciated the importance of a thorough investigation of our mineral wealth, to have the geological survey resumed. For this end recommendations were made in several of the messages of our Governors, and bills were introduced by Dr. Jewett, of Summit, and subsequently by General Garfield; but though the value of such investigations to the credit and industry of the State was generally confessed, and there was no considerable opposition to either bill originating in doubt of the intrinsic merit of the measure, yet, at one time because the State Treasurer had appropriated to his own uses half a million of the people's money, and subsequently because the treasury was long kept empty by the expenditures upon the State House, it was thought by the majority wiser to defer making appropriations for this, as well as various other confessedly desirable objects, till the finances of the State should be in a better condition. In all these years, however, the State was suffering a positive annual loss, felt in both its industry and credit, for the want of the knowledge a properly conducted geological survey could not fail to impart. Every financial agent of the State, located in or visiting the moneyed centres of our country or the world; agents going abroad to effect loans with which to construct our lines of railroad, all took pains to gather information in reference to our geology, and all had to deplore the fact that this information was so meagre.

Finally, the great rebellion came upon us with all its horrors, and its waste of life and treasure. For five years all the thoughts and energies of the people were turned to the arts of war, and the arts of peace were well-nigh forgotten. When, however, the struggle was over, and the nation's life, so eagerly sought and strongly imperilled, was saved, our citizen soldiers laid down their arms to return to plow and workshop, and once more the processes of creation and conservation succeeded to those of destruction.

Among the methods suggested for repairing the breaches of war, and moving faster the retarded wheel of progress, was a geological survey; a thorough investigation of the quality; quantity and distribution of each of our mineral staples with a view to the expansion of all the wealth-producing industries based upon them.

This measure was recommended to the Legislature of 1869 in the annual message of Governor Hayes, and was made the subject of a bill introduced into the House of Representatives by Capt. Alfred E. Lee, of Delaware county. This bill was subsequently passed in March, 1869, by a large majority, irrespective of party, in both branches, and became a law, of which the following is a copy:

LAW PROVIDING FOR A GEOLOGICAL SURVEY OF OHIO.

SECTION 1. *Be it enacted by the General Assembly of the State of Ohio*, That the governor is hereby required to appoint, by and with the advice and consent of the senate, a chief geologist, who shall be a person of known integrity and competent practical and scientific knowledge of the sciences of geology and mineralogy; and upon consultation with said chief geologist and the like concurrence of the senate, the governor shall appoint one or more suitable assistants, not exceeding three in number, one of whom shall be a skillful analytical and agricultural chemist, the said chief geologist and assistants to constitute a geological corps, whose duty it shall be to make a complete and thorough geological, agricultural and mineralogical survey of each and every county in the state.

SEC. 2. The said survey shall have for its objects:

1st. An examination of the geological structure of the state, including the dip, magnitude, number, order and relative position of the several strata, their richness in coals, clays, ores, mineral waters and manures, building stone and other useful materials, the value of such materials for economical purposes, and their accessibility for mining or manufacture.

2d. An accurate chemical analysis and classification of the various soils of the state, with the view of discovering the best means of preserving and improving their fertility, and of pointing out the most beneficial and profitable modes of cultivation. Also a careful analysis of the different ores, rocks, peats, marls, clays, salines and all mineral waters within the state.

3d. To ascertain by meteorological observations the local causes which produce variations of climate in the different sections of the state. Also to determine by strict barometrical observations the relative elevation and depression of the different parts of the state.

SEC. 3. It shall be the duty of said chief geologist in the progress of the examinations hereby directed, to collect such specimens of rocks, ores, soils, fossils, organic remains and mineral compounds as will exemplify the geology, mineralogy and agronomy of the state, and shall deposit said specimens, accurately labeled and classified, in a room provided by the state board of agriculture, to be carefully preserved under the supervision of said board.

SEC. 4. It shall be the duty of the chief geologist, on or before the first Monday in January of each year, during the time occupied in said survey, to make a report to the governor of the results and progress of the survey, accompanied by such maps, profiles and drawings as may be necessary to exemplify the same, which reports the governor shall lay before the general assembly.

SEC. 5. When the said survey shall be fully completed, the chief geologist shall make to the governor a final report, including the results of the entire survey, accompanied by such drawings and topographical maps as may be necessary to illustrate the same, and by a single geological map showing by colors and other appropriate means the stratification of the rocks, the character of the soil, the localities of the beds of mineral deposits, and the character and extent of the different geological formations.

SEC. 6. The annual appropriations which may be made by the general assembly for carrying out the provisions of this act, shall be expended under the direction of the governor upon the certificate of the chief geologist, approved by the governor, and the warrant of the auditor of state, as follows:

For salary of chief geologist, three thousand dollars.

For salaries of assistants, not more than eighteen hundred dollars each.

For chemicals, five hundred dollars.

For contingent expenses of the survey, including actual traveling expenses of geological corps and hire of local assistants, five thousand dollars.

SEC. 7. No money shall be paid for the purposes of said survey until the chief geologist and his assistants shall have entered upon the discharge of their duties as prescribed by this act.

SEC. 8. The survey shall be commenced by the first of June next, or as soon thereafter as practicable, and shall be completed within three years from and after the time of its commencement.

SEC. 9. This act shall take effect and be in force from and after its passage.

In the performance of the duty assigned to him by this act of the Legislature, the Governor nominated the following persons members of the Geological Corps; and these nominations were confirmed by the Senate:

J. S. NEWBERRY, Chief Geologist.
E. B. ANDREWS,
EDW. ORTON,
JOHN H. KLIPPART, } Asst. Geologists.

In addition to those whose names are enumerated above, a number of persons were employed as local assistants, for whom also provision was made in the law, namely:

REV. H. HERTZER,	ANDREW SHERWOOD,
M. C. READ,	R. D. IRVING,
FREDERICK PRIME, Jr.,	W. A. HOOKER,
W. P. BALLANTINE,	W. B. POTTER,
G. K. GILBERT,	HENRY NEWTON,

H. A. WHITING.

Of these Mr. Hertzer, who had been for many years a diligent student of Ohio geology, and had discovered the most interesting series of fossil remains yet found within our territory—was paid from the salary of the Chief Geologist, as a compensation to the State for any time devoted by him to other duties. Mr. Prime, a graduate of the School of Mines of Freiberg in Saxony, was engaged for three months, at $50 per month. Mr. Read, who had also had considerable geological experience, was paid $100, and Mr. Ballantine $50 per month, during the season when field work was practicable. Of the other members of the corps, Messrs. Gilbert and Sherwood were geologists who had devoted much time to practical geology in New York and Pennsylvania, and who, for the purpose of adding to their experience, volunteered their services for no other compensation than their traveling expenses. The five remaining names on the list are those of graduates of the School of Mines of Columbia College, who brought to our work a thorough preparation in chemistry, mineralogy and metallurgy, and who also gave their services during the summer, with no other compensation than their expenses.

The law providing for the Geological Survey requires a careful agricultural survey to be made, and as Mr. Klippart, one of the Assistant Geologists appointed by the Legislature, had for many years devoted himself to the study of agriculture, and since 1856 had filled the position of Secretary of the State Board of Ariculture, the agricultural department was committed to him.

The purely chemical work of the Survey, a most important department, was committed to Prof. T. G. Wormley, of Columbus, one of the best chemists in the country.

The law authorizing the Geological Survey provides that such survey should begin on the first of June, 1869, "or as soon thereafter as practicable." In accordance with this provision, the members of the Geological Corps entered upon their duties at this date.

The first duty required by law of the Geological Corps was the accurate determination of the geological structure of Ohio. This was a necessary prerequisite to all the subsequent work of the Survey. During the many years that had passed since the former Board was disbanded, geological surveys had been maintained, with more or less thoroughness, in New York, Pennsylvania, Kentucky, Indiana, Illinois, Missouri, Arkansas, Kansas, Iowa, Wisconsin, Michigan and Canada, and the observations made by the geologists of those States in different and widely separated localities, had presented discrepancies that had given rise to long, earnest, and, sometimes, bitter discussions. Before the diverse conclusions of these various observers could be harmonized, and the succession and distribution of the rocks represented in our geology be fully made out, it was necessary that these views should be compared in Ohio; that observations made east, west, north and south should here be connected. Ohio thus, in some sort, formed the key-stone in the geological arch reaching from the Alleghanies to the Mississippi; and for many years geologists in our own country and abroad, had been looking forward with great interest to the time when the geological survey in Ohio should supply this key-stone, and render our whole geological system complete and symmetrical. It was also necessary that our work should be first of all blocked out in its generalities; that we should learn precisely what formations were represented in the State, their order of superposition, their mineral character and contents, their thickness and the geographical areas occupied by their outcrops.

To accomplish this work, our field was divided into four districts, consisting of the north-east, the south-east, the south-west and the north-west quarters of the State, all cornering at Columbus. The immediate supervision of the work in the north-eastern section was assumed by myself; that of the south-eastern quarter by Prof. Andrews; of the south-western by Prof. Orton; of the north-western by Mr. Hertzer and Mr. Gilbert. To Prof. Andrews were assigned Messrs. Ballantine and Irving as assistants; to Prof. Orton, Messrs. Newton and Whiting. Messrs. Read, Sherwood, Hooker and Potter were occupied in the northern half of the State, and Mr. Prime devoted himself to the duty for which he was especially qualified—the investigation of our mines, and manufactures based upon mineral staples.

Fortunately for the success of our efforts in this portion of our duty, an excellent topographical map of Ohio had recently been made by my friend, Prof. Walling, and published by H. S. Stebbins, of New York. Of this map numerous copies obtained in the sheets were placed in the hands of the members of the corps. To economize time, and secure the benefit of a division of labor, the different formations were assigned to different observers. The younger members were made each familiar with a stratum or formation, and then, with map in hand, they followed it wherever it led, carefully tracing its line of outcrop. They were also instructed to make observations and take notes on all the subjects we were required to investigate, with the injunction to so thoroughly perform their work along each line of observation that it might never be necessary to go over the ground a second time. The scope of the observation made by our corps will be best comprehended from the following schedule of instructions placed in the hands of all:

DIRECTIONS FOR OBSERVING AND COLLECTING.

1. TOPOGRAPHY.—Note *a.*—Altitudes of important points, by barometer, or by reference to railroad or canal levels.

b.—Topographical features and cause of ditto.

c.—Get railroad or canal profiles wherever possible.

2. SOIL.—Note character (sand, clay, loam, muck, wet, dry, &c.), depth, origin, relations to underlying rock.

3. VEGETATION.—Note nature of vegetation and its relation to soil and geological structure.

4. SURFACE GEOLOGY.—Note *a.*—*Superficial Materials* (clay, sand, gravel, &c.), of local or foreign origin? stratified? thickness? fossils?

b.—*Glacial Surface*—planed? scratched? furrowed? direction of furrows?

c.—*Terraces and Lake Ridges.*—Composition, extent, altitude.

d.—*Peat Bogs and Marl Beds;* under former or present marshes. To be sought by boring. Fossils are elephants, mastadon, &c.

e.—Depth of rock-bottoms of valleys and stream beds. Often 100 to 200 feet below present streams.

5. GEOLOGICAL STRUCTURE.—Note lithological character, thickness, subdivisions, faults, dip, strike and fossils of each stratum. Trace geology on map. Take sections and sketches.

6 ECONOMIC GEOLOGY.—Note—Iron Ore—Coal—Clay—Peat—Marl—Manganese—Phosphate of Iron—Infusorial Earth—Glass Sand—Building Stones—Stone for flagging, paving, furnace hearths—Limestones—Hydraulic Limestones—Gypsum—Petroleum, (Wells, Springs, Sections of Wells)—Mineral Springs—Salt Springs, Licks, Wells—Gas Springs—Mineral Paint—Calcareous Tufa—Water Supply, Springs, Wells, (Sections of Wells)—Note quality, quantity and accessibility of all of the above economic minerals met with. If mined or manufactured, the quantity or quality of the mined or manufactured article.

7. INDIAN RELICS—Note mounds, earthworks, inscriptions—Excavate and survey—Collect, arrow-heads, axes, spears, pottery, &c.

8. MANUFACTURES (of Mineral Staples).—Note, source, quality and cost of material—Quantity, quality and price of product—Construction of works—Statistics of 1868, 1869. Get suits of raw and manufactured materials.

10. MINES.—Note geographical position and accessibility—kind, quantity and quality of product—plan of mines and works.

11. COLLECTING SPECIMENS. — Of rocks of each formation and important stratum—with and without fossils—collect ten sets 3x4x1 inch. Coal, iron ore, clay, &c., 3x4x1 inch. Fossils, as many good ones as possible.

Label or number each specimen in the field. Wrap in soft paper; pack in boxes, if possible of not over two cubic feet capacity, flat specimens on edge. Fill the box. Tack on addressed card, with district, locality and number of box, and name of collector. Ship by express or freight, taking receipt.

SKETCH OF THE GEOLOGICAL STRUCTURE OF OHIO.

The general results of our summer's work upon the geological structure of the State, are given in the map and section now published. In the section are represented all the formations yet recognized in the State, with the relative position and thickness of each; some such a section, in fact, as would be made by sinking a shaft about 4000 feet in depth, on the eastern margin of the State, where the highest members of our series form the surface rocks. To make this map and section intelligible, I will briefly review the different formations represented on them.

THE SILURIAN SYSTEM.

Commencing at the bottom of the section, it will be seen that the first step in our geological staircase is formed by what is called the Cincinnati group, the Blue Limestone series of the former Geological Corps, and the equivalent of the Trenton and Hudson River groups of New York. These lie near the base of the series of unchanged fossiliferous rocks, found on our continent, and belong to the Silurian system. Below all these lies the great group of crystalline rocks—once stratified sedimentary beds, but now upheaved and metamorphozed—which form the Eozoic system, composed of two groups, the Laurentian and Huronian. These rocks are exposed in a broad belt, extending from Labrador to Lake Superior, and thence north to the Arctic Sea; a portion of our continent not only composed of the oldest rocks of which we have any knowledge, but the oldest portion of the earth's surface known to us; one that has never been submerged beneath the ocean since a period anterior to the formation of our oldest palæozoic strata.

We have evidence that at one time a broad continental area filled a large part of the space now occupied by our North America, and was composed of the same rocks that now constitute the Canadian highlands. In process of time this continent began to sink, and the sea gradually encroached upon its surface, ultimately covering all except the belt I have described. From this sea, in its various advances and retrocessions, our different geological formations have been deposited. These consist of sandstones, shales, limestones, or some commingling of these different rocks. The mode in which these strata have accumulated may be described in a few words. All continental surfaces are constantly suffering erosion by the influence of rain, rivers and shore waves, and the material comminuted by these agencies is carried into the ocean basin and deposited along the shore, frequently in distinct belts. The shore itself is composed of rocks undergoing processes of comminution, gravel or sand. In deeper water accumulates the finer material, washed from the shore itself, or contributed by rivers. This settles in a belt parallel with the first, and when examined is found composed of fine sand or clay. Outside of this second belt, and beyond the point where the wash from the land reaches, there is constantly accumulating a stratum derived from the decomposition of the various structures belonging to the animate forms inhabiting the ocean. Most of these organisms are provided with calcareous shells, and so their debris forms a calcareous mud; that which is known to sailors as ooze, and such as is brought up on the lead in all deep sea soundings. Now it will be evident that when the sea invades the land each of these belts will be extended inland; the sheet of sand and gravel reaching continuously as far as the submergence progresses, the finer mechanical sediments nearly, but not quite, as far and overlapping the first; the organic sediments being deposited above the others and only in the open sea, or where it receives but little wash from the land. These strata, which we have thus seen forming, when consolidated by pressure, heat, and the deposit of soluble silica or carbonate of lime, are conglomerate from gravel, sandstones from sand, shale from clay, and limestone from ooze. In just this way all the sedimentary rocks have been formed.

In the State of Ohio, the first of the series of strata deposited on the old sunken continent, is not visible—as it is covered and concealed by those which overlie it—but going northward to the Canadian highlands, or the Adirondacks of New York, we reach portions of the old continental surface which, as I have said, have never been submerged. Here the series is complete; the lowest, and that resting on the crystalline rocks, being a sandstone named the Potsdam sandstone. Above this occurs the formation, composed for the most part of a mixture of lime, sand and clay, called from this fact the Calciferous sandrock. Over this again lies the great group of limestones, of which the Trenton limestone is the most conspicuous, and therefore called the Trenton group, which includes the Blue limestone, the lowest stratum exposed in the State of Ohio.

From what has been said it will be apparent that these three groups of Lower Silurian strata are the products of the first invasion by the sea of the old continent. Each of them forms a sheet underlying the entire valley of the Mississippi. Of this we have evidence, not only in what we see in the Ozarks and Alleghanies—that have been upheaved in such a way as to bring up and expose the older rocks—but also in borings made at St. Louis, Louisville and Columbus. In all these wells the older Silurian rocks have been reached. Our Ohio well was sunk to a depth of 2,775 feet 4 inches. I am thus accurate because I was once called upon to report upon the probability of getting from the well the hoped for artesian flow of water. The boring was discontinued, perhaps at my suggestion, as it seemed to me that the structure of this portion of our State was not favorable to a flow of water to the surface, and as proved by the observation of Dr. Wormley, the temperature of the well at the bottom was 91 degrees—that of our hottest summer weather. The water was also salt. Hence had a water-bearing crevice been struck at a greater depth, the flow from it of hot and salt water could hardly have been suited to the purpose it was intended to serve—the supply of the State House and Capitol grounds.

However unsuccessful as regards the purpose for which it was bored, this well gave us interesting evidence of the nature of the strata underlying those which are exposed to sight in our State. These were plainly the Calciferous sand rock (here containing much more lime and magnesia and less silica than in New York) and the Potsdam sandstone, which had not been passed through when the work was arrested.

THE CINCINNATI GROUP.

The Cincinnati or blue limestone group is exposed in the southwestern corner of the State (that surrounding the city of Cincinnati), and extends southward into what is called the Blue-grass region of Kentucky. The reason why over this area the Lower Silurian rocks are exposed, while all the country about them is occupied by more recent formations, is that it lies on the line of a great arch or fold of the strata, which runs parallel with the folds of the Alleghany mountains, and was doubtless produced by the same cause. Subsequently to the elevation of this arch, the rocks forming its summit were extensively removed by surface erosion, and thus the lower strata were exposed to view.

The thickness of the Cincinnati group is about 1,000 feet. It is interesting both from the number and variety of the fossils which it contains (mollusks, corals, crinoids and crustacea), and also for the fertility of the soil it has furnished. By reference to the map it will be seen that the margin of the blue limestone area is extremely ragged and irregular. This is an accurate representation of nature, however, for Prof. Orton has traced this line with the greatest care. Its sinuosities are due to the excavation and removal of the overlying rocks by all the tributaries of the Little Miami; thus the valley of each stream forms a narrow or wide prolongation of the blue limestone surface, while the divides are composed of more recent rocks.

THE CLINTON AND NIAGARA GROUPS.

These are parts of the Upper Silurian system, and are mostly limestones, the Clinton from 10 to 100 feet thick, according to the locality where it is observed, the Niagara about 80. The lines of outcrop of these rocks are nearly parallel with each other and to the margin of the blue limestone, and along this line the Clinton makes its only appearance in the State; but the over-lying Niagara, concealed in the central portion of the State by over-lying strata, presently to be mentioned, reappears on the lake shore and forms the crown of the arch to which I have referred, down nearly as far as Bellefontaine. The Clinton group will be remembered by many when I say that it forms the cliffs bordering the Genesee below the falls, at Rochester; the Niagara, that it composes the shelf over which the water pours in the great cascade from which it is named.

The Niagara limestone has considerable economic value, inasmuch as it furnishes much of the lime used in building in various portions of the State, and is the rock so highly esteemed in southwestern Ohio, known as the Dayton-stone.

THE SALINA AND LOWER HELDERBERG FORMATIONS.

The Niagara is succeeded in the ascending scale by the Salina and Water-lime groups which form the summit of the Silurian system. These strata are so named, because the first and lowest contains the salt and gypsum of central New York; while the upper, as its name implies, is characterized by the presence of hydraulic lime, and is the formation which furnished the hydraulic cement manufactured in Western New York and Louisville, Kentucky. These two limestone beds, with two others and a bed of sandstone which overlie them, and the Clinton and Niagara below, were united under the name of the Cliff limestone, in the reports of the former Geological Board. One of the results of our past summer's work has been to resolve this Cliff limestone into its component parts, and to show that it includes seven distinct formations, belonging to two great geological systems. Up to the time of the organization of the present survey, it may be said that only one of the formations composing the "Cliff" had been distinctly recognized—the Corniferous limestone, that of which the State House is constructed. Evidence of the presence of the Niagara had been obtained, but nothing definite was known with regard to its geographical position, thickness, or relations to the associated rocks.

The manner in which the water-lime group was identified will serve to illustrate the way in which the different members of our geological series have been investigated and their ages determined. It is now a well-recognized truth, that palæontology is an indispensable aid to the study of our sedimentary rocks. Each formation is characterized by a greater or less number of fossils, which are found only in them.

In the identification of the water-lime group, I was guided entirely by its fossils. The most easterly of the islands in Lake Erie, Kelley's Island, was, I knew, composed of the corniferous limestone, as it is full of fossils characteristic of that formation; but the more westerly islands, Put-in-Bay, North and Middle Bass, &c., are wrought out of a hard gray limestone, generally without fossils, and apparently quite different from any portion of the "Cliff," as seen in the southern part of the State. In this rock, after much search, I discovered a little bivalve crustacean, having the form and size of a bean. This was at once recognized as *Leperditia alta*, a fossil of the water-lime portion of the Upper Silurian of New York. With the *Leperditia* at the East are associated two or three other fossils, found only in the water-lime, and, for confirmation of the indication one of the group had afforded, the others were diligently sought, and at length were all found. Three of these are small shells, the fourth a very peculiar crustacean, *(Eurypterus remipes)* having somewhat the form of a scorpion, but from 6 to 12 inches in length. In these fossils we have irrefragible evidence of the identity of the rock forming the islands I have named with the water-lime of New York. Just beneath this stratum lies the Salina group, which contains the Onondaga gypsum and that of Sandusky. We subsequently found the water-lime to form the surface rock over a large area in the interior of the State. In several places it embraces strata that have hydraulic properties, and by an examination of its outcrops we shall hereafter doubtless find, if that has not already been done, an abundant supply of this useful mineral, for which we now pay more than $100,000 annually to our neighbors.

The Salina contains gypsum not only at Sandusky but at Sylvania and doubtless at many other localities; though this formation is so generally covered by the Water-lime that the gypsum is less frequently accessible than could be desired. This is also a great salt-bearing stratum, and evidence has already been gathered which indicates that where not penetrated by surface water it will furnish brine of the requisite strength, and probably in sufficient quantity to make it an important item in our mineral resources.

THE DEVONIAN SYSTEM.

The great group of rocks represented in the geology of Ohio is that called the Devonian system,—so named from its development in Devonshire, England,—and a group well known to most intelligent persons at the present day, through the glowing descriptions written by Hugh Miller, of one portion of it—the Old Red Sandstone—and the wonderful fossil fishes it contains. In England fishes are first met with in the Upper Silurian—the equivalent of the Niagara lime-stone—but in this country no traces of vertebrates are found till we ascend to the Devonian. Here, however, they occur in large numbers, and the rocks of Ohio have furnished some of the largest and most remarkable of all these strange forms of ancient life.

THE ORISKANY SANDSTONE.

In New York, the lowest member of the Devonian System is the Oriskany standstone, a formation until the last year not recognized in Ohio, but one which we have now identified in a number of locatities, principally in the north-western quarter of the State. It is here represented by a white saccharoidal sandstone, not more than twenty feet thick, generally destitute of fossils, but furnishing a pure quartzose sand that is destined to be largely employed in the arts for the manufacture of glass, &c. Some of the characteristic fossils of the Oriskany, *spirifer arenosus*, &c., have been found in Indiana, near the Ohio line.

THE CORNIFEROUS LIMESTONE.

Above the Oriskany comes a stratum of buff limestone, fifty feet in thickness, generally crowded with fossils, corals, shells, crinoids, &c., and in some localities altogether made up of masses and branches of coral, representing, in fact, the coral reefs of the Devonian seas. Such is its character on the islands of Lake Erie, and at the falls of the Ohio. This formation is known to geologists as the Corniferous limestone, a name given to it in New York, from the nodules of flint or hornstone which it contains. The Corniferous limestone forms two lines of outcrop in Ohio, one on each side of the great anticlinal axis to which I have before referred. Of these outcrops, the most easterly includes Kelley's Island, Marble Head and the country about Sandusky; thence running nearly southerly to the Ohio River, but in the central portion of the State extending toward the west so as to include the region around Bellefontaine. In the southern part of the State the Corniferous outcrop is gradually narrowed; the formation diminishing in thickness as it approaches the Ohio, where it disappears altogether.

On the other side of the anticlinal axis the corniferous belt crosses the State line at Sylvania, thence sweeps round to Fort Defiance and passes into Indiana at Antwerp. This is the rock upon which Columbus stands and of which the State House is built. Its economic value is very great, as is the interest attached to its fossil remains. It is perhaps the most extensively employed for the manufacture of lime of all the rocks of the State, and in certain localities it furnishes a building stone not inferior in beauty and value to any other. The quarries of Mr. Clemens, on Marble Head, and those of Mr. Clark, of Delphos, Paulding county, may be referred to as the source from which building stones are procured of special beauty and excellence.*

The fossils contained in the Corniferous limestone are so varied and numerous that I can only mention a few of the most interesting, the fishes, to which I have already referred. These fishes form several genera and species, one of which, *Macropetalichthys Sullivanti*, was first obtained from the quarries of Mr. Joseph Sullivant, near Columbus, and was named in his honor. This was a large buckler-headed fish, of which the cranium, composed of articulated plates, was sometimes fifteen inches in length, and closely resembled that of the sturgeon. Another still more

---

* These and all other important building stones of the State are represented in the collections made by the Geological Corps during the last summer, in blocks eight inches square and four inches thick.

remarkable fish of the Corniferous limestone, is one of the many interesting discoveries made by Mr. Hertzer. This I have called *Onychodus*, from the claw-like form of its teeth. The most striking feature in this great fish was presented by the under jaws, which were as broad as one's arm and from twelve to eighteen inches in length, thickly set with teeth; while inclosed between their anterior extremities—in what anatomists call the symphysis of the jaw—was a single crest of seven large conical-hooked teeth, so set as to act like the prow of a ram. Like most of these ancient fishes it had a tessellated cranium, composed of plates covered with a beautiful tuberculated and enameled surface. The Corniferous limestone also contains some interesting fossil plants, among which are two remarkable tree ferns, the oldest land plants yet found on this continent.

THE HAMILTON GROUP.

In New York the Corniferous limestone is overlaid by the Marcellus shale, and a compound mass of limestones and shales of very considerable thickness, to which the name of the Hamilton group has been given. This formation is quite largely developed in Michigan, but has never been heretofore known to exist in Ohio. During the past summer, however, we have discovered its representative in a band of bluish, marly limestone, never exceeding twenty feet in thickness, resting upon the Corniferous limestone where that is overlaid by more recent rocks. From this marly limestone we have obtained many of the characteristic fossils of the Hamilton group, such as *Spirifer mucronatus*, *Strophodonta demissa*, *Phacops bufo*, etc.

THE HURON SHALE.

Above the Hamilton beds comes the great mass of black, bituminous shale, designated by the former Geological Board as the "Black Slate." This is a very remarkable formation, not only from its wide distribution, but from its peculiar lithological character. Its outcrop forms a belt from ten to twenty miles in width, reaching from the Lake shore at the mouth of the Huron River, almost directly south to the mouth of the Scioto. It is everywhere a black rock, and by its resemblance to coal has given rise to innumerable mining schemes; all of which, however, have ended in disappointment, as, though useful for the production of oil by distillation, it can never be successfully employed as fuel. The Huron shale is on an average 350 feet thick, and containing at least 10 per cent. of combustible matter, its carbon is equivalent to that of a coal seam forty feet in thickness; a greater aggregate of combustible material than is contained in all the coal-bearing strata of the State. Doubtless the time will come when this great store of power will be in some way made available, but for the present its utilization seems for the most part beyond our reach. By reference to the geological map, it will be seen that all the north-western corner of the State is colored with a dark tint, to correspond with that of the Black shale belt between the Lake and the Ohio. This is so colored, because we have lately learned that the Huron shale forms the surface rock in this region over an area of several counties. In all geological maps made previous to the one now published, the Huron shale is represented as forming the Lake shore from near Sandusky to Conneaut, and it has generally been supposed to be the equivalent of the Hamilton group of New York. During the progress of the explorations of the last summer, however, we discovered that east of Avon Point, this black shale nowhere makes its appearance in the State, but that the shore of the Lake on the Reserve, is composed of another and more recent group of shales. We have also obtained, in various localities, fossils which prove that this formation represents, in part at least, the Portage group of New York; and that it is all more recent than the Hamilton.

Much of the doubt which has hung around the age of the Huron shale, has been due to the fact that it has been confounded with the Cleveland shale, which lies several hundred feet above it, and that the fossils (without which, as we have said, it is generally impossible to accurately determine the age of any of the sedimentary rocks) had not been found. Yet, with diligent search, we have now discovered not only fossils sufficient to identify this formation with the Portage of New York, but the acute eye of Mr. Hertzer has detected, in certain calcareous concretions which occur near the base, at Delaware, Monroeville, &c., fossils of great scientific interest. These concretions are often spherical, are sometimes twelve feet in diameter, and very frequently contain organic nuclei, around which they have formed. These nuclei are either portions of the trunks of large corniferous trees allied to our pines, replaced particle by particle by silica, so that their structure can be studied almost as well as that of the recent wood, or large bones. With the exception of some trunks of tree ferns which we have found in the Corniferous limestone of Delaware and Sandusky, these masses of silicified wood are the oldest remains of a land vegetation yet found in the State. The Silurian rocks everywhere abound with impressions of sea-weeds, but not until now had we found proof that there were, in the Devonian age, continental surfaces covered with forests of trees similar in character to, and rivaling in magnitude, the pines of the present day.*

The bones contained in these concretions are those of gigantic fishes,

* Prof. J. W. Dawson, of Montreal, has made known a very rich and interesting flora —similar to that of the coal period—found in the upper Devonian rocks of New Brunswick; and has described many other land plants, from New York and Canada, obtained from strata, some of which are of Hamilton age.

larger, more powerful, and more singular in their organization than any of those immortalized by Hugh Miller. These fishes we owe to the industry and acuteness of Mr. Hertzer, and in recognition of that fact I have named the most remarkable one *Dinichthys Hertzeri*, or Hertzer's terrible fish. This name will not seem ill chosen when I say that the fish that now bears it had a head three feet long by two feet broad, and that his under jaws were more than two feet in length and five inches deep. They are composed of dense bony tissue, and are turned up anteriorly like sled runners; the extremities of both jaws meeting to form one great triangular tooth, which interlocked with two in the upper jaw seven inches in length and more than three inches wide. It is apparent from the structure of these jaws that they could easily embrace in their grasp the body of a man--perhaps of a horse—and as they were doubtless moved by muscles of corresponding power, they could crush such a body as we would crack an egg-shell.

THE ERIE SHALE.

The mass of shale to which I have referred as forming the Lake shore is on the eastern border of the State, several hundred feet in thickness, but, like most of our rocks composed of mechanical sediment, it thins out toward the west, and in central Ohio has entirely disappeared. This formation also for many years formed debatable ground to geologists, but during the past summer we have been able to gather from it numerous fossils *(Spirifer Verneuilii, Leiorhynchus mesacostalis*, &c.) of species which prove the beds containing them to be the equivalent of the Chemung group of the New York geologists. The Erie shales are bluish or greenish in color, but, though in some places four hundred feet thick, they include less of interest or value than perhaps any other formation in our series, and therefore need not detain us. They form, as we now know, the summit of the Devonian formation, and immediately underlie the most interesting and valuable division of our geology.

THE CARBONIFEROUS SYSTEM.

As is known to most persons, the Carboniferous formation is so named from the beds of coal it contains in Europe and America, where our geological nomenclature originated. Researches in other countries, made within a few years past, have, however, proved that more recent groups of rocks—as the Triassic in China and the Cretaceous and Tertiary in our western territories—include an equal amount of combustible matter, and perhaps as well deserve the name Carboniferous.

In Europe the Carboniferous formation is divided into three great groups; the Lower Carboniferous or Mountain Limestone, the Carboniferous Conglomerate or Millstone Grit, and the Coal Measures, or the strata containing the workable seams of coal. In many parts of our country this is precisely the structure of the Carboniferous series, but in Ohio the Lower Carboniferous rocks consist mostly of mechanical sediments—sandstone, shale, &c.—and the Mountain Limestone is almost entirely wanting.

The lowest member which we possess of the Carboniferous group is that well known to most persons under the name of the "Waverly sandstone," a name derived from the town of Waverly, in Pike county, where famous quarries are located upon it. By referring to the map, it will be seen that the south-eastern third of the State is colored of a uniform dark brown tint. This represents the Coal Measures. Parallel with the margin of this dark area is a narrow belt of red, which represents the Carboniferous Conglomerate. Outside of this a still broader belt of yellow occupies the position of the outcrop of the Waverly group—that which we are now considering. In southern Ohio this formation, according to Prof. Andrews, is 640 feet in thickness, composed mostly of sandy shales and ochery sandstone. Aside from the band of building stone to which I have referred, called the City Ledge, some five feet in thickness, and a stratum of highly bituminous shale just below it, sixteen feet thick (distilled for oil, and rich in interesting fossils), the group here possesses few elements of economic value. In the northern part of the State, however, it is much less homogeneous, and is composed of the following elements:

	Feet.
Cuyahoga Shale (dove-colored shale and fine blue sandstone)	150
Berea Grit (drab sandstone)	50
Bedford Shale (red and blue clay shale)	60
Cleveland Shale (black bituminous shale)	20-60

Of these the Berea Grit is one of the most valuable elements in our geological series, inasmuch as, quarried at Amherst, Berea, Independence, &c., it is a source from which we derive, in the form of grindstones, building stone, &c., at least a million of dollars annually. The value of this stone for the purposes I have enumerated is too well known to require amplification. It is not only largely employed within our State, but exported both east and west, and is being used for the most beautiful and expensive public and private buildings in all our great cities.

This Waverly group is a vast storehouse of fossils, many of which, especially the fishes, are of great interest. These have been collected in considerable numbers during the past season, and the study given to them has enabled me to decide the long-mooted question of the age of the formation containing them. By most geologists this has been considered as a portion of the Devonian formation, and the equivalent of the Chemung and Portage of New York; but, as I have shown, these groups are represented by the Erie and Huron shales, which underlie the

Waverly; and the fossils to which I have referred prove beyond all doubt that the latter group is a portion of the Carboniferous system.

These fossils are *Palœoniscus* 2 species, *Ctenacanthus* 3, *Gyracanthus* 2, *Orodus* 2, *Helodus* 2, *Polyrhizodus* 1, *Cladodus* 3; all Carboniferous forms, with great numbers of mollusks and crinoids, of which many species have been found elsewhere in the Lower Carboniferous, and some in the Coal measures. Among the latter I may cite *Spirifer cameratus*, *Productus semi-reticulatus*, *Streptorhynchus umbraculum*, and others.*

We have also discovered that the species found in this formation, claimed by some geologists to be identical with those characteristic of the Devonian of other States, have all been wrongly named, and that so far as now known, no Devonian species occur in the Waverly.

THE CARBONIFEROUS CONGLOMERATE.

This rests upon the Waverly and forms the floor of Coal measures; its line of outcrop forming a narrow belt, encircling all the coal area. It is generally a coarse sandstone interstratified with beds of greater or less thickness, composed mostly of rolled quartz pebbles, and constituting a typical pudding stone. The average thickness of the Conglomerate is perhaps one hundred feet, and it contains large numbers of fossil plants, generally similar to those found in the Coal measures. In some localities it also furnishes very beautiful building stone; perhaps the most beautiful in our country. The places where it exhibits its best phases, are Akron and Cuyahoga Falls in Summit connty, and Mansfield, Richland county. The rock quarried at the first-named place, is of a deep purplish red, and has been used in the construction of same of the finest residences in the State.

THE COAL MEASURES.

The Coal measures consist of a series of sandstones, shales, limestones, fire clays and beds of coal, of which the latter are the most important and interesting. The geographical area occupied by the coal rocks, as has been stated, comprises the south-eastern third of the State. As the general dip of all our rocks east of the great anticlinal is towards the east, the Coal measures, which form the highest member of our series, grow thicker in that direction. In the vicinity of Wheeling, near the centre of the Alleghany coal basin—of which our coal area forms a part—the Coal measures have a thickness of about 1,500 feet, and include, perhaps, ten workable seams of coal, under each of which is a stratum of fire clay. These latter also contribute their quota to the great economical

* Prof. Winchell, State Geologist of Michigan, who has studied the mollusks of the Michigan equivalent of the Waverly, has for some years asserted that it was of Carboniferous age.

value of this part of our geology. Many of the sandstones of the Coal measures furnish excellent building material; the limestones are useful for quicklime, and in the localities where they contain an uuusual percentage of clay, they can be used for the manufacture of hydraulic cement.

The coal rocks are full of the remains of animal and vegetable life. In the many years which I have devoted to the study of the geology of the Coal formation in Ohio, I have collected several hundred species of these fossils, of which a large number are new to science. Some of the more interesting species are represented in the drawings which have been submitted with the other materials forming our first report.

With the plants, which constitute the most characteristic fossils of the Coal measures, we have found many shells, fishes and amphibians, and it is apparent that in this group of rocks we have a store of material which in its richness is pretty certain to exceed our means of illustration.

The economical value of the mineral staples contained in this portion of our geological series, is such as to demand somewhat fuller exposition than I have given of the other subjects touched upon in the preceding hasty sketch of the geology of our State. I shall therefore venture to devote several pages each in the chapter on Economic Geology, to topics so important as COAL and IRON; since they constitute the *kraft und stoff*, the force and matter of modern material progress.

THE DRIFT.

The materials known as the Drift deposits are beds of sand, gravel and boulders, which form the surface of a large part of our State, and which have received the name of Drift, because they are generally foreign to the localities where they are found, and have been transported (drifted) sometimes hundreds of miles from their places of origin.

In Ohio we have no geological formations intervening between the Coal measure and the Drift, and therefore have no representatives of the Permain, Triassic, Cretaceous or Tertiary. The reason of this is simply that about the close of the Carboniferous period the Alleghany Mountains were raised, carrying up all the area lying between the Mississippi and the Atlantic. Since that time no considerable portion of this region has been submerged, and therefore no deposits were made upon it during the ages I have enumerated. West of the Mississippi the land has been long and often below the ocean level since the Carboniferous period, and there all the newer formations are well represented.

The phenomena presented by the Drift are very varied and interesting, and it is evident that the Drift period formed one of the strangest and most important chapters in all our geological history. Like most of the formations enumerated in the preceding pages, the Drift deposits have been discussed at considerable length; and while it is true of the other groups, that a few words may suffice to convey a clear idea of them, or at least of the new things we have learned about them, the Drift phenomena are too complicated, too little known and too interesting to be so summarily dismissed. Hence I am compelled to quote considerably at length from my report in order to impart any definite conception of the subject.

The most important facts which the study of the Drift has brought to light, are briefly as follows:

1st. Over the northern half of North America, and down as low as Dayton, in Ohio, *we find, not everywhere, but in most localities where the nature of the underlying rocks is such as to retain inscriptions made upon them, the upper surface of these rocks planed, furrowed, or excavated in a peculiar and striking manner, evidently by the action of one great denuding agent.* None who has seen glaciers and noticed the effect they produce on the rocks over which they move, upon examining good examples of the markings to which I have referred, will fail to pronounce them the tracks of glaciers.

Though having a general north-south direction, locally the glacial furrows have very different bearings, conforming in a rude way to the present topography, and following the direction of the great lines of drainage.

2d. *Beneath the Drift deposits the rock surfaces are, in many localities, excavated to form a system of basins and channels, often cut several hundred feet below the lakes and rivers that now occupy them.*

These channels frequently exhibit traces of ice action, and we may say that they have generally been modified, if not produced by ice, and date from the Ice period, or an earlier epoch.

These valleys form a connected system of drainage at a lower level than the present river system—lower, in many places, than the surface of the ocean—and hence lower than could be produced without a continental elevation of several hundred feet. A few examples will suffice to show on what evidence these statements are based.

Lake Michigan, Lake Huron, Lake Erie and Lake Ontario are basins excavated in undisturbed sedimentary rocks. Of these, Lake Michigan is 600 feet deep, with a surface level of 578 feet above tides; Lake Huron is 500 feet deep, with a surface level of 574 feet; Lake Erie is 204 feet deep, with a surface level of 565 feet; Lake Ontario is 450 feet deep, with a surface level of 234 feet above the sea.

An old, excavated, non-filled channel connects Lake Erie and Lake Huron. At Detroit the rock surface is 130 feet below the city. In the old regions of Bottewell and Enniskillen from 50 to 200 feet of clay overlies the rock. What the greatest depth of this channel is is not known.

At Toledo the rock surface is 140 feet below the lake. An excavated trough runs southward from Lake Michigan to the north line of Iroquois county, Illinois; thence south-west through Champaign county, beyond which point it has not been traced. Its western margin is very sharply marked at Chalsworth, Livingston county, where it has a depth of 200 feet, and reaches to the Cincinnati group. Farther north its bounding walls are composed of Niagara limestone, which forms buried shoulders on the Calumet and Kankakee rivers. At Bloomington this trough acquires a depth of 230 feet, and it then contains one or more strata of carbonaceous earth, with trunks of trees supposed to represent ancient soils. Where penetrated in other localities the depth of this channel is from 75 to 200 feet, and it is filled with clay, sand, gravel, etc., (Prof. J. H. Bradley.)

The rock bottoms of the troughs of the Mississippi and Missouri, near their junction or below, have never been reached, but they are many feet, perhaps some hundreds, beneath the present stream beds.

The borings for oil in the vallies of the western rivers have enabled me not only to demonstrate the existence of deeply buried channels of excavation, but, in some instances, to map them out. Oil Creek flows from 75 to 100 feet above its old channel, and that channel had sometimes vertical and even overhanging cliffs. The Beaver, at the junction of the Mahoning and Shenango, runs 150 feet above the bottom of its old trough. The Ohio, throughout its entire course, runs in a valley which has been cut nowhere less than 150 feet below the present river.

The Cuyahoga enters Lake Erie at Cleveland more than 100 feet above the rock bottom of its excavated trough. The Chagrin, Vermillion, and other streams running into Lake Erie exhibit the same pheuomena, and prove that the surface level of the lake must once have been at least 100 feet lower than now.

At New Philadelphia the Tuscarawas is running 175 feet above its ancient bed. At Cincinnati the gravel and sand have been found to reach over 100 feet below low water mark, and the bottom of the trough has not been reached. At the junction of the Anderson with the Ohio in Indiana a well was sunk 94 feet below the level of the Ohio before rock was found (Hamilton Smith.) At Steubenville the railroad bridge across the Ohio is built on cribs, the rock bottom of the channel not being reached. One of the piers of the St. Louis bridge was sunk in sand and gravel nearly 100 feet below the bottom of the Mississippi.

The falls of the Ohio, formed by a rocky barrier across the stream, though at first sight seeming to disprove the theory of a deep, continuous channel in our western rivers, really afford no argument against it; for here, as in many other instances, the present river does not follow accurately the line of the old channel, but runs along one side of it. At the Louisville falls the Ohio runs across a rocky point which projects from the north side into the old valley, while the deep channel passes on the south side, under the low lands, on which the city of Louisville is built.

The importance of a knowledge of these old channels in the improvement of the navigation of our larger rivers and lakes is obvious; and it is possible that it would have led to the adoption of other means than a rock cutting for passing the Louisville falls had it been possessed by those concerned in this enterprise.

If it is true that our great lakes can be connected with each other, and with the ocean, both by the Hudson and Mississippi, by ship canals—in making which no elevated summits nor rock barriers need be cut through—the future commerce created by the great population and immense resources of the basin of the great lakes may require their construction.

3d. *Upon the glacial surface we find a series of unconsolidated materials generally stratified, called the "Drift Deposits."*

Of these the first and lowest are blue or red clays (the Erie clays of Sir William Logan), generally regularly stratified in their layers, and containing no fossils but drifted corniferous wood and leaves. Over the southern and eastern part of the lake basin these clays contain almost no boulders, but towards the north and west they include scattered stones, often of large size, while in places beds of boulders and gravel are found resting directly upon the glacial surface.

In Ohio the Erie clays are blue, nearly 200 feet thick, and reach up the hill-sides more than 200 feet above the present surface of Lake Erie. On the shores of Lake Michigan these clays are, in part, derived from different rocks, and they then include great numbers of stones.

On the peninsula between Lake Erie and Lake Huron the Erie clays fill the old channel which formerly connected these lakes, having a thickness of over 200 feet, and containing a few scattered stones.

Above the Erie clays are sands of variable thickness and less widely spread than the underlying clays. These sands contain beds of gravel, and near the surface teeth of elephants have been found, sometimes water-worn and pounded.

Upon the stratified clays, sands and gravel of the drift deposits, are scattered boulders and blocks of all sizes, of granite, greenstone (diorite and dolerite), siliceous and mica slates, generally traceable to some locality in the Eozoric area north of the lakes. Among these boulders have been found many masses of native copper, which could have come from nowhere else than the copper district of Lake Superior.

Most of these transported stones are rounded by attrition, but the large blocks of corniferous limestone scattered over the southern margin of the lake basin in Ohio show little marks of wear. Some of these masses—10 to 20 feet in diameter—have been transported from 100 to 200 miles southeastward from their place of origin, and deposited 300 feet above the position they once occupied.

Above all these drift deposits, and more recent than any of them, are the "lake ridges"—embankments of sand, gravel, sticks, leaves, etc., which run imperfectly parallel with the present outlines of the lake margins. Of these the lowest on the south shore of Lake Erie is a little less than 100 feet above the present level of the lake; the highest some 250 feet. In New York, Canada, Michigan, and on Lake Superior a similar series of ridges has been discovered, and they have everywhere been accepted as evidence that the waters of the lakes once reached the points they mark; that they are nothing else than ancient lake beaches I shall hope to prove further on.

In the southern half of the Mississippi Valley the evidences of glacial action are entirely wanting, and there is nothing corresponding to the wide-spread drift deposits of the north. We there find, however, proofs of erosion on a stupendous scale—such as the valley of East Tennessee—which has been formed by the washing out of all the broken strata between the ridges of the Alleghanies and the massive tables of the Cumberland Mountains—the canons of the Tennessee 1600 feet deep, etc. Here, also, as in the lake basin, the channels of excavation pass below the deep and quiet waters of the lower rivers, proving by their depth that they must have been cut when the fall of these rivers was much greater than now.

The history which I derive from the facts cited above is briefly this:

1st. At a period probably synchronous with the glacial epoch of Europe—at least corresponding to it in the sequence of events—the northern half of the continent of North America had a climate comparable with that of Greenland; so cold, that wherever there was a copious precipitation of moisture from oceanic evaporation, that moisture was congealed, and formed glaciers which flowed by various routes toward the sea.

2d. That the causes of these ancient glaciers corresponded in a general way with the present channels of drainage. The direction of the glacial furrows proves that one of these ice rivers flowed from Lake Huron along a channel now filled with drift, and known to be at least 150 feet deep, into Lake Erie, which was then not a lake, but an excavated valley, into which the streams of Northern Ohio flowed, 100 feet or more below the present lake level. Following the line of the major axis of Lake Erie to near its eastern extremity, here turning north-east this glacier passed through some channel on the Canadian side—now filled up—into Lake Ontario, and thence found its way to the sea, either by the St. Lawrence or by the Mohawk and Hudson.

Another glacier occupied the bed of Lake Michigan, having an outlet southward through a channel now concealed by the heavy beds of drift which occupy the surface about the south end of the lake passing near Bloomington, Illinois, and by some route yet unknown reaching the trough of the Mississippi, which was then much deeper than at present.

3d. At this period the continent must have been several hundred feet higher than now, as is proved by the deeply excavated channels of the Hudson, Mississippi, Columbia, Golden Gate, etc., which could never have been cut by the streams that now occupy them, unless when flowing with greater rapidity and at a lower level than they now do. Similar submarine troughs lead out from the mouths of the Chesapeake and Delaware Bays, showing that the Susquehana, Potomac, York and James rivers were once branches of a single stream, which, like the Schuylkill, had its mouth face to the east of the present coast line.

The depth of the trough of the Hudson is not known, but it is plainly a channel of erosion, now submerged and become an arm of the sea. This channel is marked on the sea bottom for a long distance from the coast and far beyond a point where the present river could exert any erosive action, and hence it is a record of a period when the Atlantic coast was several hundred feet higher than now (J. D. Dana.)

The lower Mississippi gives unmistakable evidence of being—if one may be permitted the paradox—a half-drowned river; that is, its old channel is deeply submerged and silted up, so that the "Father of Waters," lifted above the walls that formerly restrained him, now wanders lawless and ungovernable, whither he will in the broad valley.

4th. The Ice period—a period of continental elevation and of active erosion—was followed by a *water* period, when the continent was depressed five hundred feet or more below its present level; when the climate was much warmer than before; when the glaciers retreated northward and were gradually replaced, in the basin of the great lakes, by an inland sea of fresh water. In this period were deposited the fine, laminated clays (Erie clays) which cover so much of the glacial surface in the interior of the continent, and the "Champlain clays," that hold the same relative position in the Atlantic slope. The Champlain clays contain abundant marine, arctic shells, but the Erie clays are not certainly known to contain any fossils except floated trunks, branches and leaves of corniferous trees—pines and spruces—now growing on the northern part of the continent.

5th. After the deposition of the Erie clays, sand, gravel and boulders in large quantities were transported from the region north of the lakes, and spread over a wide area south of them. That these materials were not carried by currents of water or glaciers is certain; as either of these transporting agents would have torn up the Erie clays, which now form an unbroken sheet beneath them. We are therefore forced to the conclusion that they were *floated* to their resting places, and that by icebergs. Icebergs are always formed by the rupture of the end of a glacier protruded into the sea; and they always carry boulders, gravel and sand from their places of origin, and deposit them when they melt. When our lake-basin glaciers had retreated to the highlands north of the lakes, icebergs were detached from them, and floated southward, sowing sand, gravel and boulders broadcast over the southern shallows, just as they are now doing over the banks of Newfoundland and the bottom of the Antarctic ocean.

6th. During the water period, the old, deeply excavated channels of our river system were silted up—in many cases entirely obliterated—and up to a certain level all the asperities of the surface smoothed over by the Drift deposits, just as minor inequalities are effaced by a fall of snow.

7th. Following the water period, ensued an era of continental elevation, which progressed until the present level was reached, and the Champlain clays and the other Drift deposits were raised several hundred feet above the ocean level. By this elevation of the continent most of the old lines of drainage were re-established, and the rivers began the work of clearing out their old channels. In most cases this work is not yet half done, and in many—as the Genesee, at Portage, New York, Rocky River, in Cuyahoga county, O., and others too numerous to mention—the line of lowest levels taken by the new streams did not follow their old routes, and new channels were formed. Some of these have been cut down one hundred feet or more in the solid rock, so that this, the last phase in the Drift phenomena, has consumed ages of time.

8th. The last emergence of the continent took place slowly, as we know, and its progress was marked by periods of repose. In these intervals of rest our terraces, old shore-cliffs and lake ridges were formed, and this may be properly designated as the Terrace epoch. Local and minor terraces are formed by constantly deepening streams swinging from side to side in their valleys, but all the great and general terraces were formed by the arrest in dead water of the materials transported by flowing water. Old shore-cliffs are beautifully shown in many places along the lines of outcrop of the Conglomerate and Berea Grit in Lorain, Medina, Cuyahoga, Geauga, Lake, &c. The lake-ridges mark old shore lines, on a sloping surface composed of drift materials. Just such are now being formed around the south end of Lake Michigan, between Cedar Point and Huron, on Lake Erie, and in a thousand places along the Atlantic coast, especially in Virginia and the Carolinas. In the north-western portion of Ohio the lake-ridges form a series of curves, imperfectly parallel with each other and the present lake shore. From the nature of the material composing them, and their elevation above the surrounding surface, they are always well drained, so that the roads of that section are often located on them. The "ridge roads" are well known, and they mark the lines of the principal ridges.

The formation of these ridges was the last act in the drama of the Drift. When the upper ones were formed, the whole lake basin and much of the country bordering the upper Mississippi was submerged by one great inland sea. Even when the ridge which ran through the city of Cleveland was formed, the water of Lake Erie stood one hundred feet higher than now, and all our great lakes formed a single sheet of water broken only by a few scattered islands. The depression of the water level was apparently caused by the cutting down of the outlets. That process is perhaps going on as rapidly now as ever. The last hundred feet of depression of the water surface, we know, has been effected by the cutting down of the Niagara barrier, and every day now must witness something removed from it by the torrent that rushes over it. Larger lakes than those on which we now pride ourselves have been emptied, in the western part of our country, by thus cutting down of the gorges of the Columbia, Klamoth and Sacramento, and it is evident that, if present causes continue to operate, at no very remote period, geologically speaking, all our lake basins will be converted into vallies traversed by rivers.

9th. In the retreat of the shore line from the contraction of the water surface to its present area, every part of the slope between the present and highest ancient lake levels—*i. e.*, all within a vertical height of three hundred feet—must have been submitted to the action of the shore waves, rain and rivers; by which these loose materials were rolled, ground, sorted and shifted until little was left of the original bedding. The fine materials—clay and sand—must have been washed out and carried farther and still farther into the lake basin, to form, in short, the upper sandy layers of the Drift.

In this "modified Drift," especially in the old river deltas, the remains of elephant and mastodon are frequently found; never, so far as yet known, in the older, true Drift.

I have said that the erratic blocks, of northern origin, which stud the surface over so large a space south of the lakes, were the last of the Drift deposits. That the lake ridges are of later date is proven by the fact that, while the ridges often traverse surfaces strewed with boulders, none of these are ever found on them.

In all the changes of elevation and climate which the valley of the Mississippi experienced during the Drift period, its general structure and main topographical features remained the same; yet the character of its surface suffered very important modifications, and such as deeply affected its fitness for human occupation. Going back to the later Tertiary ages for a starting point, we find the following sequence of events recorded:

a. In the Miocene and Pliocene epochs: The continent several hundred feet lower than now; the ocean reaching to Louisville and Iowa; great lakes in the country bordering the Upper Missouri; a sub-tropical climate prevailing over the lake region; the climate of Greenland and

Alaska as warm as that of southern Ohio now, (palms growing as far north as Lake Superior); herds of gigantic mammals, elephants, mastodon, rhinoceras, &c., with great cats and other carnivorous, corresponding in size and numbers to their prey, the herbivorous, all now extinct, ranging over a fertile and beautiful surface.

b. A pre-glacial epoch of gradual continental elevation, in which the erosion of our lake basins and river valleys, began long before, was continued with increasing energy as the elevation of the surface became greater, giving greater falls to the streams, and supplying, by greater breadth of surface and better condensers, an increased flow of drainage. Accompanying this elevation and in part dependent upon it, but mainly due to astronomical causes, was a depression of temperature which culminated in the "Glacial Epoch," when the continent was many hundred feet higher than now, the climate of Ohio was similar to that of Greenland at present, and glaciers covered a large part of the surface down to the parallel of 40 degrees. These glaciers planed down much of the more level surface, but along the drainage lines widened the valleys of the water-courses, and excavated the basins of our great lakes. By the cold of the "Glacial Epoch," the Arctic flora and fauna were brought down to our latitude; the tertiary flora and fauna driven southward and to a great degree destroyed.

c. The ice period was followed by another interval of continental subsidence, characterized by a warmer climate, by melting glaciers, by an inland sea of fresh water filling all the lake basins, and by the deposit of the clays, sands and boulders of the drift (Erie clays, Champlain clays, &c.)

d. Another epoch of elevation, probably still progressing, in which the water surface has been much diminished, the silted-up valleys of the streams partly cleared, the terraces and lake ridges formed, and a wide territory, covered with the drift deposits, opened to human occupation

Much of the topographical monotony which characterizes the northwestern part of the State, is due to the spread of the drift clays over all the irregularity of the underlying rocks. The system of agriculture pursued in all this region has followed as a necessity the deposition of these clays; so that they have not only determined the occupation of a large portion of our people, but have affected all their modes of thought and action, and they may almost be said to underlie the manners and morals, as they do the farms and towns, of all the dairy districts.

ECONOMIC GEOLOGY.

COAL.

Coal is entitled to be considered as the mainspring of our civilization. By the power developed in its combustion, all the wheels of industry are kept in motion, commerce is carried with rapidity and certainty over all portions of the earth's surface, the usual metals are brought from the deep caves in which they have hidden themselves, and are purified and wrought to serve the purposes of man. By coal, night is in one sense converted into day, winter into summer, and the life of man, measured by its fruits, greatly prolonged. Wealth, with all the comforts, the luxuries and the triumphs it brings, is its gift. Though black, sooty and often repulsive in its aspects, it is the embodiment of a power more potent than that attributed to the genii in oriental tales. Its possession is therefore the highest material boon that can be craved by a community or nation. Coal is also not without its poetry. It has been formed under the stimulus of the sunshine of long past ages, and the light and power it holds are nothing else than such sunshine stored in this black casket, to wait the coming and serve the purposes of man. In the process of formation it composed the tissues of those strange trees that lifted their scaled trunks and waved their feathery foliage over the marshy shores of the carboniferous continent, where not only no man was, but gigantic salamanders and mail-clad fishes were the monarchs of the animated world.

On this picture, however, we have no time to dwell; our present purpose is to consider coal in its utilitarian aspect, and to show what it is and for what it can be used.

That the assertions I have made in regard to the economic value of coal are not exaggerations, will be apparent by a glance at the present material condition of the civilized world.

Of all the nations of Europe, England is the most powerful, because she is the richest. Though occupying a group of islands insignificant in area, she has spread her power over the entire globe, and it is her boast that the sun never sets on her possessions. It is well known to the political economist that the source of England's wealth has been her manufacturing industry; and the main-spring of her industry has been her stores of coal. In this respect she enjoys a great pre-eminence over all the nations of Europe. The United Kingdoms have a coal area that has been reckoned at 10,000 square miles, while in round numbers Belgium has 500, France 2,000, Spain 4,000, and the other nations of Europe still less. The annual coal production of Great Britain is now more than 100,000,000 tons, and a very short calculation will suffice to show what an important contribution this makes to her national wealth. The power developed in the combustion of a pound of coal, is reckoned by engineers as equal to 1,500,000 foot-pounds. The power exerted by a man of ordinary strength during a day of labor is about the same; so that a pound of coal may be regarded as equivalent to a day's labor of a man. Hence three hundred pounds will represent the labor of a man for a year. It has been estimated that 20,000,000 tons of the annual coal product of Great Britain is devoted to the development of motive power, and that this is equivalent to the labor of 133,000,000 of men. These men, in this calculation, are considered as exerting merely "brute force;" but since they may all be regarded as producers only, and not consumers—the profit on the balance of her coal product fully covering all expenses—we are safe in estimating the contribution made to the wealth of Great Britain, by her annual coal product, as equal to that of 133,000,000 of skilled operatives laboring for her enrichment.

Such being the value to a nation or community of this combustible, let us see how our nation and our State has shared in nature's gifts.

The area of the coal fields of the carboniferous age, lying within the limits of the United States, has been estimated at 150,000 square miles. The productive coal area of Ohio is not less than 10,000 square miles, or quite equal to that possessed by Great Britain, and far in excess of that of any other European nation.

I have said that the annual coal production of Great Britain is over 100,000,000 tons—a rate of expenditure of capital which is seriously alarming British economists. In Ohio the annual coal production is now about 3,000,000 tons. So it will be seen that we not only have an almost inexhaustible source of wealth in our coal fields, but that as yet we have scarcely begun to draw from this treasury. Hence I was justified in saying, as I did, that this promised to be by far the most important source of our power and material progress; and one of the most important duties pressing upon our legislators, and on us as geologists, is, by all means in our power, to promote the rapid and intelligent development of all the industries that are to spring from this source.

In order that we may more clearly apprehend the nature and capabilities of the material which has such potency, and with which we are so richly endowed, I will briefly describe some of the varieties which it exhibits, and the uses to which they are adapted.

Coal is now considered by all chemists and geologists of any standing as of organic origin, and it may be easily demonstrated that it has been derived from the decomposition of vegetable tissue. As we find it in the earth, it forms one of a series of carbonaceous minerals which represent but different stages in a progressive change from vegetable tissue as found in the living plant. In peat and lignite we witness the first step in the formation of coal. *Peat* is bitumenized vegetation, generally mosses and other herbaceous plants, which under favorable circumstances accumulates in marshes, hence called peat-bogs. *Lignite* is the product of a similar change effected in woody tissue; and because it retains, to a greater or less degree, the form and structure of wood, it has received the name it bears. Peat is the product of the present period, and lignites are found in deposits of recent geological age. In the older formations these carbonaceous accumulations, still further changed, are *bituminous coal.* Where special and local causes have operated to carry the change still farther, as where the beds of coal have been involved in the upheaval of mountains, and heat has acted upon it; it is converted into *anthracite.* Where this metamorphosis has been carried still further, the result is *plumbago*, or black lead.

Most of the mineral fuels employed by the civilized nations of the world belong to the class of bituminous coals, but in our own country, up to the present time, by far the largest quantity of coal produced and consumed has been anthracite, because our beds of coal which lie nearest the sea-board and have been longest worked, are of this character. These are, however, of the same age with our Ohio coal beds, and the peculiar phase which the coals of eastern Pennsylvania exhibit, is due to the fact that a portion of the great Alleghany coal-field was involved in the upheaval of the Alleghany mountains, and the coal, in common with the associated rocks, was greatly metamorphosed—its gaseous matter being nearly all driven off by the great heat which attended the elevation of the mountains.

The changes which vegetable tissue has suffered in passing through the various stages I have enumerated, are not only physical but chemical. They have been carefully studied by several eminent chemists, and have been so fully explained, that they may be comprehended by any intelligent person. The *rationale* of this process may be seen at a glance by reference to the following formulæ, taken from Bischoff's Chemical Geology:

Wood.			*Loss.*		*Peat.*
Carbon	49.1	—	21.50	=	27.6
Hydrogen	6.3	—	3 50	=	2.8
Oxygen	44.6	—	29.10	=	15.5

Wood.			*Loss.*		*Lignite.*
Carbon	49 1	—	18.65	=	30.45
Hydrogen	6 3	—	3 25	=	3 05
Oxygen	44.6	—	24.40	=	20.20

Lignite.			*Loss.*		*Bituminous Coal.*
Carbon	30.45	—	12.35	=	18.10
Hydrogen	3.05	—	1.85	=	1.20
Oxygen	20.20	—	18 13	=	2.07

Bituminous Coal.			*Loss.*		*Anthracite.*
Carbon	18.10	—	3.57	=	14.53
Hydrogen..........	1.20	—	0.93	=	0.27
Oxygen............	2.07	—	1.32	=	0.65

Anthracite.			*Loss.*		*Plumbago.*
Carbon	14.53	—	1.42	=	13.11
Hydrogen..........	0.27	—	0.14	=	0.13
Oxygen	0.65	—	0.65	=	0.0

From this table it will be seen that the change from wood-tissue to peat or lignite, and from these to bituminous, thence to anthracite coal and plumbago, consists in the evolution of a portion of the carbon, hydrogen and oxygen, leaving a constantly increasing percentage of carbon behind, until ultimately the resulting mineral consists of a portion of the original carbon of the plant with all its earthy matter. That portion of the original substance which is lost in this progressive change, escapes in the form of some hydrocarbon, as water, carburetted hydrogen, carbonic acid, petroleum, &c. The escape of these volatile compounds we see in the gases bubbling up from marshes where vegetable matter is undergoing decomposition; in the gases generated in our coal mines and, in my judgment, in our oil-springs, which always flow from strata charged with bituminous matter. By the application of heat, and with proper management, we can manufacture any of these mineral fuels from vegetable fibre at will. This has been done repeatedly, and although we cannot accurately reproduce the conditions under which these changes are effected in nature's laboratory, we can so closely imitate them as to demonstrate their character.

We find also that, under peculiar circumstances, nature has departed from her usual routine, and has locally effected all the changes I have enumerated, in a short space of time; as at Santa Fe, New Mexico, where a trap dyke has cut through Cretaceous strata in which are beds of soft and nearly valueless lignite, and where over a large area this outflow of melted rock has converted this lignite into a compact and valuable anthracite. So at Los Bronces, in Sonora, Triassic coals are converted into anthracite by the eruption of porphyritic rock. On Queen Charlotte's Island, south of Alaska, is a Tertiary lignite changed by a similar cause into the most beautiful and brilliant anthracite I have ever seen.

All the coals of Ohio belong to the group known as bituminous coals, but these exhibit very considerable variety in their chemical and physical characters, and the different varieties are adapted to very different uses.

Following an economic classification, our coals may be described as, first, dry, open-burning or furnace coals; second, cementing or coking coals; third, cannel coals.

The first of these includes those that do not coke and adhere in the furnace, and are such as may be used in the raw state for the manufacture of iron.

The second group, to a greater or less degree, melt and agglutinate by heat, forming what blacksmiths term a "hollow fire." This property causes them to choke up the furnace and arrest the equal diffusion of the blast through the charge. Hence they cannot be used in the raw state for the manufacture of iron, but must be "coked." This process of coking consists in burning off the bituminous or gaseous portion; which leaves them in the condition of anthracite, except that, as this change is effected without pressure, the resulting material is cellular and spongy. Coals of this character, when free from sulphur—their great contaminating impurity—are used for the manufacture of gas; the volatile portion, driven off in the retorts, serving the purpose of illumination, while that which remains is coke, and may be used as fuel.

The cannel coals have usually a more distinctly stratified structure, are more compact and homogenous in texture, and contain a larger percentage of volatile matter than the others; also the gas they furnish has higher illuminating power. Hence they would be used, to the exclusion of all others, for the manufacture of gas, only that the coke which they furnish is of inferior quality. They are therefore, for the most part, employed as household fuels—for which they are specially adapted—and, in small portions, for enriching the gas produced from coking varieties.

The marked differences exhibited by the kinds of coal I have enumerated, are doubtless due, principally, to the circumstances of their formation. The furnace coals have generally a distinctly laminated structure, and are composed of bituminous layers separated by thin partitions of a material allied to cannel, which does not coke. Hence the bitumen in them is held in cells, and cannot flow together and give the mass a pasty, coherent character.

The cementing coals have few such partitions, but show, upon fracture, broad, brilliant surfaces of pitch-like bitumen. Both these varieties are supposed to have been formed in marshes, where they were saturated, but not constantly covered by water. The cannel coals were deposited in lagoons of open water in the coal marshes, where the finely macerated vegetable tissue accumulated as carbonaceous mud. Hence they have a large percentage of hydrogen, and their gas has high illuminating power. Hence also the remains of shells, fishes, amphibians and crustacea—all aquatic animals—so generally found in them.

In Ohio, it chances that the lowest stratum in the series is generally a furnace coal. Along its northern line of outcrop this is known as the "Briar Hill coal." This coal enjoys a deserved celebrity for its adaptation to the manufacture of iron, and now furnishes the fuel by which half the iron produced in the State is made. In consequence of the structure of our coal basin, this coal stratum, underlying all the others, and dipping towards the south and east, is, for the most part, covered by the overlying rock. As a consequence, up to the present time it has been worked only along its line of outcrop, and the great area it occupies below drainage is almost untouched. It is plain, therefore, that the time is not far distant when our people will be driven to reach and work it by shafting. In Ohio we have as yet sunk but two or three shafts, to reach seams of coal, and these to no great depth; while nearly all the coal mined in Great Britain is obtained by shafting—sometimes to the depth of 2,000 feet. By carefully studying the dip of the rocks (which is not uniform, but is frequently counteracted by folds that elevate or depress the coal seams from their normal planes), we shall be able to do much to guide the efforts soon to be put forth to reach it. Some localities are already known to me where this Briar Hill seam, far from its outcrop, rises much nearer the surface than it was supposed to be. Other like localities will doubtless be discovered, upon careful search.

Another seam of coal which has this open-burning character is that known as the "Hocking Valley coal," found fifty or sixty miles southeast of Columbus, and over an area—estimated by Prof. Andrews, who has carefully studied that district—of not less than six hundred square miles, maintaining a thickness of from 6 to 11 feet, with a remarkable uniformity and purity of composition. Should this coal be capable of use in the raw state as a furnace fuel, it is destined to assume an importance second to no other in the State, and to form a basis upon which a manufacturing industry will be established in its vicinity, by which not only that section but the entire State will be enriched.

By far the greater portion or our coals are, however, of the coking variety, and while these, up to the present time, have been little used as furnace fuels, it is certain that the general estimate of their value in this connection is a mistaken one, and that by proper management they can be so used as to accomplish all the purposes of the furnace coals, so called. In the Old World, three-fourths of the iron produced is manufactured with coking coals; and it is only necessary that the processes followed there should be adopted here to insure an equally good result, except so far as affected by the difference in the price of labor. To investigate the peculiarities of the different seams of coal included in this class, and prescribe the best method to be pursued in their use, is a great and important duty to be performed by this or some other Geological Board, and one that will add millions annually to the revenues of our people. In order to show how important this work is, I will only refer to the manufacture of iron in our south-eastern counties, until recently the most important centre of iron industry in the State. Here there is an abundance of excellent ore, and forty furnaces that have been for years using charcoal for its reduction. But the supply of fuel afforded by the forest growth of a country is comparatively small, and it has there been already to a large extent exhausted. Now this region abounds in coal, though mostly of the coking variety, and it is evident that its prosperity and progress will hinge upon the intelligent adaptation of the coals found there to the purposes heretofore served by charcoal. If the mineral fuel of this portion of the State can be successfully employed in the reduction of its ores, the iron manufacture may be expanded to an indefinite extent; without this, it must not only cease to advance, but diminish.

Already an exhaustive investigation into the properties and adaptations of the different Ohio coals, has been begun by the Geological Corps. This should be continued until every owner of coal lands, in every county in the coal area, shall know with accuracy how much and what kind of coal he possesses, for what it is fit, how much it is worth, how it can be worked, and where it is to be marketed. It is not too much to expect, that, when this investigation shall have been completed, the industries of the State will be sensibly affected and very much expanded by it.

IRON.

While it is true that coal is, as we have called it, the main-spring of modern civilization, it is also true that much of its value depends upon its association with iron. In the few words I have devoted to our coal deposits, I have done nothing like justice to their richness and value; and while Ohio cannot boast of an equal endownment in iron, it may at least be said that she has fully her share of this element of wealth. In most countries certain varieties of iron ore are found associated with coal—blackband, clay-iron-stone, &c.—and in these ores Ohio is far richer than any of those States that share with her our great Alleghany coal basin. Again, our coal field is so situated, and the coal it furnishes is of such quality, that a large part of the richer crystalline ore found in other States must inevitably be brought to our territory to be smelted and manufactured.

In order that the conditions under which the production of iron is now, and is hereafter to be, carried on in Ohio, may be better understood, I will devote a few words to a description of the different varieties of iron ore found in our country, and their relation to the fuel with which they are to be smelted.

The richest of all the ores of iron is the "Magnetic oxide," which contains, when pure, 72.4 per cent. metallic iron, and 2.76 oxygen. It consists of the protoxide and sesquioxide combined, and may be recognized by its black powder and its magnetic property. This variety of ore is found in great abundance in the crystalline rocks of the Alleghany belt, in the Adirondacks, and in Canada. It is the ore brought to us under the name of the Champlain ore—from the fact of its occurrence on the shores of Lake Champlain—and is that mined so extensively in southern New York, New Jersey, and further south along the same line. From its abundance in the localities I have cited and its proximity to the anthracite coal of Pennsylvania, this ore has formed the basis of a very large manufacture in the Eastern States, and has furnished more of the iron produced in this country than any other single variety.

As found in Canada and along the Alleghanies, the magnetic ores are extremely prone to contain certain impurities, which injuriously affect the metal produced from them. These are principally phosphorous in phosphate of lime, and sulphur in the form of sulphide, or iron pyrites. Of these the phosphorous renders the iron "cold short," or brittle when cold; and the sulphur "red short," or tender at a red heat. Many of these ores contain also a large percentage of titanium, by which they are rendered refractory, and the iron made brittle. These defects in the eastern magnetic ores almost preclude their use for the finer qualities of iron and steel, and yet they are destined to form an important element in the manufacture of iron in Ohio. Iron making is, in one aspect, much like oil painting, for, as the painter gets his finest effects by skillfully blending many tints, so the ironmaker can only obtain his best results by using in the furnace several varieties of ore. The iron ores of Eastern New York and Canada may, by the cheapness of return freights, be delivered within our territory at a price so low that they will continue to be used as they now are, in considerable quantities, by our iron smelters. Some of the Canadian ores can be furnished on the Lake shore, at a very low figure, but these ores are so largely contaminated by sulphur or titanium that they are, at present, but little used. When, however, we shall have introduced the Swedish roasting furnace, which will remove, at little cost, three, and even four, per cent. of sulphur, we may expect these ores to be much more largely imported than they now are.

The ore next in point of richness to the magnetic, is that called "Specular iron," which consists, when pure, entirely of peroxide. This is a crystalline ore, generally having a metallic appearance, and takes its name from the speculum-like reflections from its polished surfaces. When free from foreign matter, this ore contains 60 per cent. of iron, and 40 of oxygen. Most of the Lake Superior ores are of this character, as are also those of the Iron Mountains of Missouri. To us the Lake Superior ores are of immense importance, as will be seen from the fact that at least two-thirds of all the ore mined in the Marquette district are brought to our State, and this ore constitutes the main dependence of all that great group of furnaces which have been constructed in the northern part of the State within the last twenty years. The product of the Lake Superior iron mines for 1868 was 507,813 tons, for 1869, 643,283 tons, and of this at least one-third is supposed to have been smelted with Ohio coal. The Lake Superior ores are almost entirely free from phosphorous, sulphur, arsenic and titanium, the ingredients which so injuriously affect iron ores elsewhere; and the magnetic ores of Michigan, of which the supply is now known to be large, are the purest of which I have any knowledge. From these facts it is evident that the Lake Superior iron ores are peculiarly adapted to the production of all the finer grades of iron and steel; and indeed it is the opinion of our most accomplished metallurgists that the manufacture of steel in future years, so far as this country is concerned, will be based almost exclusively upon these ores.

As I have before stated, the coals of the Alleghany coal field are superior to those of the West; and it is certain that nowhere can an abundant supply of mineral fuel suitable for smelting the Lake Superior ores be so cheaply obtained as in Ohio. Some portion of these ores are now, and will continue to be, smelted with charcoal on the upper peninsula of Michigan, but the supply of this fuel is so limited that it will play but an insignificant part in the iron manufacture of the future.

I have already referred to the iron ores of Missouri. These have become famous through the descriptions published of the magnificent deposits of Iron Mountain, Pilot Knob, Sheppard Mountain, &c. These are specular ores of excellent quality, and are of importance to us, since they are now used to a considerable extent in the southern part of the State, and still larger quantities are destined to be brought to our coals which outcrop on the banks of the Ohio.

The ores which I have enumerated, constitute with our native ores, the main source of supply to our furnaces. I should add, however, to this list one other variety; that which is known as the "fossil ore," a stratified red hematite, found in the Clinton group, and which forms a belt of out-crop extending, with more or less intermission, from Dodge county, Wisconsin, across a portion of Canada, entering New York at Sodus Bay, passing through Oneida county where it has received the name of the "Clinton ore," thence running down, through central Pennsylvania, Virginia and East Tennessee, into Georgia and Alabama. In this latter region it is known as the "Dyestone ore," from the fact that it has been employed by the inhabitants for imparting a reddish-brown tint to cloth. This Clinton ore is an anhydrous peroxide, containing from 40 to 50 per cent. of metallic iron, and generally a notable per centage of phosphorus. Its use in Ohio has depended upon this latter quality, from the fact that it imparts a "cold-shortness" to iron made from it, and is supposed to correct the red-shortness of sulphurous iron.

Within our own territory we have all the varieties of iron that are ever associated with coal, viz: blackband, kidney ore, stratified ore—or as it is called block ore—and, in less abundance, brown hematite, the hydrated peroxide of iron. Of these, the blackband is a bitumous shale, largely impregnated with iron, taking its name from its stratification and black color. In its natural condition it contains from 20 to 33 per cent. of iron, but, by burning off the carbon, it becomes much richer. This ore is found and largely used in Mahoning and Tuscarawas counties, and is known to exist in Columbiana. Sought for by those who know it, it will undoubtedly be discovered in many parts of the State. It smelts with great facility, making very fusible iron, and such as is especially adapted to foundry purposes. The kidney ore—an earthy carbonate of iron—generally forms balls or concretions, lying in the shales of the coal formation. Where these shales have been extensively eroded, the ore is cheaply mined by "stripping;" and was the main dependence of most of our furnaces previous to the introduction of the crystalline ores. The yield of the kidney ore in the furnance will average about 33 per cent., or three tons of ore make one of iron. This ore is found, in greater or less abundance, in every country included with the coal area. The "block" ores of the coal measures vary much in purity and abundance in different localities. They are generally strata of limestone charged with iron. In the southern portion of the State, ore of this character forms a large number of distinct beds, from two to six feet in thickness, and constitutes the principal source of supply of some forty furnaces now in blast in that district.

In certain localities, some of these stratified iron ores near their outcrops are changed from their original condition, have lost their carbonic acid and have been converted into brown hematite. The average richness of the stratified ores may be said to be about the same as that of the kidney ores—namely, 33 per cent. of metallic iron. The iron furnished by some of them is of very superior quality, as is proved by the reputation of the celebrated Hanging Rock iron made from these ores. Probably nowhere in the world are the ores of the coal measures so abundant and so rich and excellent as in the iron district of southern Ohio, to which I have alluded.

THE MANUFACTUBE OF IRON.

We have now considered briefly the principal elements—the coal and the ores—that are to form the basis of the great iron industry, which, in future years, is destined to be developed within our State. It is known to most persons that, with the fuel and ore, limestone is used in large quantity in the smelting furnaces; but, as this material is readily attain able in all localities, it need not now occupy our time. I may say, however, in passing, that a large amount of work needs to be done in our State in the investigation of the composition of our fluxes and their adaptation to the ores we most use. In this part of the iron manufacture our furnace men are working very much in the dark, and it is certain that they can receive important aid.

The ordinary process of reduction of the ore in the blast furnace is so well known that I need not dwell on it in detail. All varieties of iron ore consists of a combination—sometimes exclusively, always mainly—of oxygen and iron. This oxygen, when brought in contact with carbon at a high temperature, unites with it, and passes off as carbonic acid or carbonic oxide, leaving, as a result of this smelting process, cast iron. This is, however, not yet metallic iron, for it contains 4 to 5 per cent. of carbon, and is a carburet of iron; a hard, brittle substance, applicable to a thousand uses in the arts, but not yet malleable. The manufacture of bar iron consists mainly in the removal of this carbon. This change is effected by the agency of the "puddling process" as it is called. In this process the cast iron, or what is termed "pig," is placed in a reverberatory furnace, and there exposed, at a high temperature, to the action of an oxidizing flame. This burns out the carbon and leaves the iron pure, except as it contains a small portion of silicon, sulphur, phosphorus, &c. As the iron in the puddling furnace approaches the malleable condition, it becomes adhesive and pasty, and is worked into balls; these are taken out and passed through the squeezers and rolling-mill, where they become what is called "muck bar." Muck bar ordinarily requires still further refining, so it is cut into convenient lengths, piled, re-heated, re-rolled, and then comes out as "merchant bar." Thus we have cast iron and bar iron; the two forms in which iron is most largely used by civilized man. This peculiar and protean metal is capable, however, of assuming still another condition, in which it supplies certain of our wants much more perfectly than do either of the forms before mentioned. This we call steel; and steel differs from malleable iron only in containing from one-half to one and a half—say on an average one—per cent. of carbon. This carbon, though so minute in quantity, imparts to it peculiar properties, rendering it capable of being cast like pig iron, without the loss of its malleability, and also communicates to it the all-important property of temper, by which its hardness is immensely increased, and it is fitted for many uses that no other material known to us can serve.

The facts which I have detailed are known to most men at all educated in the iron manufacture. Hence, it may seem that this branch of industry is so simple and has been carried to such perfection that science can throw no new light upon it. And yet, as a matter of fact, there is scarce any art practiced by our people so eminently progressive, and so far from having reached perfection as this one. Indeed, our most intelligent furnace men have said to me, that there is no department of its work in which the Geological Survey is capable of being more useful to the people of Ohio, than by the assistance it can render to our iron manufacturers in improving their process.

To show the rapid changes that are taking place in the manufacture of iron, I will allude to one or two of the more important improvements that have been made in it within the last few years.

Nearly all the iron used in the world, at the present time, is manufactured with mineral fuel, and yet if reference be made to the first report, published by the former Geological Board—a little more than thirty years ago—it will be seen that the use of raw coal as a furnace fuel was then announced as a new and wonderful discovery; and the first employment of mineral fuel in Ohio dates from a period considerably subsequent to that. The old charcoal furnaces were thought to do well when they gave a yield of from thirty to fifty tons per week. Now there are several furnaces in Ohio, each of which produces three hundred tons of pig in the same time, and some of the English furnaces are producing six hundred tons per week.

Much of the improvement in our furnaces has been made within the last five or six years, and has consisted in increasing their dimensions, viz: the diameter, from ten to sixteen feet, and the height, from forty to sixty feet, by adding to the force and temperature of the blast, by close top, &c. These improvements, so potent in their influence on the productiveness of the furnaces are, however, not yet introduced by half of the furnace men in our State. By most of them, therefore, these steps of progress are to be made.

Even our best furnaces are still behind the age, as in their productiveness and economy they come far short of what is accomplished elsewhere, and what is attainable here. For example: the average consumption of our Briar Hill coal is two and a half tons to one of iron. At Massilon, three and a half to four tons of coal are used to make a ton of iron. In contrast with these figures, in the Cleveland district, in England, where coke is used, no better than some of our own, the furnace stacks are carried to a height of one hundred, and in some instances one hundred and two feet, and in them less than one ton of coke makes a ton of iron. With the resources at our command, and the ingenuity for which our people are celebrated, I think we may be sure that we shall not long remain satisfied while such comparisons can be made. It is very certain that we have not yet reached perfection in the combination of our ores, in the choice of our fluxes, in the adaptation of our fuels, nor in the dimensions and models of our furnaces. The advantages which the foreign manufacturer possesses consists of improved processes, cheaper labor, and greater capital. To balance these advantages, we have better and more varied materials, three thousand miles less transportation, and a high tariff. By the aid of these, our furnace men, with little capital, dear labor, and wasteful methods, are able to maintain themselves in the competition, and are prospering. The time is not distant, however, when the protection to our industry afforded by our present tariff will be removed. I don't say it should be, for I don't believe it should, but simply that it will. For this impending storm our iron men must trim their sails. All the light of foreign experience must be thrown on our processes, while the problems presented by the ores, fuels and fluxes of each locality are to be carefully worked out, and capital concentrated so that our furnaces may consist of several stacks, carried on by one set of machinery, and one set of officials instead of several, thus simplifying and cheapening all branches of the art. When this shall be done, whatever political wind may blow, our iron industry will be always prosperous, ever expanding, and our greatest source of wealth.

THE ELLERSHAUSEN PROCESS.

In the manufacture of bar-iron and steel, the evidences of progress is still greater than in the art of reducing the ore, and it is not impossible that our present methods of manufacture, in five years from this time, will be entirely revolutionized. In the manufacture of bar-iron, the most striking invention that has been introduced of late years, is that of the Ellershausen Process. This is due to a man by the name of Ellershausen, who was a lumber merchant in Canada. When he had nearly stripped his timber lands, and had acquired a fortune in so doing, his attention was attracted to the ledges of iron ore which his property contained, and abandoning the lumber trade, he went into the manufacture of iron. The ore he used, like so much of the Canadian ore, proved to be impure, and the enterprise was unfortunate and entailed the sacrifice of the fortune he had acquired. In his efforts to surmount the difficulties he encountered, Ellershausen thought and read widely on the subject of iron-making, and ultimately he devised a method by which, as he thought, the ordinary process would be greatly shortened. Going to New York with his plan, he there met with little encouragement, and thence turned his steps to Pittsburgh, the greatest centre of iron industry in the country. Here he fell in with my friend, T. S. Blair, of the firm of J. H. Shœnberger & Blair, one of the most intelligent and thoroughly-educated of our iron men. By him Ellershausen was given the opportunity to test his method, and the ultimate success he attained is due, in no small part, to the suggestions he received from Mr. Blair.

The Ellershausen process may be explained in very few words. We have seen that pig-iron consists of pure metallic iron, with four to five per cent. of carbon, while the richer iron ores consist mainly of iron and oxygen. Ellershausen's theory was that iron ore could be mingled with cast iron in such a way that the oxygen of the ore would unite with the carbon of the pig metal, and, passing off as carbonic oxide, leave the iron of both elements in the combination in the metallic state. The experiment was first tried by drawing a ladle of molten iron from the fur nace, and stirring into it a quantity of iron ore. The change anticipated began at once, and the iron assumed a pasty condition, which rendered it impossible to stir it with a bar. Substituting a wooden rod, the materials were mingled and were made to form a ball similar to that collected in the puddling furnace by the rabble. This ball heated, squeezed and rolled, was found to furnish a fair article of bar-iron. Subsequently there was substituted for the ladle a wheel, eighteen feet in diameter, bearing on its margin a series of boxes. This wheel was made to revolve beneath a stream of molten iron and pulverized ore that crossed each other at right angles. By the rotation of the wheel the boxes were gradually filled with layers of iron mixed with ore. When each contained a sufficient quantity the sides were removed and the blooms transferred to the puddling furnaces, these reheated until the slag they contain was "sweated" out, then squeezed and rolled into bars. These bars, without piling or re-rolling, are found to exhibit all the properties of first class iron. The Ellershausen process has now been in operation for a year in the establishments of J. H. Shœnberger & Co., and Lyon, Shorb & Co., in Pittsburg, where it may be witnessed by any who have a desire to investigate it.

Many other methods besides that of Ellershausen, have been devised for cheapening the cost of bar-iron; consisting for the most part in efforts to reduce the time and expense of the laborious and costly process of puddling, as now practiced. Several of these methods promise well and deserve investigation, but I will only refer to a single one, the "Mechanical rabble," a device for performing the ordinary work of a puddler by machinery. This is now practiced in several foreign establishments, and if it could be made generally successful, would be much more valuable in America than in Europe, as labor is so much dearer here than there. After all, it seems to me we should look for the greatest improvement in the manufacture of bar-iron, in a complete change of the process followed. All these to which I have alluded have been based upon a supposed necessity of first reducing the ore to the form of pig-iron, and then, by a second manipulation, obtaining malleable iron from this by eliminating the four or five per cent. of carbon which cast iron contains. But it is possible to produce malleable iron direct from the ore. This is called, by metallurgists, the "direct process," because it follows a direct line and avoids the roundabout through the blast furnace. This is the method practiced in what is called the Catalan Forge; and many thousand tons of iron are annually manufactured by this forge in America and elsewhere, but by no plan yet devised, has iron been made more cheaply by this direct way than by the other. It is, however, by no means certain that the limit of possibility in this direction has been reached; but, on the contrary, it is confidently believed, by some metallurgists, that not many years will elapse till all our bar-iron is manufactured by some direct process. The ground of this confidence is the peculiar property that carbonic oxide has of reducing the oxide of iron at a comparatively low temperature. If we put a few grains of pulverized iron ore with some carbonaceous substance, in a test tube, and heat this over a spirit lamp to a red heat—1000° or 1200°—the ore is immediately decomposed, its oxygen uniting with the carbon, and grains of metallic iron become visible. This is the theory of the Renton process, the process of Dr. Smith, and what is known as Chenot's process, but up to the present time all these methods have been practically unsuccessful, from a difficulty in regulating the temperature; for it is a remarkable fact that when the temperature is raised above 1400° fusion begins, silicates are formed, and the mass is agglutinated together in such a way as to be unmanageable, while the access of the gas to the ore is prevented. Several eminent metallurgists are, however, at work on this problem, and it seems to me that their efforts must ultimately be crowned with success. I need not dwell upon the benefits that would accrue to society and civilization by a diminution of say one-half in the cost of production of bar-iron. So great would be this benefit that there is hardly a family in any civilized community who would not sensibly feel it. As we have seen the great improvements that have taken place within the last twenty years in the manufacture of cast iron have cheapened this material to half its former cost. On the other hand, the Bessemer process has reduced the price of steel in an equal degree, and now the cheapening of bar-iron has become the great metallurgic desideratum. It would be very strange if when the inventive faculty of our people, combined with the experience of the world, are brought fully to bear upon the problem that its successful solution should not be reached.

THE MANUFACTURE OF STEEL.

THE BESSEMER PROCESS.

Perhaps the best illustration of the progressive character of the iron manufacture is furnished by recent improvements in the manufacture of steel. It will be remembered that steel is iron with one per cent. of carbon, or cast iron from which three-fourths of the carbon have been removed. Fifteen years ago all our steel was made by what is called the "cementation process," so well known that I need not describe it. About this time Mr. Bessemer, an English iron-master, conceived the plan of forcing common air into melted pig-iron, and thus, by bringing its oxygen in contact with the carbon, to induce the formation of carbonic acid, eliminate the carbon and produce malleable iron; or, by arresting the process at a certain point, to leave the fluid metal in the condition of cast steel. Upon trial the injection of even cold air into molten iron, instead of chilling it, as many predicted, produced active ignition and intense heat. This was the germ of the famous Bessemer process for the manufacture of steel, a process by which fully one-half of the steel now made is produced, and by which, as has been stated, the cost of steel has been reduced at least one-half. Many years elapsed before Mr. Bessemer succeeded in overcoming all the mechanical difficulties which stood in his way, and in silencing the opposition which the conservatism of the iron manufacture offered. Now the process may be said to be not only a success, but a triumph; and its author deserves to be regarded as one of the greatest benefactors of the human race. For the production of steel, Mr. Bessemer first proposed to arrest the combustion of the carbon in the iron so as to leave about one per cent. unconsumed. This point was found difficult to hit, and he ultimately adopted the method of adding, after the process was complete, the requisite quantity of carbon in the form of *spiegeleisen*, a highly carbonized cast iron. This is the course now generally adopted; and steel is being thus made in large quantities, not only in Europe, but in our own country and our own State. A very complete establishment for the manufacture of Bessemer steel has been erected by Messrs. Stone, Chisholm & Jones of Cleveland, and there this interesting and important improvement in iron making may be at any time seen in successful operation.

The objection has been made to the Bessemer process that it contained too many elements of uncertainty, that it failed to give constant and uniform results. This objection has, however, been removed by a very simple method—suggested by my friend, Dr. Schmidt, and now constantly practiced at the Troy Steel Works—of dipping out and testing a sample from each five-ton charge, then adding carbon or oxygen as necessary.

THE SIEMENS-MARTIN PROCESS.

This process, invented and largely employed in France, has lately been introduced into this country by Messrs. Cooper & Hewitt, at Trenton, N. J., and has proved here, as abroad, an entire success. It consists in melting down, in a Siemen's furnace, a quantity of pig iron, then adding to this sufficient malleable iron to dilute the carbon in the mass to any desired percentage, and thus produce any required grade of steel. The point aimed at is reached invariably by testing, from time to time, the quality of the metal, and adding pig iron or bar iron as required. This is a simple and perfectly manageable method of producing steel, but it is doubtful if it can rival in simplicity and cheapness the process of Mr. Bessemer.

The two modes of steel making which I have briefly described are capable of producing, at a price scarcely greater than that of bar iron, steel adapted to all the coarser purposes for which steel is used; and it is by one or the other, or, what is better still, both combined (one using up the other's scrap) that all the steel rails, now so largely substituted for iron, are made. But for all the finer grades of steel—that used for cutlery, &c.—we are still compelled to depend upon the old and expensive process of cementation. There seems to me, however, to be a strong probability that improved and cheaper processes will also soon supply us with our finer steels.

THE BARRON PROCESS.

This is a new method, and one perhaps not yet beyond the condition of an experiment, but it has at least sufficed for the production of steel of as fine a quality as has ever been made by any other means. The whole process consists in exposing malleable iron to the action of gaseous hydro-carbons at a temperature just below that of fusion. Under these circumstances the iron rapidly and regularly absorbs the carbon of the gas, and becomes steel. By the Barron process, shapes of iron are converted into steel without change of form, and this is the most satisfactory application of it I have seen. For example: tools or implements of any kind may be moulded and cast, these shapes made malleable by the ordinary process, and then, by impregnation, converted into steal, coming out as scissors, knives, axes, or other implements of the very best quality, with no forging whatever. Whether this method is capable of effecting, cheaply the conversion of large masses of iron, is not yet demonstrated, though it is claimed; but from the fact that a piece of iron may by this means be covered with a sheet of enamel, or coated with a layer of any desired thickness of steel, while yet retaining all the toughness of its iron core, and that by a coating of clay, the absorption of carbon may be limited to any portion of the surface acted upon, it is evident that this method is destined to have extensive application in the arts.

The quality of steel made by this process is such as leaves nothing to be desired. With tailors' sheers, cast in form, made malleable, and then converted by the Barron process, I have cut Florence silk so nicely as to prove the edge perfect; then with these same shears have cut up sheets of tin and untempered steel; returning to the silk have found the edge wholly unimpaired, and this after a repetition of the trial more than twenty times.

There are various other methods of manufacturing steel, which, if I had unlimited space, it might be well to allude to; but I have already said enough upon this subject to show what activity and progress there is in the improvement of the methods of manufacturing iron, and I have been led to dwell upon the subject, perhaps even now longer than was in good taste, carried away by my sense of the immense importance this industry is to assume in our State, when our resources are properly investigated and brought into use.

SALT, OILS, CLAYS, ETC.

There are many other mineral staples found in our State, to which, did time permit, I should be glad to call attention, citing the proofs we have gained of their existence, their promise as regards quality and quantity, and the investigations proposed for determining their abundance and value. But I have already passed the limits I had assigned myself. Within a few months a fuller report of our work will be published, and in that report will be given the details of such matters as are referred to now, as well as much information of interest in regard to some subjects not here alluded to. I have, in the preceding pages, attempted nothing more than an outline sketch of the duty assigned to the Geological Corps, and what has been done toward its performance. In order that this may be more clearly understood, I will very briefly recapitulate the work accomplished by the survey during the last summer and fall, and state what is our plan of operations for the future.

In many instances it has happened that the first season's work of a Geological Survey has been mainly consumed in organization and preparation for the future. I think I have shown that we have accomplished something more than this. In addition to our organization, we have made a general, and, for the most part, thorough investigation of the geological structure of the State; have studied each of the formations found in our geological series, and have determined the relative position, age, thickness and lithological characters of each; have settled the doubts that have long hung over some of them; have added to the list several not before known to exist here, and have marked the areas occupied by the surface exposures of each on a geological map. This map has been made altogether from new and original observations, and may be accepted as far more minute and accurate than any geological map of Ohio before published.

More careful studies have been made of certain districts: as that of the Straitsville coal-field, by Prof. Andrews; of Greene and Montgomery counties, by Prof. Orton; of Cuyahoga and Erie counties, by myself; thus beginning the detail work of the survey, which it is proposed to carry through all the counties and townships of the State. We have also made a good beginning on our Economic Geology. Prof. Wormley, our chemist, has made a large number of very carefully conducted analyses of our coals, iron ores and limestones, earning many times over the small sum that we were able to appropriate to his department. I have also had made, at my own cost, a still larger number of analyses, and have had a dozen different varieties of hydraulic limestones not only analyzed but practically tested by special apparatus which Gen. Gilmore was kind enough to loan me for the purpose. These investigations have been carried far enough to enable us to compare nearly all the varieties of lime used in the State, and to deduce from this comparison some conclusions which will have a practical value to all our architects and builders. Most of our building stones have also been examined, the composition and strength of some of them determined, and nicely dressed blocks of each placed in the State collection. Many of our clays have been collected, and investigations begun for the determination of their composition and their adaptation to the manufacture of pottery, fire-brick, common brick, &c. Already a great industry is based upon this material in our State—one that is capable of indefinite expansion, and one that especially needs the aid which applied science can afford it. In the article of fire brick alone, an immense gain would be secured to our furnace-men by supplying them (as they may readily be supplied) with a good article of home manufacture at half the cost of the imported. The Amboy brick cost us $65 a thousand, and Mr. Alexander, of Akron, has demonstrated that an equally refractory brick can be made and sold here for $35. The imported Dinas brick cost in this country $100 a thousand; we can make in Ohio an equally good brick for less than $50.

The conditions of the iron manufacture in northern Ohio have been investigated with considerable care. All the furnaces in that region have been visited, and, in most instances, plans of the works, statistics of production, and suits of raw and manufactured materials have been obtained. I have already alluded to the evidence furnished by these investigations, of the necessity and possibility of improving this branch of industry. In another year it is proposed to carry this line of inquiries still further, and to extend the investigation to other parts of the State, where there is a still more important work for us to do.

A State Cabinet has been not only begun, but has grown until it has filled the room assigned to it in the State House. Over fifty boxes of rocks, fossils, ores, coals, clays, oils, building stones, &c., have been unpacked there, and in the series of specimens are duplicates for our colleges.

In our examination of the geology of the State, large numbers of fossils have been found, many of which are new, and some are of unusual scientific interest. Of these, with others in my possession before, drawings have been made sufficient to form fifty plates; these have been made without expense to the State, and are included in the material already submitted as our first report.

And now a word in regard to our future, and I shall have done. Should the Geological Survey be continued under its present management, the investigations now begun will be extended until they shall have covered all our area, and have embraced the agricultural capabilities, the geological structure in all its details, and all the mineral staples; determining their quality, quantity, distribution and adaptation. It is also hoped that, without any considerable expense to the State, experts in these departments shall give us fuller information than is now possessed by our people in regard to our plants and animals. My judgment is that all this information should be made as concise and practical as possible; should be published in volumes of modest dimensions and moderate cost, so as to be brought within the reach of all those who can make intelligent use of them; that they should be made of such a character as to be of real utility to our people, and of greater value to those who pay for them than to residents in other countries. My idea of a geological report is, that it shall be an embodiment of all the important facts in natural or applied science that immediately concern the inhabitants of the area it covers, so that it may be a book of constant reference to the manufacturer, the mechanic, the architect, the farmer, the teacher, the parent; one that may always be at hand to answer any question that may be asked in regard to geological structure, economic minerals, fossils, plants or animals. The investigations necessary to prepare such a report will require time and money; but most the nations of the Old World, and many of our sister States, have expended sums for such purposes which, if well directed, would more than serve our purpose. I can hardly think that Ohio, third in the Union, as she is, in wealth and population, and so rich in undeveloped resources, will rest satisfied with anything short of a full and thorough exposition of her gifts; such an one, in fact, as her pride and interest alike dictate.

Not having an opportunity of reading the proof of this report, I find in it many typographical errors. Such as have been noticed are indicated in the following table.

J. S. N.

ERRATA.

Page 5.	Line 38,	for "analysis, read "analyses."
" 11.	" 15,	for "elephants," read "elephant."
" 11.	" 15,	for "mastadon," read "mastodon."
" 11.	" 29,	for "or," read "and."
" 19.	" 29,	for "corniferous," read "coniferous."
" 23	" 31,	for "Permain," read "Permian."
" 24.	" 42,	for "old," read "oil."
" 24.	" 42,	for "Bottewell," read "Bothwell."
" 25.	" 5,	for "Chalsworth," read "Chatsworth."
" 25.	" 9,	for "then," read "there."
" 25.	" 12,	for "Prof. J.," read "Prof. F."
" 26.	" 16,	for "their," read "thin."
" 26.	" 17,	for "corniferous,,' read "coniferous."
" 26.	" 25,	for "then," read "there."
" 26.	" 34,	for "pounded," read "rounded."
" 26	" 38,	for "Eozoric," read "Eozoic."
" 27.	" 29,	for "causes," read "courses."
" 28.	" 9,	for "face," read "far."
" 29.	" 29,	for "in," read "on."
" 29.	" 32,	for "corniferous," read "coniferous."
" 30.	" 12,	for "Klamoth," read "Klamath."
" 31.	" 2,	for "elephants," read "elephant."
" 31.	" 3,	for "rhinoceras," read "rhinoceros."
" 31.	" 3,	supply "animals," after "carnivorous."
" 31.	" 9,	for "falls," read "fall."
" 32.	" 4,	for "usual," read "useful."
" 33.	" 18,	for "has," read "have."
" 39.	" 36,	for "60," read "70."
" 39.	" 37,	for "40," read "30."

PART II.

REPORT OF PROGRESS IN THE SECOND DISTRICT,

BY PROF. E. B. ANDREWS,

ASSIST. GEOLOGIST.

REPORT OF THE GEOLOGICAL SURVEY OF OHIO.

SECOND DISTRICT.

To PROF. JOHN S. NEWBERRY, *Chief Geologist of Ohio:*

SIR: In the organization of the Survey, the Second District was assigned to me. This District has for its northern boundary the line of the Central Ohio Railroad; for its eastern and southern, the Ohio river; for its western, the western limits of the Great Black Slate, extending from Columbus to a point on the Ohio river a few miles above Rome, in Adams county. Nearly twenty-three counties are included within these limits.

I entered at once upon my work. I have had for assistants William G. Ballantine, A. B., a graduate of Marietta College; Roland D. Irving, of New Brighton, Staten Island, N. Y., a graduate of the School of Mines Columbia College, New York City, and Wm. Ward, of Marietta. Each rendered valuable service. Mr. Ward continued with me about two months, and rendered me much aid. Mr. Irving remained with me until about the 1st of September. His labors were of great service, especially in working out the sections of the Black Slate and Waverly sand-stone, along the Ohio river, in Adams and Scioto counties. These labors, and those of Mr. Ward, were none the less efficient, nor less cheerfully given, for being entirely gratuitous, the State only paying their necessary traveling expenses. Mr. Ballantine received a small remuneration. He remained with me until after the middle of November. A large number of the sections taken in Perry county and portions of other adjacent counties were the product of his indefatigable and skillful labor.

GENERAL FEATURES OF THE SECOND DISTRICT.

The surface is generally hilly. The only exception to this is in the northwestern part of the District, where, in Franklin and Pickaway, and portions of Fairfield and Licking counties, most of the surface is comparatively level and smooth.

The whole district slopes to the south and southeast, and consequently the drainage is to the Ohio river.

The Ohio river flows in a long, trough-like depression, made, doubtless, at the time of the uplifting of the Alleghany mountains. This was subsequent to the formation of the coal measure rocks, as these are lifted up, and form the summit of the mountains in portions of Pennsylvania and

---

NOTE.—The delay of this report is due to the Engraver of the Sections. The author had no opportunity to see the proofs and correct the mistakes.

West Virginia. The Ohio basin does not show a uniform slope towards its centre downward in the direction of its major axis. It is undulating, and often exhibits areas of considerable extent, with a northern slope and drainage. In West Virginia, the Monongahela flows northward to meet the Alleghany at Pittsburg. In the Second District, I find small areas with a similar slope and drainage. Several of the smaller tributaries of the Muskingum river flow in a northerly direction. The principal rivers in the District are the Muskingum, Scioto and Hocking, all flowing into the Ohio river. Between the Scioto and the Hocking are several smaller streams, the Little Scioto, Pine creek, Symmes' creek, Indian Guyandotte creek, Raccoon creek, Leading creek, and Shade river, all emptying into the Ohio. Between the Hocking and Muskingum is the Little Hocking. Above the Muskingum, the principal tributaries of the Ohio are Duck creek, Little Muskingum river, Sunfish and Captina creeks. The Little Muskingum river flows, during its entire course, in a basin parallel to the Ohio river, and only eight or ten miles from it. The Indian Guyandotte creek flows in a basin similarly parallel to the Ohio.

In the northern part of the district there is a pretty large area, with a northwestern slope. This area is drained by Wills' creek, which flows northward through Noble and Guernsey counties, and then westward and empties into the Muskingum river above Dresden, near the north line of Muskingum county.

The south fork of the Moxahala creek drains a considerable valley which slopes to the north. This fork rises in the high lands between Oakfield and Bristol, in the southern part of Perry county, and flows northward for twenty miles. The Moxahala empties into the Muskingum two or three miles below Zanesville. The south fork of the Licking river flows to the northeast. Wolf creek, which rises in the northern part of Morgan county, flows in a valley which shows a remarkable parallelism with that of the Muskingum. It maintains an average distance of five or six miles from the Muskingum for twenty miles, and then, as the Muskingum turns and flows northward, in Windsor township, Morgan county, it also bends to the north and northeast in Wesley and Palmer townships, Washington county, and enters the former near Beverly, in Waterford township, in the same county. The south fork of Wolf creek rises within two or three miles of the Ohio river, in Warren township, Washington county, and flows to the northward. Nearly all of the western part of Washington county is drained by that creek, and consequently slopes to the north. These facts are of great significance as showing original undulations of the surface, before the present work of drainage began. How far the underlying strata show corresponding undulations will hereafter be determined as the different parts of the District are studied in detail. Very limited observations made in the valley of the Moxahala appear to indicate that in portions of the valley, at least, the dip of the rocks is conformable to the original northern slope of the surface.

It is an interesting fact that the Muskingum river, which drains no inconsiderable part of Eastern Ohio, has its bed during its whole course above the level of Lake Erie. The height of the surface of Lake Erie, at Cleveland, above tide water, as given by Col. Charles Whittlesey, is 564 feet, while the elevation of the mouth of the Muskingum is 571 feet, as given by Col. Charles Ellet, Jr., in his contributions to the Physical Geography of the Mississippi Valley, published by the Smithsonian Institution. This makes the mouth of the river 7 feet above the average level of Lake Erie. This is probably 4 or 5 feet too great.

The mouth of the Scioto is 90 feet below the level of the Lake, while the Ohio river, at Wheeling, W. Va., at low water, is 56 feet above. Thus it will be seen that the plane of the surface of Lake Erie, if continued, will pass below the surface of nearly the whole area included in the Second District.

Col. Ellet gives the fall of the Scioto, from Columbus to Portsmouth, to be 302 feet. This river would therefore pass below the level of the surface of the Lake at a point 27.8 miles above Portsmouth. This supposes, however, that the fall of the river is uniform throughout its course. The Muskingum river, according to Col. Ellet, falls between Zanesville and its mouth, at Marietta, 104 feet. This makes that river, at Zanesville, about 111 feet above the level of the Lake. The Scioto, at Columbus, is 212 feet above the level of the Lake, or 101 feet above the Muskingum, at Zanesville.

The valleys of all the principal streams in the District are generally deep and well defined, and the work of aqueous erosion has been immense. The immediate valley of the Scioto is the broadest, as it is the most fertile; and next to this, in width and fertility, is that of the Muskingum. All the streams have innumerable small tributaries, which have cut for themselves deep channels. A correct topographical map of Southeastern Ohio would present the peculiar and beautiful dendritic aspect belonging to all regions where the valleys are eroded and the drainage rapid. The erosion has been entirely produced by the flow of waters which have fallen upon the surface of the State, the only exception to this in the Second District being in the more level region in the northwestern part, where doubtless there have been at work, in the remote past, erosive agencies which have acted on a vast horizontal scale. As, in the course of ages, the Ohio deepened its bed, the largest affluents felt the effects of the increased declivity, and increased the depth of their channels, and with this came the gradual deepening of all their smaller tributaries. Hence, with ample time given for the work, we should expect to find what we now see—the whole District completely eroded into a vast and wonderful system of ramifying valleys. The hills and ridges are simply the remnants of what were once continuous rock strata. In many sections, the ever-toiling water, in rain drops, and streamlets and rivers, has sculptured the hills in rounded and graceful forms, while in others, the streams have cut for themselves channels with almost perpendicular sides, giving to the scenery a bold mural character. The latter characteristics are more often seen where the streams flow over the heavy sand-rock strata. Between Lancaster and Logan, the Hocking river flows in a valley, bordered by high cliffs. Some of the tributaries have eroded channels so deep and narrow that they may be properly termed canons. The Licking river has excavated a similar channel in the vicinity of Black Hand. In many places we find a cliff on one side, and rounded hills on the other. This is well seen on the Marietta and Cincinnati railroad, in the vicinity of the Cincinnati Furnace, in Vinton county.

In many sections we find the hills beautifully terraced. This is due to the different degrees of hardness in the strata. Shales are more easily disintegraded and removed than harder rocks, and the latter consequently show a more perpendicular front. Sometimes a highly soluble limestone dissolves away, leaving harder rocks in bolder front above. These terraces are often of great assistance to the geologist in enabling him to see at a glance the range of certain strata along the sides of distant hills.

DRIFT.

After the valleys were eroded as they now exist, many of them were filled with what is geologically termed "drift" materials, which are chiefly waterworn pebbles and bowlders, sand, and sometimes clays. The principal outspread of the drift is in the northwestern part of the district, in the Scioto Valley, and near the sources of the Hocking and Licking Rivers. In this region, the surface of the earth is almost wholly covered with superficial deposits brought from the north. Some of the materials are not found in place within the State, but come from beyond the lakes. Limestone bowlders and gravel show, from their contained fossils and lithological character, that they originally came from the Corniferous limestone, a formation well developed in the northern part of the State. All the streams which have their sources within the great drift region of the central and northern portion of the State, have carried down more or less of the drift materials, and deposited them in vast sandbars and sandy flats. These now constitute the well known terraces of the Scioto, Hocking and Muskingum rivers. The Ohio river is also bordered by these terraces, the materials having been largely brought to it by its northern affluents. The tributaries to the Ohio from the south, as the Little and Great Kanawhas, have no such terraces. The same is true of all the smaller Ohio tributaries, such as Raccoon, Little Muskingum and Duck creek, which do not have their heads in the central drift region.

In the terraced drift we find two classes of materials—the hard and the comparatively soft. The former is composed of diorytes and other granitoid forms, quartzites and other metamorphic rocks, and the cherty portions of limestones. The latter is made up of softer sandstones, slates and bituminous coals. I have found small bowlders of fine grained Waverly sandstones, which for fineness of texture, and softness under the chisel, and perfection of color, I have never seen surpassed. Their original home was in the Waverly formation, and not very far to the north; for such is the softness of the material, that they could not long have survived the friction of rolling in currents of water, surrounded by harder bowlders, much less the more wasting friction of propulsion by glaciers, under enormous ice-pressure. We sometimes find similar soft material only very slightly eroded.

In the large terrace formed at the confluence of the Muskingum and Ohio rivers, on which the town of Marietta is built, we often find large quantities of pebbles of bituminous coal. Bushels could sometimes be taken from a single spot, of all sizes, from four inches in diameter downward. Bituminous coal being soft and easily eroded, the coal of these pebbles must have been torn from its native seam at some point in our Ohio coal measures but a short distance up the Muskingum, probably not above Zanesville. It has been estimated that lumps of coal of medium size, dropped into the Ohio River from steamboats and barges, are worn away to nothing in rolling on the bottom, a distance of from fifty to one hundred miles. Pebbles and bowlders of Ohio coal measure sandstone are also often found in the drift terraces on the Muskingum. It will be remembered that this river holds its course chiefly within the limits of the coal formation.

No careful instrumental surveys of the altitude of the terraces above the streams has as yet been made, but they probably range from 40 to 80 feet above the present average level of the waters. The terraced drift is never found far up any of the tributaries of the streams which have carried down the materials. It is sometimes crowded a short distance into the mouths of tributaries. We sometimes, however, find the drift some distance from the present channels of the rivers, and back of the immediate river hills; but in all the cases of the kind I have examined, the drift is in old channels, or in new ones formed at the time by very high water. An example of this may be seen in the so called "plains" between Salina and Athens, in Athens county. Here an old channel, west of the Hocking river hills, was entirely choked up by the drift. Another and less marked exhibition of this is at Newport, Washington county, on the Ohio river. While the materials of the drift terraces are more often gravels and sand, we find sometimes layers of fine clay. A layer of fine blue clay is found in the terrace at Marietta. This was a fine sedimentary deposit from quiet water. From the location of this clay, it might have been dropped from the still water of an eddy made by the meeting of the two rivers. In the same terrace I have seen a large rounded bowlder of coal measure sandstone, twenty inches in diameter, imbedded in a fine yellow clayey sand. It was as much isolated, so far as other adjacent coarse material is concerned, as a granite bowlder on a western prairie.

The drift in the northwestern part of the District constitutes an almost continuous sheet, covering the whole surface, and in this unbroken condition extends itself for some distance down the valleys of the Scioto and Hocking rivers; but, as the valleys become more narrow, the continuity is broken, and the drift is found only in isolated sandbars and drift plains. At no point in these valleys, nor in that of the Muskingum, do I find any striation of the underlying rocks, such as, in the more northern portions of the State, is attributed to the action of glaciers.

The highest elevation on which I have found drift bowlders is on the summit of Flint Ridge, in Licking county, which is 170 feet above the adjacent valley. To this add 50 feet as the estimated elevation of the base of the ridge above Newark, and we have bowlders 220 feet above Newark, and 374 above Zanesville, and 490 above Marietta, and 729 above Cincinnati. On the hills in Kentucky, in the neighborhood of Ashland, Greenup county, more than one hundred miles south of Flint Ridge, I saw drift bowlders 200 feet above the Ohio river, and, in one of the deep valleys of Scioto, Brush creek, in Adams county, Ohio, I have seen bowlders of Lake Superior rocks, which had evidently been brought over the high ground to the north. This high ground cannot be much less than 700 feet above the Ohio river at Cincinnati. There will doubtless be many similar examples of this kind brought to light during the progress of the survey. How came these bowlders to be thus left upon these high hills? If glaciers had reached such elevations, we should expect to find large accumulations of glacier-worn materials, whereas we find, in fact, only a very few isolated bowlders. More probably they were transported by floating ice, but we are yet to find corroborative proof of the existence of so vast a body of water, filling the Ohio Valley at Cincinnati to the depth of at least 730 feet. Such a body of water must have constituted an arm of a gulf, filling the Valley of the Mississippi. It could have had little current, and contained little sedimentary matter brought in from rivers, since we find neither trace of current action nor deposited sediments. The explanation of our *river terraces* requires the movement of strong currents along our valleys by which the gravel and sand were accumulated in vast sand-bars and flats. Water in the streams from 80 to 100 feet higher than at present would make the terrace. If we should accept the glacier theory to explain the spread of the drift over the central and northern part of the State, then the final melting of a vast body of ice would fill, with torrents, all the streams down the slope to the Ohio river, and these sweeping currents would carry down the materials in the drift terraces. It would appear then, that it is possible to refer the origin of the drift terraces, and the deposit of occasional bowlders on high hills, *to different and very distinct causes.*

The terrace in the olden time presented great attraction to the mound-builder race. We everywhere find on them earthworks, in the form of mounds, elevated squares, walls and ditches. Being dry and sandy, the surface could be easily removed and accumulated in their various structures. To the profound questions of the ethnologist, who the mound-builders were, whence they came, and whither they went, we can only reply that they once lived here, here cultivated the soil, here worshiped, perhaps with the solemn rites of human sacrifice, here planned and executed mighty works of organized labor, and then passed away. We find their temples, and fortresses, and tombs.

The character of the soil of the river terraces and plains depends upon the nature of the materials composing it. In the Scioto valley much of the gravel is of limestone origin, and hence the remarkable fertility of the Pickaway plains and the other terraced benches in that valley. The Hocking valley, below Lancaster, is generally narrow, but the soil of the terrace often contains much of the drift limestone. The Muskingum river terraces contain less limestone gravel, but the soil is generally fertile, and is much esteemed for ease of working and the earliness of its crops.

The coarse gravel of the terraces is much prized as a material for the making of railroads. The Marietta and Cincinnati Railroad Company finds on its line, in Warren township, Washington county, on the Ohio river, a fine body of terrace gravel, which has been largely used as a ballast for the road-bed. After leaving the Ohio river, no more coarse gravel is found until the road enters the valley of the Hocking. Passing the valley no more gravel is reached until the road enters the valley of the Scioto. Railroads located longitudinally within these terraced valleys have rare facilities for making a most perfect road-bed. The Hocking Valley Railroad is thus located, and, although a new road, is one of the smoothest in the State.

OUTLINES OF THE GEOLOGICAL FORMATIONS.

The rocks formed in the 2d District are in ascending order—the Great Black Slate, the Waverly Sandstones, the Conglomerates, and the productive Coal Measures. This is also the order in which they appear in the district, as we pass from the western line eastward. Each of these formations dip to the east and south-east, and they consequently overlie each other as shingles upon a roof.

The general outlines of these several formations have been studied and mapped. In the hilly region in the southern part of the State, it is most difficult to determine the outlines with entire exactness, without much longer time for the work than has yet been at my disposal. The general outlines, however, are given, and more minute details will be added hereafter, as the several counties through which these lines pass are separately studied. As the Ohio river crosses the different formations, careful determinations have been made of the points where most of the formations show themselves on its banks, and dip beneath its bed.

The Conglomerate in my district is very uncertain. It is not often found in its true place, and instead of constituting a uniform and wide-spread floor, on which the coal measures rest, it is found only locally, being deposited where strong currents swept, while in the more quiet waters of the period firmer grained sandstones were accumulated, which I have provisionally called the Logan Sandstones. In the provisional map of the outlines of the formations I have given a more continuous Conglomerate than the facts will probably warrant, rather out of a sort of geological courtesy and reverence for the "traditions of the elders" than any other reason.

THE OHIO BLACK SLATE.

The "Ohio Black Slate" is the lowest formation in the geological series found in the 2d District. It is finely exposed, in Ohio river hills, in the neighborhood of Rockville, Adams county, and in nearly all the hills which range to the north. The upper part of it is well seen in the hills at Chillicothe, underlying the Waverly Sandstone group. It spreads itself across the Scioto valley in its upper part, and is found resting upon the Corniferous limestone in the immediate vicinity of Columbus.

Thickness.—It was carefully measured by the barometer, in the Ohio river hills, near the mouth of Big Sulphur creek, Green township, Adams county, and found to be 320 feet in thickness. Here its limits were distinctly seen, as it rested upon the limestone—the "Cliff Limestone" of Dr. Locke—and upon it reposed the Waverly sandstone. This formation is probably less thick in its northern extension from the Ohio river, although no measurements have been made. Prof. Orton, of the 3d District, who has observed the Black Slate on the waters of Paint creek, west of Chillicothe, thinks the formation considerably thinner in that region than on the Ohio river. Although only half as thick as the Waverly, it often covers as much horizontal surface as the latter, sometimes more. This is because the hills west of the Scioto project it west, and the valley throws it east.

Bitumen.—The black color of this slate is derived from the large amount of bitumen it contains. Prof. Wormley, Chemist of the Geological Survey, reports the volatile matter (bitumen chiefly) as 8.40 per cent. This is nearly one-fourth as much as we find in some bituminous coals. We have, therefore, in the 320 feet of Black Slate, bituminous matter enough to furnish, with the requisite bitumen, a seam of coal nearly 80 feet thick.

The conditions under which this formation was deposited, involved comparatively quiet waters, charged with a constant supply of fine sediment, with which there was at all times commingled organic matter, which alone could have furnished the bitumen. The even distribution of the bitumen throughout the entire mass of the sediments, would imply that the water abounded with the minute forms of vegetable or animal life. Thus far, search for their forms has been unrewarded. After a failure by myself, I placed samples of the slate in the hands of Prof. Wormley, whose skill in microscopic researches is well known, and whose instruments are of the most perfect kind. Thus far his search for distinct organisms has been unsuccessful. It is reasonable to suppose that the organisms contained no silica or lime, and that in their decomposition and bituminization all organic structure was destroyed.

Petroleum.—The Black Slate is an evident source of rock oil or petroleum. It affords oil readily by artificial distillation, but we find abundant evidence that it is distilled naturally. At numerous points we find springs of oil at the top of the slate. Generally they are in the lowest layers of the overlying Waverly sandstone as if the ascending oil (for oil being lighter than water is upward in its tendency), had been intercepted by the sandstone and had flowed out between its more open layers. Such oil springs abound in the western part of Scioto and eastern part of Adams counties. On Churn creek, a branch of Scioto Brush creek, is an oil spring affording a thick, heavy oil from which more or less oil has been gathered in the summer time and used by the citizens for medicinal purposes. This is in the Waverly sandstone, only a few feet above the Black Slate.

On the Rocky fork of Scioto Brush creek is a cluster of oil springs. The largest is called the Hazelbaker Spring, on a little tributary called Oil run. From this spring oil is constantly flowing. It is thick like most spring oil, the more volatile portion having been evaporated through surface exposure. This oil flows out from between layers of the Waverly sandstone only a few feet above the black slate. Around the points of the hills near this spring I found several places where the oil has once flowed out from crevices in the sandrock and become inspissated. The places of outflow had exactly the same stratigraphical position just above the Black Slate. On Bear creek, a tributary of the Scioto river, in Scioto county, we found similar oil springs. Oil springs are found on the Kinnickinnick creek, in Kentucky, in the same geological position. No one, after an examination of the various localities, can doubt that the oil originated in the Black Slate. Other interesting facts tending to verify this conclusion will be given in connection with the description of another black slate desposit found interstratified with the Waverly sandstone.

There are occasionally found interstratified with the layers of slate thin layers of asphaltum. They have a highly resinous lustre. They are, however, very limited in extent, and appear to have spread themselves, as if at one time they had been pressed out of the slate in a viscid condition.

In the Black Slate are often found septaria, or large concretionary forms, which are generally hollow and contain crystalized calcite and often shining globlules of asphaltum. Similar concretions in the Black Slate, near Delaware, contain the remains of fishes of the most remarkable size and form. No search has yet been made for these strange fishes in the Second District, but scales of small ganoid fishes are abundant in the slates, especially in the upper part.

Lingula sub-spatulata, M. and W.: Discina, capax? White, are also found, the Lingula in great abundance. Careful search has been made for other mollusca, but thus far in vain. Near Latham, on Sunfish creek, Pike county, was found a stratum of very hard fire clay 1 ft. 2 in. thick, situated fifty feet above the base of the black slate. This is the only break in the continuity of the slate anywhere observed. It may be only local, but it indicates that for a short time the waters in that region were free from the usual organic matter, while at the same time they dropped an exceedingly fine clay sediment.

Uses of the Black Slate.—Oil is easily distilled from it, but the yield is not large and such distillation will be unprofitable while the earth yields petroleum so bountifully.

The slate, when burnt or pulverized, is said to answer an excellent purpose for roofing when mixed with coal-tar. Capt. James Patterson, of Rockville, has prepared the material and it is said to be useful and durable. The slate is first de-bituminized by heat and afterwards ground into powder to be mixed with the tar. The process of baking the slate has hitherto been done in retorts. Should the slate be found capable of being burnt in open heaps,a great expense would be saved. There is no limit to the supply of slate in the hills.

The slate is also used for covering walks in place of gravel. It rapidly crumbles and covers the walk so compactly as to prevent the growth of grasses. The sulphate of iron from the decomposed sulphuret also tends to kill vegetation. The slate is largely used for this purpose in the cemetery at Chillicothe. In time it will disintegrate and form blue clay.

Vertical Joints.—In the bed of Blue creek, Adams county, vertical joints in the layers of the black slate were well exhibited over a space some 60 yards in length. They were generally parallel and the small pocket compass showed their direction to be N. 32° E. Two miles above Blue creek, another observation gave the same direction, viz: N. 32° E. In a stratum of the slate a little higher, the direction was N. 10° W.

WAVERLY SANDSTONE.

A group of sandstones and shales, measuring on the Ohio river, 640 feet in thickness (from the Black Slate to the base of the Sub. Carboniferous Limestone in the Kentucky hills), rests conformably upon the Black Slate. It takes its name from the town of Waverly, in Pike county, where the stone has been extensively quarried. It extends from the Ohio river in a somewhat northeasterly direction through the 2d District. Its lithological character changes greatly in its northern extension, it being much coarser to the north. A careful section was made of it on the Ohio river, especially of those portions which are of the most economic value. The best exposures are in the river hills at Rockville, Adams county, and between that point and Portsmouth. For a section of the whole group, see map.

SECTION OF THE WAVERLY SANDSTONE GROUP.

The lower part of the section was taken at the cut of the inclined railway at the quarry of the Hon. W. J. Flagg, on Lower Twin creek, Scioto county. At this place the fifty feet directly above the Black Slate were not seen, but were found exposed at other points, although no minute measurements were made. The shale partings are of a light bluish color, and are often quite arenaceous. There is a remarkable exception to the general character of the Waverly group, in a stratum of highly bituminous black slate, which is found about 137 feet above the base. It is 16 feet thick, and remarkably persistent in the Waverly, and is said by my associates to be found in the northern part of the State. It is not easily distinguished in appearance from the great Black Slate below. It is found to be somewhat richer in bitumen. Prof. Wormley reports it to contain 10.20 per cent. of volatile matter, and to have a specific gravity of 2.262.

It contains the same mollusca, genera and species, as the Black Slate viz., Lingula sub-spatulata, M. and W., and Discina capax. ? White. It also contains similar scales of small ganoid fishes. Besides these fishes there are remains of larger fishes. A collection of these larger fish remains was made by Capt. Jas. Patterson, of Rockville, who takes an intelligent interest in all such matters, from this slate, at Fairview, Kentucky, a little below Rockville. Through the generosity of Capt. P. I obtained some fine specimens this summer at Rockville. They are yet to be studied and described. This black slate in the Waverly is said to be a fish-bed throughout its entire extent through the State.

The conditions under which this slate was formed must have been very similar to those existing when the great Black Slate was deposited, viz., quiet water and a commingling with the sediments of a vast amount of minute organic matter. No trace of bitumen is elsewhere seen in any other part of this great formation.

This Waverly Black Slate is evidently a very wide-spread stratum. It is not only found extending through the Waverly formation to the north, but it evidently accompanies the Waverly rocks in their dip under the coal measures. I have little doubt that the deep oil wells in the West Virginia uplift pass through it. While this uplift is located in the center of the great coal basin, it brings to the surface the strata of the lowest part of the productive coal measures. At Burning Spring, Wirt county, West Virginia, the lowest seam of coal is brought up. Below this coal the oil producers begin to bore. No true conglomerate is found, but the sandstone and shales of the Waverly are considerably thickened, as we should expect in going from Ohio eastward. All the wells, so far as I can learn, which are sunk to the requisite depth, pass through from 15 to 20 feet of "black slate," which I cannot doubt is the black slate of the Waverly. I give a section of a well bored at Burning Spring, by A. B. McFarland, Esq., an intelligent citizen of Parkersburg. (See Fig. 1.)

Over the black slate we find, on the Ohio river, 1 ft. 7 in. of compact blue clay, upon which rest 3 ft. 9 in. of blue and drab shales imperfectly laminated. Then comes the famous stratum of sandstone called the "city ledge." It was first quarried nearly forty years ago by the late John Loughery, Esq., and the same stratum is still very largely quarried by Messrs. W. L. Caden & Bro., Mueller, Adams, Flagg, and others, in vicinity of Rockville and Buena Vista, on the Ohio river. Near Rockville the stratum is 3 ft. 5 in. thick. The same "city ledge" on W. J. Flagg's land is 4 ft. 6 in., and at another place 3 ft. 11 in. At the latter place there is an under layer 2 feet thick, separated by 3½ inches of blue sandy shale. Here the lower layer is quarried. On Upper Twin creek the same stratum is found, although it is not here wrought. One-fourth of a mile east of Stony Run, 3¾ miles below Portsmouth, the equivalent of the city ledge is quarried. Here are three layers, measuring 1 ft. 9 in., 1 ft. 9 in., and 2 ft. 10 in., separated by thin layers of shale 3 inches thick.

It is a fortunate fact that everywhere the rock over the city ledge is a comparatively soft shale. This greatly facilitates the work of stripping off the superincumbent material. These overlying clay shales afford a fine material for brick, and excellent pottery, it is said, can be made from the finer parts of them. A section of the "city ledge" and the shales is here given. (See Fig. 2.)

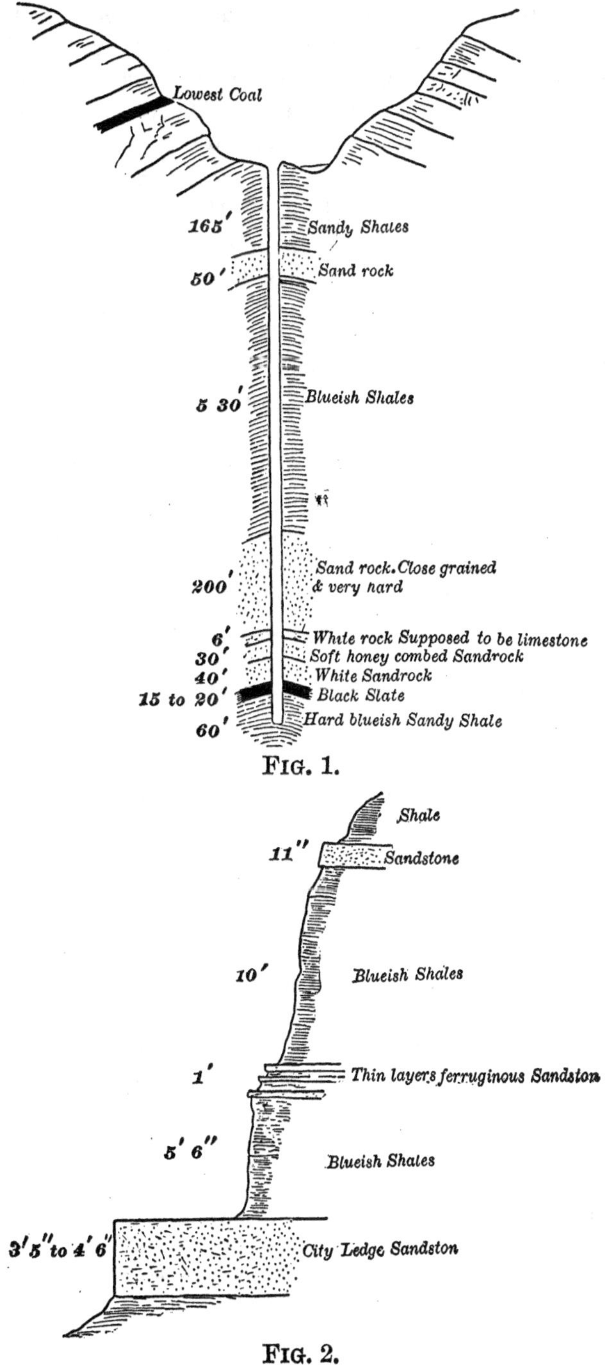

FIG. 1.

FIG. 2.

The stone quarried at Buena Vista and neighborhood is remarkable for its durability and resistance under pressure, the ease with which it is wrought for all architectural purposes, and for its uniform and beautiful color—a delicate bluish drab, sometimes called "French drab." The stone in the quarry is remarkably even-bedded, and is split out in blocks of a very uniform size, averaging about 45 cubic feet each. These blocks are sawed into slabs and pillars most economically. This stone is used in Cincinnati for all the finer architecture, and it has no superior in the country.

The top of the "city ledge" layer is covered with Spirophyton cauda galli, and other species, and with innumerable stems and stalks of marine plants. Occasionally the leaf of a Spirophyton extends down into the stone, to the injury of its compactness and strength. These plants show no carbonaceous structure. There is not even a black stain upon leaf or stalk, so completely have the carbon and hydrogen of the ancient plants escaped. This escape was doubtless due to the fact that the plants were only imperfectly submerged. The opinion has been expressed that petroleum originated from marine vegetation. In the Waverly we have the proof of a vast marine flora, but in no case do we find any oil traceable to this source, nor the slightest tendency to bituminization in any of these plants. What might have been the case had the fucoids been covered by clays or other impervious material, it is impossible to say. These Waverly plants are accumulated in comparatively shallow water, probably very near the surface, since we find on the under side of some of the sandstone layers casts of well-marked striæ, such as might be made by the movement of shore ice along a muddy bottom. So far as could be ascertained, the casts of ripple marks run at right angles to the direction of the striæ. This seemingly corroborates the supposition that ice causes the striæ. Mr. John Miller, superintendent of Mr. Mueller's quarries at Buena Vista, thinks the striæ lie in the direction of N. E. and S. W., while the ripple marks are from N. W. to S. E. These striæ are remarkably uniform and parrallel. The mud was often planed down quite smooth, and yet the tool-marks are ever discernible. Upon the mud, thus prepared, the sandy layers were deposited. If the different layers of the sandstone should generally be found to contain upon their under surfaces these casts, we might perhaps infer from this the periodicity of the winter ice, and the succeeding deposits of the sandy sediment brought

---

NOTE.—W. L. Caden & Bro. quarry and sell annually 150,000 cubic feet of this stone, taken from the city ledge stratum. Much of this is prepared for use in their large steam saw-mill. Mr. Mueller quarries about 200,000 feet, all, or nearly all, taken from the city ledge seam. Mr. J. W. Adams also quarries the city ledge stone largely. In addition to his own quarries, he rents those of Hon. W J. Flagg, on Lower Twin creek, together with his railroad. It should be added, that Mr. Mueller has a fine railway to his quarries, on which he uses locomotives.

down periodically from the continent of that period. This would make the accumulation of the Waverly rocks a rapid one, yet there could not have been a very strong current to move the materials of the formation, as it is developed near the Ohio River, for they are too fine and too much mingled with clay. To the north, in Fairfield county, and in that region, the Waverly sandstone is very coarse, and required much stronger currents for the accumulation of the materials.

About 47 feet above the "city ledge" is a group of layers, lying so horizontally and so evenly bedded as to arrest attention. This group was named by Dr. Locke in the old reports—the "Beautiful Quarry." The position of these layers is indicated in the general section. They have never been quarried to any considerable extent, but doubtless the choicer layers will be wrought at some future day. The same group is well exposed on the road to the residence of Hon. Wm. J. Flagg, on the high hill between Upper and Lower Twin creeks. Although no other layer of sandstone than the "city ledge" is now wrought, to any extent, in the neighborhood of Buena Vista, it is not because there is not a vast amount of excellent stone besides. The "city ledge" has a great reputation, and as it is easily wrought for all architectural purposes, it is in great demand. Such has been the competition among the owners of quarries, that they feel compelled to supply their patrons with the "city ledge" stone. Could the stone from other layers be once fairly introduced, I have no doubt of its value and popularity.

The stone of the "city ledge" is sometimes contaminated with petroleum, but this is in exceptional localities. Many of the large blocks of the stone used in the supension bridge over the Ohio river at Cincinnati show the tarry oil, as the sun's heat has caused it to exude and run down These were blocks not deemed worthy, I suppose, to be used in the finer stone works in the city. A limestone quarried in the suburbs of Chicago is charged, in a similar way, with petroleum. A Presbyterian church on Wabash avenue in that city, built of this stone, presents the appearance of having been covered with dripping tar. The oil in the "city ledge" stratum has evidently originated in the highly bituminus slate which immediately underlies it. In confirmation of this supposition, the lowest sandstone layers of the Waverly group and which rest directly upon the Great Black Slate, contain oil and constitute a horizon of oil springs.

The upper Waverly sandstone are nowhere extensively quarried along the Ohio river, so far as I could learn, except on Carey's run, between Stoney run and Portsmouth, where there is a pretty extensive quarry of Waverly layers, situated above the horizon of the "city ledge." No measured sections of the rocks were here made. The stone is now being quarried for the piers of the railroad bridge between Cincinnati and Covington, Ky. Generally they are not sufficiently firm and durable for building purposes, and yet, upon more careful examination, there will doubtless be found portions of the formation of excellent quality.

A careful examination of the quarries in the Waverly group in Pike county has not yet been made. Stone from the town of Waverly and vicinity is extensively used for building purposes in all the cities and towns on the Ohio Canal, at Chillicothe, Columbus, &c. A fine grained stone from Pike county, of a very rich, dark yellow drab, has recently been introduced into Columbus. The block of stores of Peter Hayden, Esq., on Broad Street, has its front of this stone. For large buildings, and especially for churches, this stone is admirably fitted to gratify the tastes of those who prefer rich dark hues in eclesiastical architecture. A stone from the Waverly group, quarried at Newark, of a lighter yellow and much courser in texture, is also prized for building purposes. The new Roman Catholic Cathedral at Columbus is being built of it.

Quarries are opened in the Waverly rocks in the Hocking valley. The stratigraphical position of some of these quarries will be given hereafter.

The upper Waverly sandstones on the Ohio river section contain less interstratified shales than the lower portion. The whole rock is generally softer and of a more yellow color, due to the presence of iron. At many points, the iron ore, a hematite, forms a coating on the sandstone two or three inches think. We have here the dawn of the coming iron ore period of the lower coal measures. The ore was nowhere seen of suitable thickness for practical use.

Direction of Vertical Joints.—In the bed of Stony run, four miles below Portsmouth, vertical planes appear with unusual distinctness, dividing the horizontal strata into rhomboidal blocks. Directions of joints, N., 30 deg. E., and S., 82 deg. E.

In the Waverly, in the bed of Pond creek, one mile from the Ohio Canal, vertical joints are very distinct, cutting the horizontal strata into triangular, trapezoidal and rhomboidal blocks. Directions, N., 38 deg. W., N., 6 deg. W., N., 50 deg. E., N., 52 deg. E. and N., 70 deg. W.

In the Waverly just below the "16 feet" or "Waverly black slate," on Rocky Fork of Camp creek, Camp Creek township, Pike county, the direction of joints is N. 32 deg. E. and N. 68 deg. W.

In the "Waverly black slate" at Patterson's quarry, below Rockville, the direction is N. 50 deg. W. In the "Logan sandstone," (upper Waverly) at Scott's Creek Falls, Hocking county, the direction of joints is N. 82 deg. E. Also, in the same, below the bridge, in the bed of Hocking river, N. 86 deg. E.

Vertical joints in the upper Waverly, top of Springville hill, Ky., opposite Portsmouth, N. 84 deg. E.

The vertical joints in the fire clay at Taylor's quarry, three miles above Portsmouth, N. 50 deg. E. This clay rests upon the top of the Waverly.

The hills along the Ohio river, in the Waverly formation, are very high and steep. The following altitudes were taken by the barometer: Butterworth's hill, four miles north of Rome, Adams county, 543 feet above the bed of Stout's run. On the Longhery hill, east of the mouth of Rock run, at Rockville, Adams county, the stratum of fossiliferous sand rock is 440 feet above the bed of the run, and there are probably 50 or 60 feet of the hill above that stratum, making the hill at least 500 feet high. The altitude of the picturesque dwelling of Hon. W. J. Flagg, on the hill between the two Twin creeks, Scioto county, is 505 feet above the lower Twin creek bridge. This corresponds very nearly with an instrumental survey made by Mr. Flagg for the location of a road.

Raven Rock hill, about three miles below Portsmouth, was found to be 508 feet high. On the top is a cairn of stones. The highest point in the range of the high and picturesque hills in Kentucky, directly opposite Portsmouth, is 527 feet above the alluvial bottom as the base.

The height of the first Ohio river hill on the Ohio side above Portsmouth, is 402 feet. This is not high enough to take the coarse coal measure sandstone. On the top are the remains of an Indian or mound-builder lookout. On the next hill to the east, the coarse coal-measure sand rock shows at an elevation of 416 feet, where it is 15 feet thick. Forty-five (45) feet below the sand rock is a stratum of blue fire clay, from three to four feet thick. This is doubtless the equivalent of the seam of fire clay worked by Mr. Taylor, one mile further east. Mr. Taylor's hill is 388 feet above the alluvial bottom. His clay is one foot seven inches thick, and lies 22 feet below the top of the hill. This clay is doubtless the same in geological position with that extensively quarried on the hills near Sciotoville. The finer grained upper Waverly rocks show themselves 10 feet below Mr. Taylor's fire clay.

The height of the hill back of Josiah Merrill's landing, in Kentucky, 10 miles above Portsmouth, is 330 feet. The sub-carboniferous limestone is extensively deposited in the hill, and measures 46 feet thick. It is 215 feet above the base of the hill.

FOSSILS OF THE WAVERLY.

The Waverly group contains impressions of marine plants throughout its whole vertical range. They are the Spirophyta of Hall, in several species and stems of numerous fucoidal plants. The Spirophyta abound in the productive coal measures, as will be shown hereafter. A small fragment of a Dictophyton, Hall, was found at Buena Vista, in the "city ledge" sandstone. The upper Waverly contains several forms of marine plants, as yet undescribed. The lower Waverly, on the Ohio river, is found to be very barren of animal fossils. Not a single one of any kind was found in the 137 feet of sandstones and blue sandy shales lying below the Waverly black slate. The black slate contains, as has already been stated, two forms of brachiopoda, Lingula sub-spatulata and Discina capax, and fish remains. There are also great numbers of a minute fossil form, resembling the dental arrangements of gasteropods. In the "city ledge" layer, a single indistinct form of a cyathophylloid coral was obtained. In the clay shale directly above the "city ledge," a fragment of a very indistinct form of goniatites was found. As this is probably the horizon from which Dr. Hildreth's specimens came—which were described by Dr. Morton—I searched the shales carefully, but found nothing but a mere fragment. Dr. Hildreth's goniatites came from a shaft, at Munn's run, above Portsmouth, sunk to the Waverly black slate, in expectation of finding it coal. One hundred and twenty-seven feet above the "city ledge" is a sandstone rich in fossils. About 114 feet above this is another stratum of sand rock covered with iron ore, also rich in fossils. This stratum was not found in place, but the fragments were found near the top of Mr. Flagg's hill, near Buena Vista, and the place of the stratum proximately estimated. Fossils were formed in large iron stone concretions in a sandstone near the mouth of the Little Scioto, at Sciotoville, above Portsmouth. The collections of the Survey have not yet been studied. In a private collection made by myself some years since at Rockville (in the first fossiliferous sand rock stratum above the "city ledge"), and at Sciotoville, Prof. A. Winchell, of Michigan, has identified the following forms:

Rockville.—Fenestrella, sp?; Producta semi-reticulata, Flem.; P. arcuata, Hall; Chonetes geniculata? White; C. Illinoisensis, Worthen; Hemipronites umbraculum, Sch.; Orthis Michellini, Lev.; Spirifera carteri, Hall; S. biplicata? Hall; Spiriferina solidirostris, White; Pleurotomaria vadosa, Hall; Nautilus trisulcatus, M. and W.; Phillipsia Doris, Hall, sp.; Cythere crassi-marginata, Win.

Sciotoville.—Zaphrentis ida? Win.; Trematopora? vesiculosa, Win.; Trematopora? Sciotoensis, n. s., Win.; Crinoid stems, 2 species; Fenestrella sp?; Producta semireticulata, Flem.; P. morbilliana, Win.; P. Cooperensis? Swallow; P. concentrica, Hall; P. gracilis, Win.; Hemipronites umbraculum, Sch.; Orthis sub-eliptica? M. and W.; Spirifera Carteri, Hall; S. Marionensis, Shumard; S. subrotundata, Hall; Spiriferina solidirostris, White; Syringothyris typa, Win.; Spirigera Hannibalensis, Swallow; S. Ohioensis, Win.; Rhynconella Sageriana, Win.; R. Missouriensis, Shumard; Centronella? flora, n. s., Win.; Aviculapecten caroli, Win.; Perno-pecten lineatus? Win.; Sanguinolites Marshallensis, Win.; Sanguinolaria, sp?; Pleurotomaria vadosa, Hall; Murchisonia prolixa, M. and W.; M. quadricincta, Win.; Conularia Newberryi, Win.; Orthoceras Indianense, Hall.

SOIL OF THE WAVERLY HILLS NEAR THE OHIO RIVER.

Hon. W. J. Flagg, who owns a large estate in these Waverly hills, and who has devoted much time and thought to fruit culture, as well as to the development of the building stone, has sent the following interesting and valuable statement relative to the region:

Concerning the economic value of the hills of Adams and Scioto counties in the neighborhood of the village of Freestone, which is on the Ohio river, near the point where the line dividing those counties touches it:

These hills being steep and rough are hardly cultivated at all, except for fruit. The peaches from the orchards of Mr. Loughery, overlooking the villages, have a high reputation in market, and what little wine has been produced from a few vineyards near by, has been of uncommon delicacy of flavor and richness. Without any analysis of the soil to inform us, we know that it abounds in silex, is deficient in lime, has some clay, and a good deal ot iron, as well as potash. Comparing it with the soil of one of the best vineyards in one of the chief wine districts of Europe, Lafitte in Medoc, we find the latter to contain—

Silicious pebbles	629	parts.
Fine sand	283	"
Pure silex	62	"
Humus	13	"
Alumina	7	"
Lime	40	"
Iron	86	"

In the limestone soil of the Burgundy wine district, the proportion of iron is from ten to thirteen per cent., and of silica about thirty per cent. These show that for the production of wines of fine quality, lime in large quantity is not an essential constituent, and that in two, at least, of the great French vine districts, the soil, like that of the hills of Adams and Scioto, abounds in silica and iron.

The timber is chiefly white oak, poplar, chestnut, beech, hickory, sugar tree and locust, of remarkable strength and durability, as compared with the growth of the plains and valleys.

Ginseng, sarsaparilla and other medicinal plants of marketable value, are found in the woods, and are gathered and disposed of in considerable quantities.

Mineral springs of real or supposed virtue in healing disease, issue in many places from the bases of the hills. One of these, in Adams county, has already become an established resort for invalids.

The upper parts of the hills are formed of a very even and compact stratafication of what are known as the Waverly sandstone, interlaid with clayey shales. Though capable of yielding an inexhaustible supply of very good building material, and though formerly quarried for that purpose, to some extent, these sandstones are now abandoned in favor of the harder and more beautiful ledge lying below them.

Immediately beneath the Waverly ledges comes a very thick bed of fine bluish grey clay, excellent for brick, tile and potters' ware An English potter finds in this clay the very material that has made Staffordshire what it is, the pottery of the world. It is not of such clay that the fine white ware and porcelain we get from Staffordshire are made, but those wares must be enclosed, when baked, by a kind of matrix, to supply which so large a bulk of common clay is needed that the finer substances of which the ware itself is formed, and of which not a tenth as much is needed, can better be transported to it than it to them. Hence potteries are always established near the clay beds. The clay in question is quite pure and free of grit.

Next below is the "city ledge," so called, a stratum of close-grained greyish-drab sandstone, from three feet to four feet thick, from which the fine building stone now generally used in Cincinnati and other cities of the valley is obtained. Usually no other is quarried, but lately a ledge, two feet thick, lying immediately under it, and of the same color and general composition, has been introduced to the market and been received with favor.

The price of these stones at Cincinnati is fifty cents per cubic foot, less than one-third that of the brown stone so much used in New York and other eastern cities, but which is, nevertheless, no stronger, nor more durable, nor any easier worked, nor, in common estimation, more beautiful than what is here so cheaply and abundantly afforded. Accordingly, in all buildings constructed in Cincinnati, during the last fifteen years, where anything like elegance is attempted, whether public or private, for residence or business, the "Buena Vista Free Stone," so called, is the material used. And owing to its cheapness it is put up in more massive blocks, and forming thicker walls than is common in the East.

Close below the city ledge comes a bed of black bituminous slate or shale fifteen feet thick.

This in turn rests upon a series of layers, in all about 125 feet thick, of fine cream colored sandstone, separated by thin deposits of clayey shale. One or two of these layers near the bottom of the series are of beautiful appearance, quarry and work well, and seem well adapted to the finest building purposes, but as they are locked down by so heavy a mass of what has at present no merchantable value, they are not worked. Ultimately, however, the whole must come into use to build up the great and beautiful cities that are, and are to be, in the valleys of the Ohio and Mississippi.

Next we come to a second bed of black bituminous slate of the thickness of from three hundred to three hundred and fifty feet, and known in geology as the Hamilton Shale. Like the upper bed, this slate is highly bituminous. Numerous issues of petroleum from its surface and above it caused oil seekers to bore several wells in the neighborhood in question, during the years 1865 and 1866, but without valuable result. It is also rich in sulphur, and is said to contain, besides considerable lime, phosphorus and potash.

In other countries much thinner and poorer beds of bituminous matter than these, have, for many years, been worked and distilled for the production of oil. And though at present all the distilleries that have been put up for that purpose in the vicinity of Freestone, are lying idle, or being dismantled, yet if ever the time shall come when a short supply or extended consumption of petroleum shall raise its price to double or treble what it now is, resort must be had to some such basis of supply as we find at the foot of the hills of Adams and Scioto counties, in that immense bituminous deposit.

Many fruit growers and especially grape growers of the eastern shores of Lake Erie, and others on the borders of Crooked lake, New York, attribute their remarkable success to the presence in the soil of their orchards and vineyards of this same slate. To it they have lately been led to trace not merely the large and regular crops they have obtained—so abundant and so certain as to have run up the price of land to speculative rates—but also their very great immunity from the vine disease. They find in the slate an abundance of sulphur, which is the well known remedy for that disease. It is stated that vine growers in the north of

France, who use as a manure a black earth highly charged with sulphur, also escape the ravages of the malady and attribute their escape to the sulphur. Experiments are furthermore being made on an extensive scale to test the value of the slate when ground to a fine flour and applied in the same way as a substitute for ground plaster.

The same flour mixed with coal-tar as a kind of mastic and applied on a sheathing of woolen paper, has of late been considerably employed for roofing. When well put on it makes a good roof, capable possibly of almost indefinite renewal of painting with a fresh coat of the mixture.

Other elements of value are supposed to lie within the rich body of slate, among them the elements of sulphuric acid and alum.

All which brings us down to the limestone at low water mark. Richer hills there are, but where can any be found so thoroughly valuable from top to bottom as these?

W. J. FLAGG.

The Waverly hills in Southern Ohio are heavily timbered, and the day is not far distant when all the accessible forests will be needed and used as fuel for the production of iron. For many purposes charcoal iron is a necessity, and it will always command an extra price. The number of charcoal furnaces is rapidly diminishing, while that of stonecoal furnaces is increasing. Charcoal iron will, therefore, be relatively more valuable in the future than now. There are, however, few districts in the State where woodlands can be obtained sufficiently cheap for furnace uses. This is not the case in the Waverly hills below Portsmouth, for lands are much cheaper here than in any other part of the State. Iron ores from Missouri are already largely used by furnaces higher up the river, and also limestone for flax is carried up the river from the Silurian limestone formation in the vicinity of Manchester, Adams county. Ores for mixture, or to be used independently, could be obtained on the line of the Portsmouth Branch of the Marietta and Cincinnati Railroad.

I have not been able to study the Waverly rocks carefully at points north of the immediate valley of the Ohio river, and nowhere have I made a complete section.

On the Marietta and Cincinnati Railroad, we pass, in going west, the base of the productive coal measures in the vicinity of the Cincinnati Furnace five or six miles west of Hamden, in Vinton county. Here are ledges of coarse sandrock of great thickness, giving a picturesque mural character to that part of the "Hungry Hollow" valley. At the base of the coarse sandrock, I find in the railroad cuts to the westward, alternate layers of conglomerate and fine grained sandstone, the latter, however, greatly exceeding the former in thickness. Under these, the rocks become uniformly fine grained, and both in texture and color resemble the layers of the middle and lower Waverly strata, at Buena Vista, on the Ohio river. I have not yet measured the group between the coal measures above and the undoubted Waverly below, but there are probably one hundred and fifty feet of these intermediate beds. The railroad descends pretty rapidly from Cincinnati Furnace to Raysville (77 feet), and the rocks dip in the opposite direction; hence there may be more than one hundred and fifty feet of these rocks. In the fine grained blue Waverly sandstone at the base of the conglomerate group, I find Producta semireticulata, Orthis Michelini, Rhynchonella Sageriana, a Myalina, and several other undetermined species of fossils. The lower fifty feet of the conglomerate group, or more properly beds of passage, greatly resemble the fifty feet seen in a cut on the Columbus and Hocking Valley Railroad, on the farm of James Francisco, Marion township, Hocking county, of which I give a section elsewhere.

In passing from the coal measures in Hocking county down to the Waverly, we find in place of the coarser rocks at Cincinnati Furnace, a group of comparatively fine grained buff colored sandstone, one hundred and thirty-three and a half feet thick. These rocks contain marine plants, Syirophyton, cauda-galli, &c.; Producta, 3 species; Rhynchonella, Orthis, &c. Below this group which I have called, for convenience of designation, the *Logan Sandstone*, are eighty-five feet of alternate fine grained Waverly-like seams and conglomerate. The fine grained sandstone is often blue and rich in fucoids after the manner of the Ohio river Waverly. Beside the marine plants are Producta; Chonetes; Syringothyris, typa; Orthis, &c. Below this conglomerate group we find the coarse sandstone and conglomerate which form the chief Waverly in the hills in the Hocking Valley. The Waverly is found to be entirely changed in its lithological character. It is always coarse with the single exception of twelve feet of fine grained rock seen at the base of the hills near Sugar Grove, Fairfield county. Often it contains pebbles of the size of a hickory nut. At Mount Pleasant, a bold hill near Lancaster, some two hundred feet high (by estimate), there is a bluff exposure on the south-western side. The rock here varies in no respect from a common coal measure conglomerate. It ranges all the way from a hard compact sandstone to a coarse conglomerate filled with quartz pebbles. In color it ranges from white through various shades of yellow to dark ochre and even to lively brick red. Generally, however, it is a coarse yellow loose grained sandrock. There is much false bedding, and an exact section would be impossible. In many places the face of the cliff presents a curiously honey-combed appearance from unequal disintegration by weathering. The typical Waverly look was nowhere seen. If a layer of fine grained Waverly-like stone seen between Sugar Grove and the mouth of Clear creek, continues to the north-west, its place would be in this hill. The Lancaster stone is quarried for building purposes, and the new court house now in process of erection at Lancaster, is being built of it.

Four miles below Lancaster, in Berne township, the Waverly sandrock is quarried by Messrs. Sharpe and Carlisle. The quarry is something over a hundred feet above the Hocking canal, and is opened in a hard compact but coarse grained sandrock about twenty feet in thickness and of excellent quality. Above this were exposed about fifteen feet of loose laminated sandrock.

Just below the village of Sugar Grove, on the east side of the canal, is the quarry of Robert L. Sharpe, Esq., in the same geological range as the quarry last mentioned. Fossils are rare. I saw only an indistinct spirifer. The section is as follows. (See Fig. 3.)

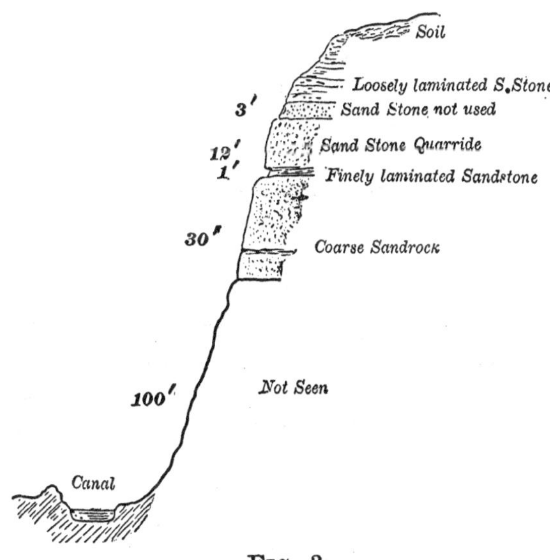

Fig. 3.

The stone from the two quarries last named has been principally used for locks and bridge piers, and is said to give good satisfaction. On the Ohio and Erie canal this stone was used in rebuilding locks at Lockbourne and at Lockville, making about twenty-five locks in all. It was also used in the acqueduct and locks at Circleville. It has also been used at various points on the Hocking canal. The stone has been thus used for some thirty years, and on the Ohio canal for fifteen years, and is reported to stand the test admirably. Mr. Sharpe reports the gross sales from the lower quarry last year at $12,000. The present year will probably show $15,000 from the two quarries.

The following is a section showing the alternation of conglomerate and fine grained blue sandstone as we ascend in the Waverly series. Being taken in a deep railroad cut where no measurement could be made of the perpendicular sides, the figures are only estimates. The section was taken on the farm of James Francisco, Marion township, Hocking county. (See Fig. 4.)

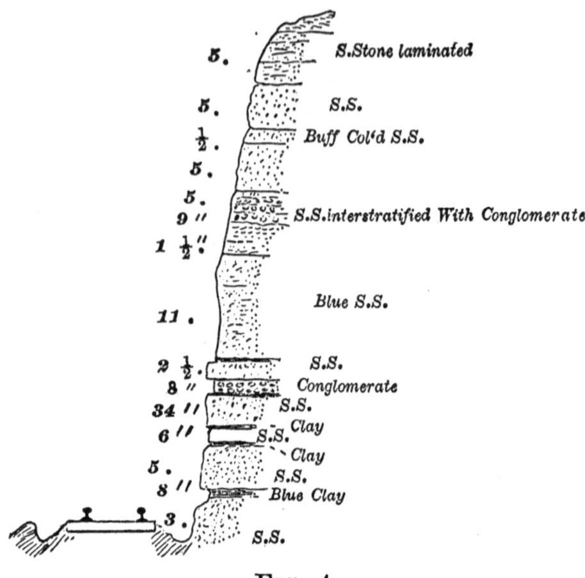

Fig. 4.

These layers, though generally fine grained blue sandrock, and much resembling, lithologically, the typical Waverly of the Ohio river, show at nearly all the seams a tendency to the coarseness of conglomerate. There is the evidence that at times the water currents swept along with sufficient force to carry very coarse gravel, while, at other times, the waters were more quiet, and deposited fine sand intimately mixed with clay. It is in the finer material that the marine plants (fucoids) are found, while the animal fossils, such as the Syringothyris, typa; are often found in the coarser deposits. Beautiful impressions of flexible stalks of fucoids are here seen. One species shows a peculiar system of transverse ridges much resembling those seen in the stems of the Rusophycus of the Clinton rocks.

There are several distinct species of these curious flexible stems to be found in the conglomerate and Logan Sandstone groups. The same are found in the upper Waverly, in the one hundred and fifty feet of fine-grained sandstone lying next below the Sub-carboniferous limestone in the Kentucky hills opposite Wheelersburg, Scioto county.

Above the group of the last section come in the heavier beds of conglomerate, well exposed at the Falls of the Hocking, one mile above Logan. Here deep pot-holes have been worn in the conglomerate. There are probably twenty feet of the conglomerate at this place, although the bottom was nowhere seen. A mile below, at the mouth of Scott's creek, a higher layer of coarse conglomerate is well exposed, and above this several thin layers of conglomerate, alternating with fine grained sandstone. The following section shows these rocks. See Fig. 5.

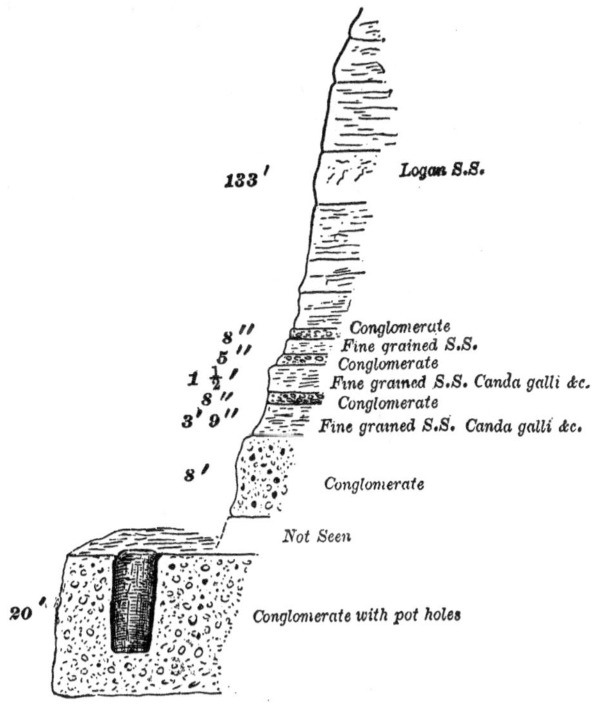

FIG. 5.

At Black Hand, near the east line of Licking county, the conglomerate is probably fifty or sixty feet thick, and over it lie, as we follow the dip to the south-east toward Zanesville, the Logan Sandstone group. The Logan Sandstone, with its characteristic fossils, is found to extend to a point between Pleasant Valley and Dillon's Falls, on the Baltimore and Ohio Railroad, C. O. Division. Many of the fossils of this group are identical with those of the upper Knobstone formation, proximate to the Sub-carboniferous limestone of Kentucky. This upper fine-grained sandstone was carefully measured near Logan, Hocking county, and found to be one hundred and thirty-three feet from the conglomerate below to the horizon of the Maxville limestone, which will be more fully noticed hereafter, and which everywhere rests upon the fine-grained sandstone of the upper Waverly.

At the top of the Logan group of sandstones, not far from Logan, Hocking county, a seam of fire-clay is reported by S. Baird, Esq., a well-known iron manufacturer, who formerly had charge of the Logan Furnace. This fire-clay has the same geological position as the fire-clay at the top of the Waverly in the Ohio river hills above Portsmouth. It has been tested, and pronounced excellent in quality, and such it appears in the samples shown me. Over the fire-clay is a seam of siderite ore in nodules, imbedded in clay, as reported by Mr. Baird.

MAXVILLE LIMESTONE.

There is above the Logan Sandstone group a limestone horizon, although the limestone is not everywhere persistent. It often gives place to sandstone of the usual coal measure grit. It was evidently formed on local basins occupied by quiet waters and cut off from the reach of the strong, sand-moving currents. But as these limestones group themselves upon one geological horizon, and always rest upon the top of the Logan sandstone group, I have no doubt that they have the same geological age, and were formed at the same time. I have called it the *Maxville limestone*, from the village of that name in Monday creek township, in Perry county, eight or ten miles north-east of Logan, where it has been extensively burned into quicklime.

The following is a section of this limestone, as seen in the land of James Tonnihill, Section 28, Green township, Hocking county. (See Fig. 6.)

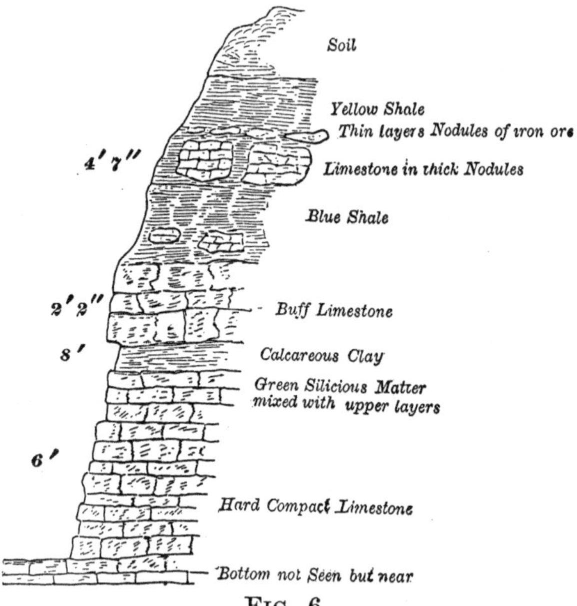

FIG. 6.

Mr. G. W. Smith is engaged in quarrying and burning this limestone at this place. He sells annually from 2,000 to 3,000 bushels of lime. The stone is also used as a flux at the Union Furnace. Mr. Smith knows nothing of the limestone west, nor, indeed, in any direction except to the north. It appears continuously northward for half a mile, and then is

NOTE.—The calcareous clay in above section is 8 inches thick, not 8 feet, as given.

said not to be seen until within two miles of Maxville. It is probable that a careful search for it, at its proper geological horizon, would be rewarded in finding it at points nearer Union Furnace, and on the Hocking river hills convenient to the canal and railroad. South and west of the Hocking river, it has not been noticed; but from recollections of explorations made by me several years since, between Jackson and the Ohio river, I am led to think that, in a few places, I saw small developments of this limestone in its true geological horizon. *The same horizon, continued across the Ohio river, would strike the Sub-carboniferous limestone of Kentucky.* I shall be able, next season, to settle this important point.* Like the Kentucky limestone, the Maxville seam generally carries a stratum of iron ore.

The following section, taken on the farm of David Hardy, near Maxville, shows the position of the Maxville limestone. (See Fig. 7.)

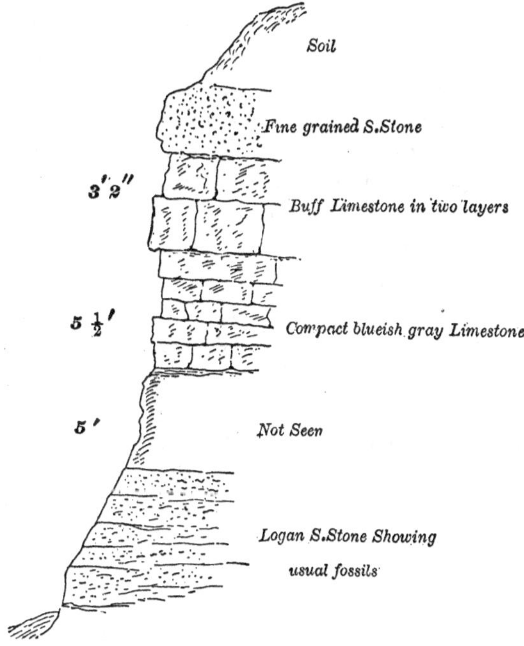

FIG. 7.

The Logan sandstone below shows the usual lithological texture and the usual fossils—fucoids (Spirophyton, cauda-galli,) etc., Productus, etc. A collection of fossils was made from the limestone. They are generally indistinct, as if the shells had been acted on by some solvent before the limestone became solidified around them. Bellerophon, Productus, Pleu-

* NOTE.—This has subsequently been verified, and the *Maxville limestone* will probably prove to be the equivalent of the *Chester limestone* of the Illinois Reports.

rotomaria, Spirifer, and a small cyathophylloid coral, etc., have been obtained.

The limestone here, as in Green township, Hocking county, appears to be of limited extent. In going south toward Logan, it is last seen in the road on Augustus Culver's land, some two miles from Maxville. Mr. Robert Ashbaugh reports that, so far as he knows, it occurs not further than a fourth of a mile west, one mile north, and not at all east of Maxville. As seen on Mr. Hardy's land, the lower five and a half feet are a bluish-gray stone, very hard and pure, breaking with a sharp conchoidal fracture, and bedded in layers of eighteen inches and under. The upper three feet and two inches contain a little iron, which causes the rock to weather buff color. In many places the buff layers are beautifully mottled with large spots of different shades of blue and green. The lower portions are preferred for the lime-kiln, and the lime is said to be of superior quality. The stone has also been quarried, and used in the Logan Furnace as a flux, for which it serves an admirable purpose. Formerly this limestone was quite extensively burned into quicklime at Maxville, but the expense of transportation by wagon renders it difficult to compete with the product of other establishments more favorably located.

At other exposures in the vicinity of Maxville, a black shale takes the place of the sandstone over the limestone, and also on the limestone there is often found a deposit of iron ore.

Following the horizon of the Maxville limestone north through Perry county, we find the stone finely exhibited in section 16, Madison township, Perry county, on the land of Edward Danison. Here the waters of Jonathan creek have excavated a deep channel, and the limestone, with perhaps fifty feet of the Logan sandstone, is exposed to view. The upper layers of the Logan sandstone are of soft, sandy shales, but contain the usual fossils of the Logan or upper Waverly group. The following section shows the position of the limestone and the associated strata. The limestone is from this point often seen in the valley, and is well exposed at Newtonville, Newton township, Muskingum county, where it lies in the bed of the stream. At Newtonville and in the vicinity a fine collection of fossils was made from the limestones, all indicating the sub-carboniferous character of the rocks. Above Newtonville, on the stream on the land of J. H. Roberts, the lower part of the limestone is buff colored. Prof. Wormley gives, of this, the following analysis:

Silica	15.20
Iron and alumina, chiefly iron	4.40
Carbonate of lime	49.80
Carbonate of Magnesia	30.65
Total	100.05

This may prove a valuable material for a cement lime.

Sec. Edward Danison's land, section 16, Madison township, Perry county. (See Fig. 8.)

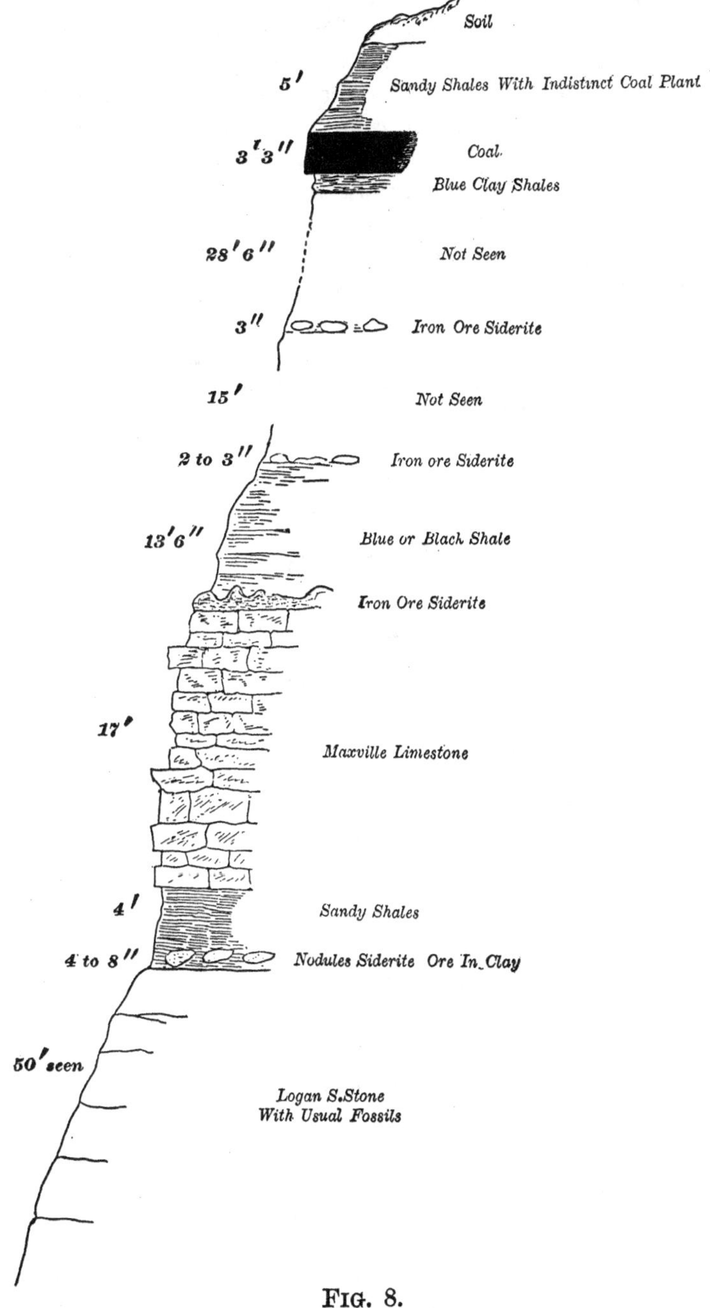

FIG. 8.

In this section there are four layers of iron ore, all believed to be of the Siderite group. The most promising is probably the one lying directly above the limestone. Of this, Prof. Wormley has made an analysis. This analysis will be found in tables on a subsequent page.

On Mr. Danison's land, 58 feet above the top of the Maxville limestone, is a seam of coal three feet three inches thick, which has been mined to a limited extent. In the sandy shales over this coal are indistinct leaves and stems of coal plants. On the slope of the hill above the coal seam are fragments of flint in considerable number.

On the farm of Joseph Rambo, section 14, Newton township, Muskingum county, a good section of the strata above the Maxville or Newtonville limestone was obtained, which is here given. (See Fig. 9.)

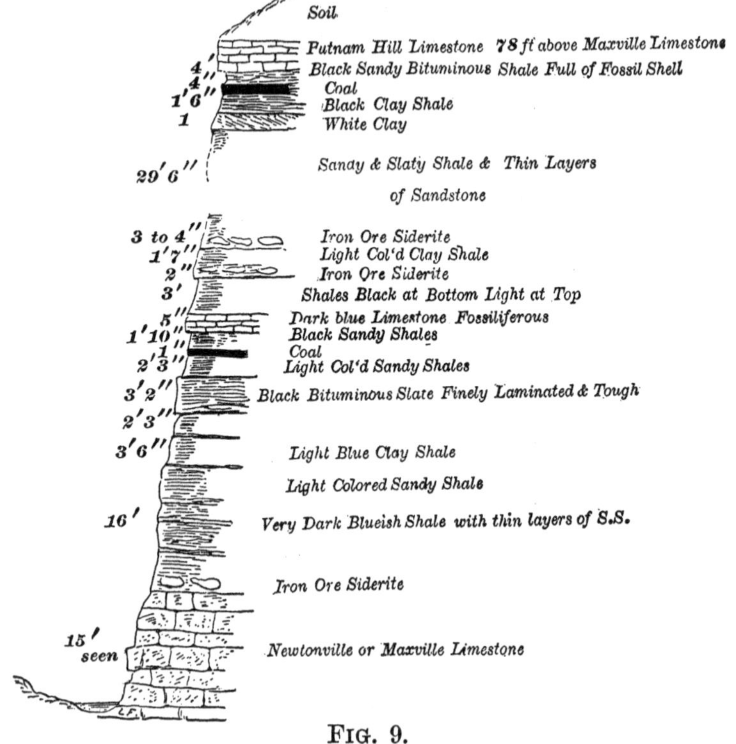

Fig. 9.

Here we have all the strata in detailed measurement up to a limestone which is generally persistent. It is 78½ feet above the great Maxville limestone. It is fossiliferous, and the sandy bituminous shales directly under it are also rich in fossils of the lower coal measure types. Although we have not traced it continuously to Putnam, opposite Zanesville, yet we are confident that it is the same as the Putnam Hill limestone, and as such we have provisionally called it. The Maxville limestone is possibly the same as the limestone in the bed of the Muskingum, at Zanesville, which will be hereafter examined.

This brings the two limestones into proper position in the geological series. I copy a section made at Zanesville, by Col. J. W. Foster, given in the report of the old Geological Survey of Ohio. (See Fig. 10.)

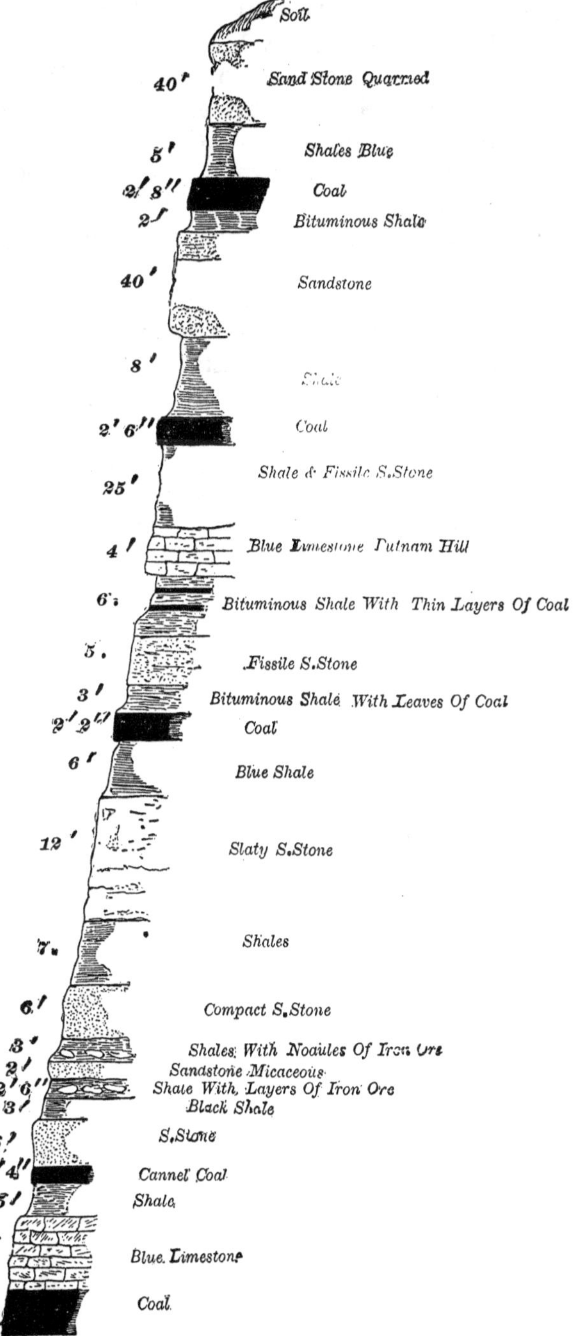

FIG. 10.

It will be noticed that Col. Foster gives a seam of coal six feet thick under the limestone in the bed of the river. It is singular that so thick a seam should never have been carefully explored.

In a section of the strata at Flint Ridge, made by Prof. Lesquereux and Dr. H. I. Salisbury, and quoted by Lesquereux in the Kentucky Reports, vol. iv., we find a seam of coal 80 feet below the blue Flint Ridge limestone, which is supposed to be the equivalent of the Putnam Hill limestone. This seam is then the equivalent of the seam under the limestone in the bed of the Muskingum, at Zanesville. The limestone, however, is not found over it at Flint Ridge. It rests directly upon the conglomerate, according to Mr. Lesquereux. It appears to be the general fact that along the base of the productive coal measures, wherever we find the Maxville limestone, we find underneath the finer grained sandrock of the Logan group. The sandstones were accumulated in basins of comparatively quiet water, and in the same basins there was often deposited, on the top of the sandstones, the Maxville limestone. I have nowhere found the Maxville limestone resting upon conglomerate.

NOTE.—At no other point in my district has coal been found below the Maxville limestone, and this fact leads me to doubt whether the "blue limestone," 8 feet thick, given by Col. Foster, is the equivalent of the true Maxville limestone. This point will hereafter be examined.

The rocks at the base of the coal measures, near Newark, are given in the accompanying section. (See Fig. 11.)

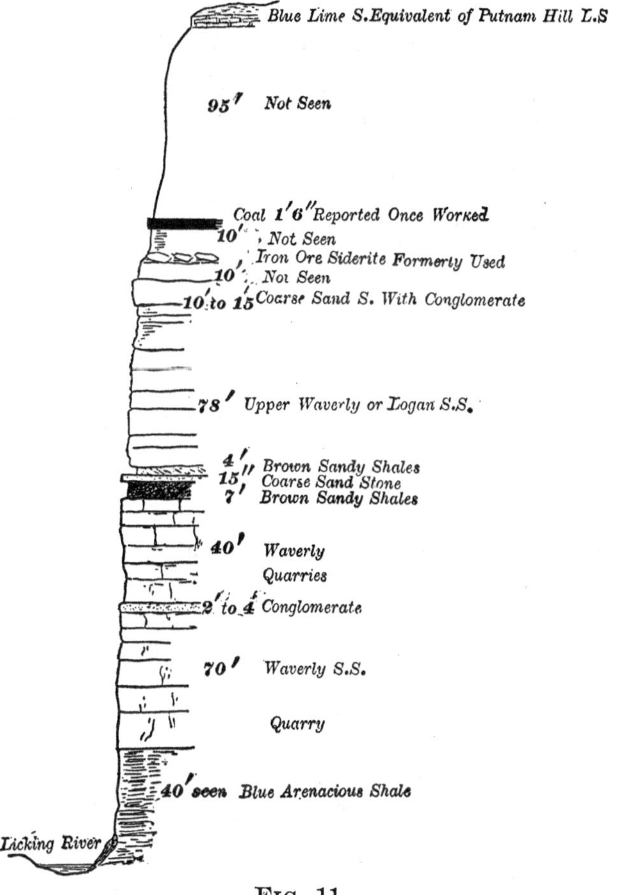

FIG. 11.

Mr. Lesquereux reports conglomerate seen at Flint Ridge, at the base of the coal measures, with a thin seam of coal lying just above it. This seam of coal has apparently the same stratigraphical position with the one at Zanesville, under the limestone found in the bed of the Muskingum, since the strata above entirely correspond.

With the exception of the small deposits of conglomerate over the Waverly or Logan sandstone, at Newark, there is little true coal measure conglomerate in that part of the second geological district, extending from the Hocking river, near Logan, to Newark. The conglomerate is found chiefly in the Waverly group.

The following is a section of the rocks in Kentucky, lying south of my district, as given by Sidney E. Lyon, Esq., in Vol. II of the Kentucky Geological Reports:

100 ft. Soft beds at the base of the coal measures in Carter county. This member varies in thickness in different localities.

75 ft. Seventy-five to 100 feet *Millstone grit.* This member, as well as the Sub-carboniferous limestone, thins out toward the Ohio river, near the mouth of Tygert's creek, where this member forms a mass fourteen feet thick, and the Sub-carboniferous limestone is only twelve feet thick.

100 ft. Calcareous muddy shale, with a few thin beds of limestone.

350 ft. Sub-carboniferous limestone, thinning rapidly toward the Ohio river.

20 ft. Twenty to seventy-five feet *grindstone grit* (upper part of Knob formation ?).

725 ft. Knobstone (Waverly sandstone of Ohio).

120 ft. Black (Devonian) slate, 100 to 150 feet.

700 ft. Buff porous limestone of Lewis, Fleming and Bath counties.

75 ft. Limestone producing red earth by disintegration.

100 ft. Slaty mudstone, thin bedded.

150 ft. Lower Silurian or Blue Limestone, forming the base of the Owingsville hill..

In this section we find the Millstone grit, or conglomerate, in its true place *above* the sub-carboniferous limestone, separated only by calcareous shales and limestones, which may perhaps be properly included with the sub-carboniferous limestone group. But *under* the great limestone there are 20 to 75 feet of *grindstone grit*, which Mr. Lyon is in doubt about, whether or not to call it a part of the upper portion of the Knob or Waverly formation.

The question at once arises whether the grindstone grit, which is probably only in local developments, as I have never chanced to see it in my examination of the Knobstone formation of Kentucky, may not correspond with theso-called conglomerate in my district, which is found in patches, sometimes conglomerate in texture and sometimes a grindstone grit, and located statigraphically at different levels from the Maxville limestone horizon down for 300 feet into the Waverly series? Should the conglomerate and coarse sandstones, which I find so scattered in their vertical range through several hundred feet below the horizon of the Maxville limestone, prove to be no true and normal conglomerate of the coal measures whatever, but simply coarse materials whose location is due to the accidents of currents, in other words, mere Waverly conglomerate, we shall be relieved from the embarrassment of finding the Waverly fauna and flora above the conglomerate.

The following is a list of fossils found in the Waverly at Newark, which have been identified by Prof. A. Winchell, of Michigan. A small part of these were sent by myself—but the larger part by Mr. Herzer: Producta semireticulata, Flem.; Chonetes pulchella, Win.; Hemipronites umbraculum, Sch.; H. inequalis ? Hall; Spirifera extenuata, Hall; Spirifera Waverlyensis n. sp., Win.; Spiriferina solidirostris White; Syringothyris typa, Win.; Conocardium pulchellum, M. & W.;

Pleurodictyum problematicum, Goldfuss; Rhynchonella Sageriana, Win.; Avicula-pecten occidentalis, Win.; A. Caroli, Win.; A. Newarkensis, n. sp., Win.; Perno-pecten limatus ? Win.; P. Cooperensis, Shumard; Sanguinolites naiadiformis, Win.; S. securis, n. sp., Win.; Orthoceras Indianense, Hall; Phillipsia Missouriensis, Shum.; Goniatites Marshallensis, Win.; G. Shumardianus, Win.; G. Ohiensis n. s., Win.; G Andrewsi n. sp., Win.; Platyceras Herzeri n. sp., Win.; P. haliotoides, M. & W.; Cypricardia rigida., M. & W.; Sedgwickia Hannibalensis, Shum.

In the sandstone layers interstratified with the shales below the "Putnam Hill Limestone," were found on the land of Mr. Rambo, of which a section has already been given, fine impressions of Fucoids of the Spirophyton cauda-galli and allied species.

This and similar facts noticed elsewhere, show a wide stratigraphical range to this group of marine plants. In New York they are found in the Hamilton rocks. In Ohio they are found in the lower Waverly in great abundance.

At Gladstone's Mill, near Newtonville, Newton township, Muskingum county, we find a limestone in the bed of the North Fork of Jonathan's creek, which is believed to be the same as the Maxville limestone. The bottom of the stone was not seen, but a well dug in the village passed through 15 feet of limestone. The upper layer show a chocolate tint. It is reported that this limestone is seen for five miles in Jonathan's creek, above Newtonville, and disappears one mile below. On Kent's run, which joins the North Fork of Jonathan's creek at Newtonville, it is said to be seen for nine miles.

About 50 feet above the limestone at Gladstone's Mill was found a stratum of sandstone 15 inches thick, on which are very fine impressions of marine plants, Spirophyton caudi-galli, &c., &c., and mingled with these were well-defined stigmariae of the coal-measure plants. They had all been drifted together and embedded in sand.

The upper limestone ("Putnam Hill") was also seen in its proper place higher up the hill, with the usual coaly matter under it.

This upper limestone has a pretty extensive range. It was seen in the Monday creek valley, on the farm of Henry Hazelton, Salt Lick township, Perry county, where was obtained the following section. (See Fig. 12.)

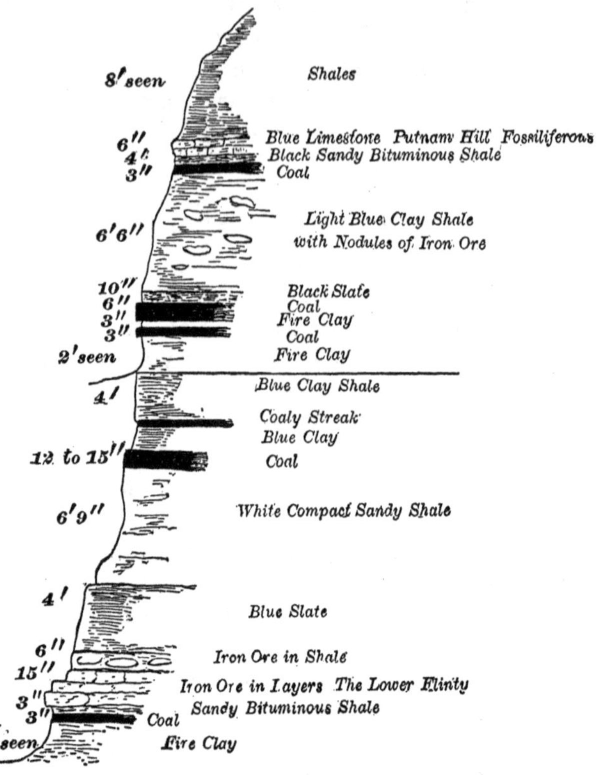

FIG. 12.

Here the "Putnam Hill" limestone, although thin, preserves its usual characteristics in stone and fossils. There are several thin seams of coal revealed in this section. They are all too thin for profitable mining, especially as the great Nelsonville or Straitsville seam is well developed in all the surrounding hills. This coal will be noticed hereafter. The iron ore given in the section has been analyzed by Prof. Wormley, and the result will be found in the table on a subsequent page.

There are, apparently, five different ore horizons between the top of the Logan sandstone group and the blue Putnam Hill limestone. Four of these are seen in the section on Edward Danison's land, given on page 83. Above them is a range of ore exhibited in the section on Henry Hazelton's land, already given. The latter is found at many points as shown by the large map of grouped sections. It is generally accompanied by limestone and often by a flint seam. At Haydensville, the group is seen in the hill directly behind the old Hocking Furnace. Here the ore is apparently of excellent quality, but it adheres so firmly to the top of the limestone rock as to make the separation difficult. On the land of Samuel Thomson, near Maxville, Monday Creek township, Perry county, our measurement gave sixteen inches, to this ore, composed of three distinct layers. Here it rests upon an earthy blue limestone. Nearly three feet below the ore is a seam of coal twenty-two inches thick. By accident, no samples of this ore were obtained for analysis. Should the quality equal that of most of the ores of the lower coal measures in this region, the ore may prove very valuable. We did not see the stratum overlying the ore at this place. Should it prove of soft material, easily mined, this ore could be obtained by the usual method of mining.

Between this ore horizon and the horizon of the Putnam Hill limestone, is a seam of coal generally thin; but on the land of Edward Danison, Section 16, Madison township, Perry county, it measured 3 ft. 3 in. It has been mined only to a limited extent.

In addition to this seam of coal, there is another directly under the Putnam Hill limestone. It is generally very thin, but in the townships of Hopewell, of Muskingum, and Hopewell, of Licking counties, it reaches a good workable thickness. My assistant, W. G. Ballantine, spent much time in tracing the range of the limestone, and is confident that the cannel coal of Flint Ridge, and the coal of Joseph Porter, on 100 acre lot, No. 16, of Hopewell township, Muskingum county, are located directly below the equivalent of the Putnam Hill limestone. The following is a section of the coal on the property of Messrs. Bradford, Pollock & Co., Hopewell township, Licking county. (See Fig. 13.)

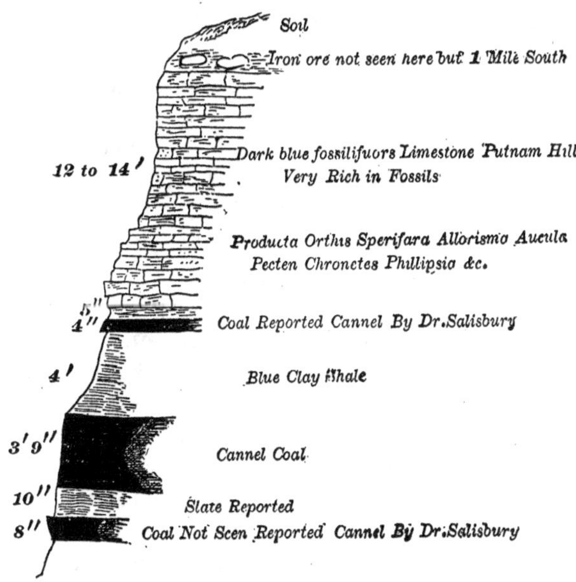

Fig. 13.

The cannel coal has been quite extensively wrought in former years for distillation into oil. The bank is now rented to Mr. Anderson, who sends a limited quality to Newark, where it is used for the parlor grate. Prof. Wormley gives the following analysis of this coal:

Specific gravity		1.298
Ash	19.95	
Volatile matter	36.80	
Fixed carbon	43.25	
Total	100.00	
Sulphur		1.31

Ash, dull white; coke, pulverulent.

At this point the cannel coal measures 3 ft. 9 in. Cannel coal is generally only a local modification of bituminous coal. The Flint Ridge cannel appears to be no exception to the general rule. The following facts were reported, viz: six hundred yards east of the present mine the cannel was only 2 ft. 9 in. One-half a mile farther east, there are 2 ft. of cannel, and a half mile still further, the coal is bitumious 2 ft. thick, while two and a half miles beyond the last point, it is cannel again, 1½ ft. thick. There were, apparently, depressions or basins on which the cannel coal was formed. These basins were filled with water as is proved by the abundance of the marine shell, Lingula, and by the great number of Stigmariæ found through the coal. I obtained a specimen of Stigmaria made up of coal itself and still retaining its cylindrical form. The Lingula and Stigmaria are, however, most abundant in the lower part of the coal, showing submergence while the coal was forming. The maceration of the vegetable matter into a pulp-like form would explain the cannel-like structure of the coal.

The limestone at Flint Ridge is separated from the coal by 4 ft. of blue clay shale, 4 in. of bituminous coal and 5 in. of bituminous slate. At the mine, the limestone is from 12 to 14 ft. thick. It is dark blue, almost black, thin bedded and contains some iron. The whole seam is highly fossiliferous and a handsome collection was made.

The following is another section showing the same limestone with a similar general grouping of strata. It was taken on the land of Joseph Porter, 100 acre lot, No. 16, Hopewell township, Muskingum county. (See Fig. 14.)

The limestone here partakes more of the nature of a highly calcareous shale than towards the extremity of Flint Ridge, ten miles west, where the last section was made. The lower part is more compact than the upper. It is very rich in fossils, of the same species of mollusca seen in the Flint Ridge limestone over the cannel coal. The seam of coal under the limestone is 4 ft. 11 in. thick, including a parting 20 inches from the bottom composed chiefly of pyrites. This parting varies from 2 to 8 inches. The upper seam of coal, in the above section, which was reported

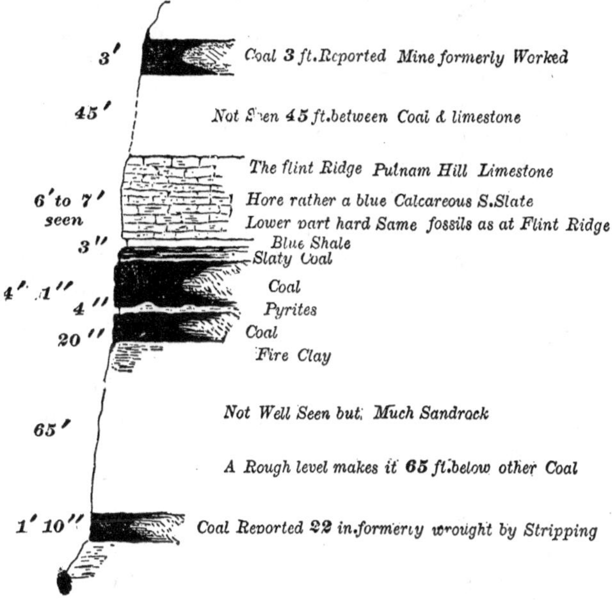

FIG. 14.

to be 3 feet thick, was formerly mined. Mr. Porter reports the coal business of Hopewell township at 120,000 bushels per annum.

The followiug is Prof. Wormley's analysis of Mr. Porter's coal:

Specific gravity		1.294
Ash	7.70	
Volatile matter	38 60	
Fixed carbon	53.70	
Total	100.00	
Sulphur		2.74

Ash, chocolate color.
Coke, compact and of metallic lustre.

A section of the rocks, taken near Cusac's Mill, on Jonathan's creek, Newton township, Muskingum county, showed an unusually bluish and fine grained sandstone about 30 feet below the limestone, believed to be the Putnam Hill limestone. It has been much quarried and used, although it has not always weathered well. As a general thing, the shales largely prevailed, and it is in consequence of this fact that we so often find that where the streams have in their work of erosion succeeded in cutting down through the Putnam Hill limestone, they have in all cases where the fall makes it possible, scored their way through the shales to the top of the Maxville or Newtonville limestone. This is very well seen in the neighborhood of Newtonville.

By reference to the map of grouped sections, it will be possible to see at a glance the lower division of the productive coal measures of this part of Ohio, extending from the top of the Logan sandstone group to the Putnam Hill limestone.

For the most part, the strata tell a story of comparatively quiet waters. At first we have a limestone-making period, during which, in limited secluded basins, limestone gradually accumulated, while at the same time in other places the stronger currents carried sandy materials, which are now found reposing at the same level of the limestone. Succeeding these we have similar scenes of quiet and also of moving waters, the former depositing fine shales and clay sediments, and the latter sandstones and sandy shales.

At a few points there were small basins in which thin layers of limestone were accumulated. There were also insular places on which the vegetation of the coal grew, which produced thin seams of coal. There was, doubtless, much vegetable matter carried into the waters, from which was evolved carbonic acid, which uniting with the iron oxides diffused in the waters and sediments, caused the formation of the common proto-carbonate or Siderite ore of iron. Some of the ores constitute regular layers, implying a regular deposition like other sedimentary strata; but for the most part the ores are in nodular form, often in large flattened discs, in which the well known laws of segregation came into play.

The iron ores, so far as they have been examined, are of the Siderite (proto-carbonate of iron) class, the exterior surfaces, which have been exposed to atmospheric agencies, only being changed to the sesqui-oxide of iron.

The carbonic acid might, in some cases, have originated in marine vegetation, which, in the form of Fucoids of the type of Spirophyton cauda-galli, was very abundant at certain periods during the formation of the strata of this lower coal-measure group.

There was a tendency to the formation of flint in connection with the layers of iron ore found about 30 feet below the Putnam Hill limestone. This stratum is far below the flint or buhr of Flint Ridge. The flint of this lower stratum was used by the aboriginal inhabitants for their weapons, and pits whence the flint was dug are not uncommon.

There is a thin seam of cannel coal a few miles south of Wolfe Station, in Perry county, on the Zanesville and Cincinnati Railroad, which was formerly mined for distillation into oil. No measurements were made, the old workings having fallen in. It belongs to the lowest part of the coal measures, but its exact stratigraghical position is not known, but will be ascertained hereafter.

Having thus given sections of the rocks of the lowest division of the productive coal-measures in the north-western portion of my District, the way is prepared to consider the strata above the level of the Putnam Hill limestone. It will be found that we have a second division with its upper member a seam of coal which is found very persistent over all the district examined. This coal is the "Nelsonville coal," the "Straitsville coal," the "Sunday creek coal," the "Upper New Lexington coal," for by all these local names is the seam designated.

The range of this coal is readily seen on the map of grouped sections. It is generally about 80 feet above the Putnam Hill limestone. In some sections, measured by the barometer, the distance was a little greater, but the instrument often gave results too great.

Another seam of coal will also be seen on the map, from 20 to 30 feet below the one last mentioned. Both of these seams have great economic value, and will hereafter be fully considered.

Between the top of the Putnam Hill limestone and the lower of these two seams of coal, we have from 50 to 60 feet of sandstones and shales. At but a very few points could we find exposures where minute and accurate sections could be made. A few feet above the limestone we find a tendency to the formation of iron ore. The largest development of ore on this horizon was seen on the branch railroad, leading from the Zanesville and Cincinnati Railroad to the Miami Company's mines, about half a mile from the mines. These mines are in Newton township, Muskingum county. Here, 5 feet over the hard blue limestone, believed to be the Putnam Hill, were some large and very fine nodules of iron ore, doubtless of the Siderite class.

There are indications of coal at a few points, but nowhere was it found to be of practical value. At one place a thin layer of limestone was seen, but sandstones and shales everywhere strongly predominate.

At an elevation of from 50 to 60 feet above the Putnam Hill limestone, it appears that the bed of the shallow ocean was made comparatively even and level, and was then brought up from below the water. On the higher and probably better drained areas, coal vegetation took root, and grew, and we have, as the result, a seam of coal. This seam is not always persistent, for the conditions of accumulations did not everywhere exist. This seam is seen at many places in the region of Nelsonville. At the mines of the Hocking Valley Coal, and Iron, Coke and Mining Company, on the land of J. W. Scott, York township, Athens county, this seam is found at a distance of 27½ feet below the main Nelsonville seam. It was not measured, but is there popularly called the "three feet vein."

Near John Fluhart's mill, Green township, Hocking county, it was seen about 25 feet below the main coal vein, but here it was much cut away by the sand rock over it.

It was also seen near Horace Hazelton's, Salt Lick township, Perry county, about 30 feet below the main seam, which is here 9 feet 4 inches thick. But at this point, also, the lower coal is much cut away by the overlying sand rock, and presents a very singular appearance. One of the best exposures of the lower seam, in the south part of Perry county, was on the land of Thomas Barnes, on Lost run, Lick township. In the immediate vicinity of Straitsville, we found no exposure showing the lower seam.

In the neighborhood of New Lexington, the lower seam is quite persistent, and has been considerably mined. At the mines of the Miami Company, on the branch of the Zanesville and Cincinnati Railroad, the lower seam is 3 feet 10 inches thick, and is largely mined. It is 22 feet below the upper coal, which is here 4 feet thick, including an inch of clay, parting near the middle.

Near the McLuney Station, Harrison township, Perry county, the lower seam, represented as four feet thick, is passed through in digging wells. Here the upper seam, four feet eight inches thick, is mined in many places.

On John Lyle's land, section 14, Newton township, Muskingum county, the lower seam, three feet ten inches thick, is extensively mined. By reference to the map of grouped sections, the general range of this coal, and its relation to the Putnam Hill limestone below, and the coal seam above, will be readily seen. It is doubtless true that in places the seam is wanting, the conditions not having been favorable to its formation.

Between this coal and the one above it we find in places valuable clay shales. Of these much pottery is made at Roseville and vicinity. There is also, a few feet below the upper coal, a layer of nodular iron ore, which will be noticed hereafter. The ore is imbedded in fine clay shales, which are everywhere found below the upper coal. These were fine sediments, which, in their deposition, evened up the bed or floor on which the coal was to be accumulated.

NELSONVILLE OR STRAITSVILLE COAL.

We now reach, in our upward progress, a seam of coal which will doubtless prove to be the finest in the State. The limits of its horizontal range I have not yet found, either in Muskingum county to the north, or in Athens county to the south. It is everywhere of good working thickness, and, over a large area, it measures from six to eleven feet. It is thinner on the north, but on Sunday and Monday creeks, in Perry county, it is eleven feet, and on the Hocking, in the vicinity of Nelsonville, it is seldom less than six feet.. There is no doubt that it is one continuous seam, as it not only holds uniform relations to the lower rocks, from the Logan sandstone up, but it has, moreover, been traced from hill to hill throughout nearly the whole distance. A glance at the large map will be more convincing than any detailed description of this point.

I have yet to trace the seam south of the Hocking hills, between them and the Marietta and Cincinnati Railroad, but I know it to extend a considerable distance south of Nelsonville. It dips below the Hocking river not far from the mouth of Monday creek, but is reached by shafts at various points as far down the Hocking as Salina and Chauncey. The description of its southern extension will be reserved until after more detailed examinations.

THICKNESS OF THE SEAM.

At Nelsonville and vicinity the coal measures from six feet to six feet four inches. The following are measured sections of the coal at the well-known mines of W. B. Brooks, Esq., and of Peter Hayden, Esq. Sec. A is that of Mr. Brooks, and Sec. B that of Mr. Hayden. (See Fig. 15.)

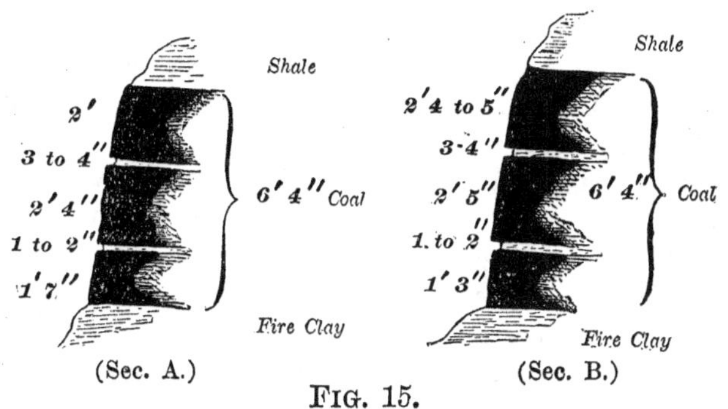

FIG. 15.

The partings are essentially the same, and the coals show the same physical structure. The partings seen in the foregoing sections are generally found to characterize the seam throughout its whole extent.

On the land of S. B. Westenhaver, Green township, Hocking county, near the north-western out-crop of the seam, the coal was a trifle thinner, measuring in total thickness five feet seven inches. Here the seam shows its usual subdivisions. The seam, in its northern and north-eastern extension, grows thicker.

At Straitsville, Salt Lick township, Perry county, the seam measures eleven feet, and shows the following subdivisions, as seen at the McGinnis bank. (See Fig. 16.)

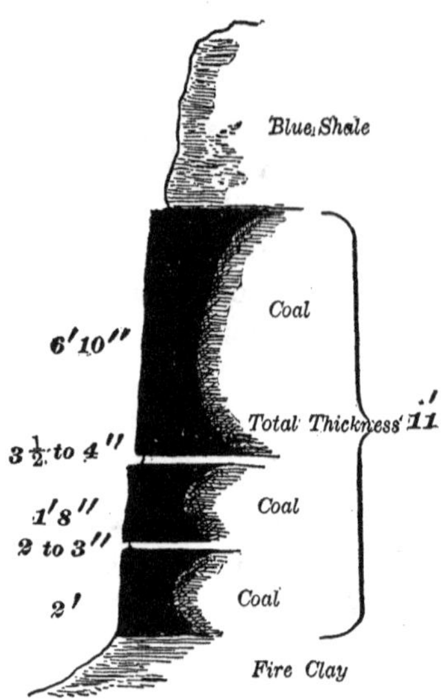

FIG. 16.

The mine of Daniel Moore, near Straitsville, was not minutely examined, but was thought to be a fac-simile of the McGinnis bank, in quantity and quality of coal.

In the same township we found the following measurements: On Thomas Barnes' land, nine feet ten inches (see section, Fig. 17); John Larue's, eight feet four inches; at Mr. Turner's drift, nine feet four inches; Horace Hazelton's, nine feet four inches; Henry Hazelton's (not well exposed), but seven feet or more. On the lands of J. Gordon and Henry Welch the coal is very heavy, but the mines were so fallen in at the openings that no measurements could be made.

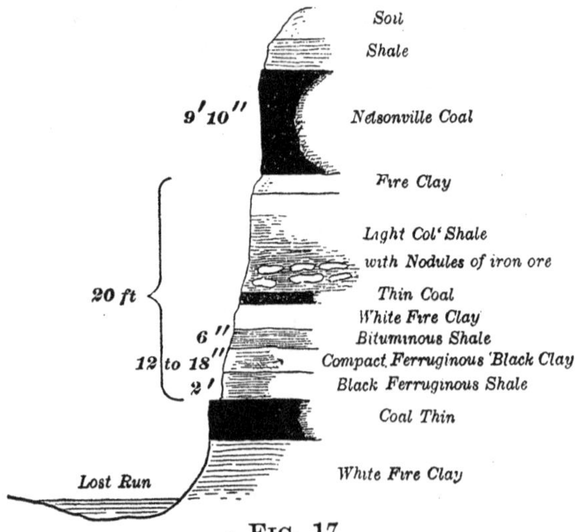

FIG. 17.

South of Straitsville, on the Snow Fork of Monday creek and its tributaries, the coal is everywhere largely developed; indeed, throughout the whole of Ward township, Hocking county, the coal is to be found in large development. It is unnecessary to designate locations; every farmer who owns hill land possesses the coal. In the valley of the Snow Fork it dips below drainage not far from the south-east corner of Ward township. The measurements on the lower part of Snow Fork showed six feet of coal. This was at James Hawkins', Sec. 3, Ward township. Higher up the stream the seam is said to increase in thickness, which I readily believe, although there were no good exposures for measurements. Near the head of the east branch, on the land of Alexander Marshall, in Sec. 35, Salt Lick township, Perry county, the "big seam" was seen largely developed. The opening was full of water, and no measurement taken. It was claimed to be eleven feet thick. From this point, crossing the high ridge to the north-east, we came down into the west branch of Sunday creek, where we found the coal in the low valley. Here it ranges from six to eleven feet in thickness. At Gaver's mill, and on the adjacent land of L. M. McDonald, Esq., near the Coal Dale P. O., Salt Lick township, the seam measures six feet two inches. The following is a section taken at the mill. (See Fig. 18.)

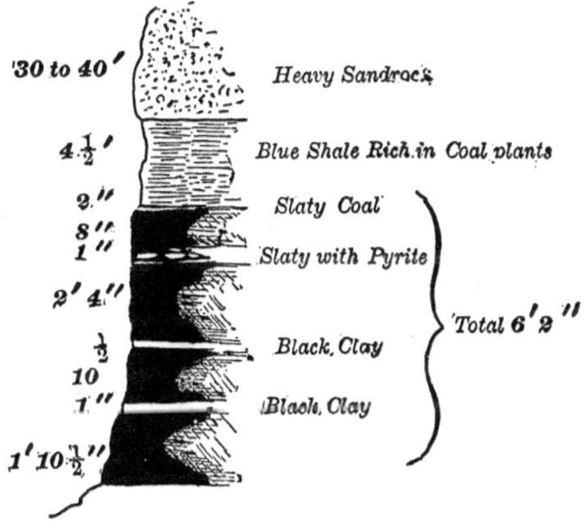

FIG. 18.

Here there is a good slate roof, very rich in coal plants. At the Lyons bank, half a mile above, the coal is 7 ft. thick, and of very excellent quality. Lower down the stream the upper slate is gone, and the sandstone has cut away the coal. At one place the coal was only 3 feet 8 inches, and at other places it was entirely gone. In that neighborhood, over a limited area, the waters, in the coal measure era, took strange liberties with the coal after it had been deposited. This will be noticed more fully hereafter.

On the farm of Benjamin Saunders, Monroe township, Perry county, on the west branch of Sunday creek, the coal measures eleven feet. Here there are two slaty partings. (See Fig. 19.)

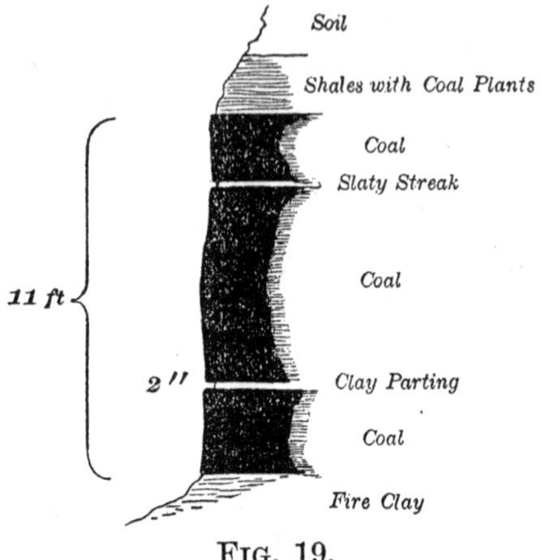

FIG. 19.

The exposure shows a magnificent body of very superior coal. The coal shows itself at other points on this branch, but no other measurements were taken. The coal in this valley generally lies low, but in mining it to the north and north-west, every advantage can be taken of the dip for easy mining and drainage.

In all the tributaries of Sunday creek which have the requisite erosion, we find the coal. In the branch which runs through the southeast section of Pleasant township, Perry county, we find the coal in full thickness, measuring at the bank of Joshua Sands, 11 feet 2 inches, with several clay partings. At the bank of William Bennett, a little above, it is probably as thick; the water preventing, at the time of our visit, a full measurement. In this neighborhood the coal lies too low for easy drainage, but the difficulty can be obviated. A vast body of coal in the hills to the north, can be mined up the dip from this valley. There is, scarcely, no limit to the coal, which is rendered accessible by the various branches of Sunday creek, in Pleasant, Monroe and Salt Lick townships. The great body of high-lands which constitute the divide between the waters flowing south and those flowing north, through Jonathan's creek, into the Moxahala and Muskingum, and west through Rush creek, into the upper Hocking, is doubtless underlaid with this coal. The coal seam constitutes a vast sheet, of 11 feet in maximum thickness on the south, but gradually growing thinner, to 4 and 5 feet, in its northern out-crop along the Zanesville & Cincinnati Railroad. The value of the upper Sunday creek valley as a coal field, cannot be over-estimated.

North of Straitsville, the higher grounds take the coal. Two and a half miles east of Maxville, on the land of Jared Danison, Monday creek township, Perry county, the coal measured, to the roof of the entry, 7 feet 8 inches. No opportunity presented itself for seeing whether there was more coal above. Here were seen the usual partings exhibited at Straitsville and Nelsonville. To the northeast, the coal extends through the hills, and was seen on the land of Levi Rarick, not far from Bristol, in Pike township. Here the thickness was 4 feet 2 inches, and the seam showed the usual partings. The coal above the upper parting is not esteemed. About 18 feet below is another thinner seam, reported to be 2½ feet thick. If this is the usual lower seam, it is nearer the upper than is common.

On James Clark's land, one half a mile north, the coal gives the same measurement. The seam is reported as worked all the way down Monday creek for some miles. From Mr. Clark's the seam was traced all the way to New Lexington, *where it is the upper seam in that neighborhood.*

In Jackson township, north of Monday Creek township, the same seam was seen on the lands of Eli Bell and Leonard Bell, in sections 34 and 35. Here the measurements were 3 feet 9 inches, exclusive of a stratum of bituminous slate, in the top, from 7 to 9 inches thick. On Emanuel France's land, Sec. 16, Pike township, the coal measured 4 feet 3 inches, with the usual partings. The upper part is held in less esteem than the middle and lower parts. Thomas McClelland's bank showed the same thickness. North of New Lexington, the mines of Judge R. E. Huston were opened in this seam chiefly; but he has mined, somewhat, the lower seam 23 feet below. No measurements could be made. Judge Huston reports the upper seam to be 4 feet, and the lower 3½ feet thick. Here the lower seam was found to be about 60 feet above the level of the railroad. The railroad, with its ascending grade, gradually rises above the two seams of coal, and at the tunnel through the ridge which divides the waters of Rush creek from those of the south fork of Jonathan's creek, it has reached an elevation of from twenty to twenty-five feet above the upper coal. The upper seam is here 4 feet 8 inches, and was formerly mined quite extensively.

On the land of Henry Jones, one-fourth of a mile southwest of McLuney Station, the seam gives a total thickness of 4 feet 8 inches. The upper part, of 13 inches, reported as not worked. Here, formerly, the coal was extensively mined.

At the mines of the Miami Company, in Newton township, Muskingum county, both seams are now largely mined, and the coal shipped by the Zanesville and Cincinnati Railroad. The upper seam measures 4 feet, and the other, which is 22 feet below, measures 3 feet 10 inches. Samples of the coals of this enterprising company failed to reach our Chemist. The coal is largely used for domestic purposes, and for the generation of steam, and is well spoken of.

Near Roseville, Clay township, Muskingum county, an old coal-working was found to be 80 feet above the Putnam Hill limestone. This is the proper place for the Nelsonville or upper New Lexington coal. No opportunity presented itself for measurement. The citizens of Roseville believe that the lower seam is wanting in that neighborhood. It is possible that the soft shales which generally overlie it, have become disintegrated, and slipped down over the out-crop and concealed it; but it may be wanting altogether, as the seam is not always persistent.

In the high ridge in Licking county, which is called Flint Ridge, we find near the top, and under the buhr or flint seam, a very thin coal seam, only 6 inches thick, which is, from its stratigraphical position, the equivalent of the Nelsonville coal. This gives us also the position of the buhr stratum.

The flint or buhr stratum, on Flint Ridge, is not found to correspond in stratigraphical position with the other layers of flint found in the district especially examined. The flint in the valley of Rush creek, near New Lexington, Perry county, lies lower in the series, and the calcareo-silicious rock of Dr. Hildreth, in the old Geological Report, found high on the hills in Section 14, Clay township, Muskingum county, lies higher in the series, as shown on the map of grouped sections. It was found difficult to determine the exact stratigraphical position of the Flint Ridge buhr, as it lies upon the top of the ridge, more like a blanket than like a rigid stratum. It conforms more or less to the undulating surface of the general top of the ridge, and is at some points many feet higher than at others.

According to a measured section at Flint Ridge, made by Leo Lesquereux, Esq., and taken from the Kentucky report, there is a thin seam of coal (6 in.) with fire clay (2 ft.) beneath, lying directly under the flint or buhr. This coal has the stratigraphical position of the Nelsonville or Straitsville coal, being 77½ feet above the "Putnam Hill" lime stone, which is found in unusual thickness above the cannel coal. This would make the place of the buhr just over the Nelsonville coal.

The buhr is of variable thickness, its maximum being perhaps 8 feet. Formerly, mill-stones were made from the rock, but the quarries have been of late years abandoned. It is claimed that the purer portions of the flint, when crushed, will serve a valuable purpose for glass making.

To the aboriginal inhabitants of the country, the layers of flint, interstratified with our coal measure rocks, were of the highest economic importance, and much of the surface of Flint Ridge has been dug over by them in order to obtain flint of the requisite quality.

These pits present a subject of great interest to all especially interested in the study of the Mound Builders. The same energetic industry which mark the building of the ancient earthworks of this mysterious race, characterize their labors on Flint Ridge.

It will be seen that the Nelsonville seam of coal, which has been traced into Muskingum county, has a very extensive range. It has been already traced over a belt of country forty miles long, and averaging twelve miles wide. To the northwest the coal rises on the hills, and disappears. To the east and southeast it dips below all the valleys. The deeper the valley, the greater the southeastern extension of the coal. Before a perfect outline of this remarkable belt of coal can be made, it will be necessary to have a careful topographical map of the region prepared. Then a geologist could fill out the outlines of this and other seams of coal, iron ores, limestones, &c., so that every land owner might, by inspection, determine the probable mineral value of his property.

A proximately accurate outline of the northwestern limit of the great Nelsonville seam, in Perry county, will be made by drawing a line through sections 27, Madison; 19, Clayton; 25, Reading; 35, Reading; 26, Reading, and 13, Jackson townships. Thence the line is probably a little west of south in Monday Creek township, on to the Straitsville region. There must be, of course, out-liers of the coal in high hills, west and northwest of this line. Where there are no guides to be found, such as the Maxville or Putnam Hill lime stones, the altitude of the hills or ridges must determine whether they take the coal.

The geographical situation, as proximate to a vast coalless district, extending west and northwest of it for hundreds of miles, its accessibility, its enormous quantity and superior quality, the rare advantages for mining and draining, make this great seam of coal worthy the attention of the people of the State and of capitalists everywhere.

QUALITY OF THE COAL.

The coal is properly classed among the dry-burning coals. The tendency to melt and cake is slight, and the free circulation of air secures the best possible combustion. Although not as highly bituminous as some other varieties of coal, yet the flame is considerable, and the coal makes a very cheerful parlor fire.

This coal, mined in the vicinity of Nelsonville, has been in use for a long time, and everywhere has the reputation of being a very superior coal for all the uses to which it has been applied. For household use it is very popular. The small percentage of ash, the unusually complete combustion—giving a fine blaze and little smoke—the large percentage of fixed carbon giving great heating power, and the small amount of sulphur to create in combustion unpleasant sulphurous fumes, all combine to render the coal of this great seam one of the very best known coals for all household use. For the generation of steam it is highly esteemed. It has been used in rolling-mills at Columbus and Marietta with strong approval. Its value for smelting iron will be considered hereafter.

The following tables of analyses by Prof. T. G. Wormley, Chemist of the Survey, will reveal in minute detail the qualities and peculiarities of the coal.

Analyses of Coal from Nelsonville and Haydenville.

	No. 1.	No. 2.	No. 3.	No. 4.	No. 5.	No. 6.	No. 7.
Specific gravity	1.259	1.285	1.272	1.284	1.271	1.258	1.340
Water	6.80	6.20	6.65	5.00	6.45	5.30	5.45
Volatile matter	33.27	31.30	33.05	32 80	32.74	30.12	29.88
Fixed carbon	57.46	59.80	58.40	53 15	58.56	63.49	55 31
Ash	2.47	2.70	1.90	9.05	2.25	1.09	9.36
Total	100.00	100.00	100.00	100.00	100.00	100.00	100.00
Sulphur	0.74	0.97	0.41	0.94	1.19	0.64	1.63
Color of ash	Dull white.	Gray.	Yellow.	Gray.	Fawn.	Fawn.	Gray.
Nature of coke.......	Pulverulent.	Compact.	Compact.	Compact.	Semi-compact.	Pulverulent.	Pulverulent.
Cubic feet permanent gas per lb. coal.....	......	3.56	3.24	4.95	......	......	......

No. 1, sample of coal from mines of W. B. Brooks, Nelsonville.
No. 2, " " " " bottom layer of seam.
No. 3, " " " " middle "
No. 4, " " " " top "
No. 5, " " Peter Hayden, bottom "
No. 6, " " " middle "
No. 7, " " " top "

Analyses of the same Seam at Straitsville, Perry County.

	No. 8.	No. 9.	No. 10.	No. 11.	No. 12.	No. 13.	No. 14.
Specific gravity...	1.291	1.239	1.307	1.247	1.248	1.244	1.241
Water	7.90	7.20	7.60	6.00	5.35	7.55	8.15
Volatile matter ...	34.63	32.29	29.65	32.15	30.48	35 61	27.46
Fixed carbon	54 29	59.44	52 77	59.41	57.21	54.90	61.73
Ash	3.18	1.07	9.98	2.44	6.96	1.94	2.66
Total	100.00	100.00	100.00	100.00	100.00	100.00	100.00
Sulphur	0.98	0.73	0.68	0.50	1.22	1.05	0.78
Color of ash	Dull white.	Reddish.	White.	Yellowish gray.	Grayish.	White.	Reddish.
Nature of coke....	Compact.	Pulverulent.	Pulverulent.	Pulverulent.	Pulverulent.	......	......

No. 8, coal from bottom layer, Straitsville, Perry county.
No. 9, " middle " " "
No. 10, " bottom of top layer, Straitsville, Perry county.
No. 11, " middle " " "
No. 12, " upper part " " "
No. 13, " second sample of middle layer, Straitsville, Perry county.
No. 14, " " bottom " " "

Analyses of same Seam on Sunday Creek, Perry County.

	No. 15.	No. 16.	No. 17.	No. 18.	No. 19.	No. 20.	No. 21.	No. 22.
Specific gravity..	1.300	1.272	1.318	1.274	1.287	1.311	1.348	1.288
Water	5.60	6.65	5.65	6.10	5.85	6.00	6.55	8.15
Volatile matter..	29.92	36.22	30.01	33.43	35.21	39.10	29.72	33.43
Fixed carbon....	62.45	53.30	57.27	55.54	53.62	51.98	52.47	54.98
Ash	2.03	3.83	7.07	4.93	5.32	2.92	11.26	3.44
Total......	100.00	100.00	100.00	100.00	100.00	100.00	100.00	100.00
Sulphur	0.76	2.00	0.67	1.46	0.51	0.51	0.47	0.64
Color of ash.....	Dull white.	Purple.	White.	Gray.	Fawn.	Fawn.	White.	White.
Character of coke	......	Compact metal'c.	Compact.	......	Compact.	Compact.	Pulverulent.	Compact.

No. 15, from Benjamin Saunders' bank.
No. 16, " Mr. Sands' bank; No. 1 from bottom.
No. 17, " " " 2 "
No. 18, " " " 3 "
No. 19, " " " 4 "
No. 20, " " " 5 "
No. 21, " " " 6 "
No. 22, " " " 7 "

Analyses of same Seam on Lost run, Ward township, Hocking County.

	No. 23.	No. 24.	No. 25.	No. 26.	No. 27.	No. 28.
Specific gravity	1.278	1.290	1.257	1.284	1.287	1.274
Water	7.15	6.80	5.85	6.15	5.80	3.05
Volatile matter	35.28	36.16	37.10	33.22	35.42	38.39
Fixed carbon	55.16	54.99	55.12	55.75	51.15	47.51
Ash	2.41	2.05	1.93	4.88	7.63	11.05
Total...............	100.00	100.00	100.00	100.00	100.00	100.00
Sulphur	1.35	1.07	1.42	1.88	1.01	4.04
Color of ash	Light fawn.	Light fawn.	Light fawn.	Gray.	Cream.	Gray.
Sulphur in the coke of given weight of coal	0.81	0.79	0.51	1.00	0.50	2.02
Percentage of sulphur in coke	1.31	1.30	0.85	1.56	0.81	3.35
Iron in coal	0.77	0.57	0.38	1.42	0.09	2.11
Percentage of sulphur theoretically required by the iron	0.878	0.650	0.433	1.620	0.102	2.408
Character of coke..........	Compact.	Compact.	Quite compact.	Compact.	Very compact.	Very compact.

The samples of coal analyzed in the above table came from the same seam on Lost run, in Ward township, Hocking county. They were taken from two different openings, but represent the seam from roof to floor.

I have thus given twenty-eight different analyses, made with great care and scientific accuracy, all representing portions of the great Nelsonville seam of coal. They are of the highest scientific interest, and of the utmost practical importance.

(1.) Let it be first remarked, that they represent the seam of coal in locations of its best development, viz., at Nelsonville, Athens county, where it measures 6 feet 4 inches; at Haydenville, Hocking county, near Nelsonville, where it measures the same; at Straitsville, Perry county, where it measures 11 feet; at two points on Sunday creek, where it also measures 11 feet; and on Lost run, in Ward township, Hocking county, where it measures 10 feet 6 inches. The coal here represented is found in six different townships and in three different counties. The locations are all accessible, and they are either already reached, or soon will be, by railroads. Nelsonville and Haydenville mines already have the advantage of railroad and canal.

(2.) Again, it is obvious that the coal in the seam is not homogeneous in quality from roof to floor. In the mine of Mr. Wm. B. Brooks, near Nelsonville, the upper part of the seam is more earthy, giving by analysis 9.05 per cent. of ash, while the average of the two analyses of the middle and lower parts of the seam is only 2.30 per cent.

In the mine of Mr. Peter Hayden, near Haydenville, the top coal gives 9.36 per cent. of ash, while the ash of the middle and lower portions of the seam average only 1.67 per cent.

The most earthy part of the coal in the Sands bank, on Sunday creek, as shown by analysis, is that taken 2 feet 2 inches from the top, which yields 11.26 per cent. of ash, while a sample taken a little above, or 14 inches from the top, gave only 3.44 per cent., and a sample taken 18 inches below gave only 2.92 per cent. A sample 2 feet 6 inches from the bottom gave 7.07 per cent. of ash.

Of the six samples obtained to represent the same seam of coal on Lost run, Ward township, Hocking county, that from the top contained 11.05 per cent. of ash, and the one next below 7.63 per cent.; while the average amount of the four remaining lower ones, representing about 8 feet of coal, is only 3.57 per cent.

The Straitsville coal is divided into three layers; and it is found that the largest percentage of ash is found near the top and bottom of the upper layer. This upper layer is 6 feet 10 inches thick in the McGinnis bank. Near the bottom of it the ash was found to be 9.98 per cent., and on the very top the ash was found to be 9.35 per cent. The latter result is not given in the table, but comes from the analyses of a single independent specimen, sent to the laboratory by Mr. S. M. Baird. The sample of the top coal, of the series given in the table for the Straitsville coal, afforded less ash, viz., 6.96 per cent. The average ash of all other samples taken elsewhere in the seam, is only 2.26 per cent.

Thus it will be seen that this great seam of coal is not uniform in regard to the ash of its several parts. There are generally two sources from which the ash of our coals is derived; first, from the inorganic matter which belongs to all vegetation, and shows itself, for example, in the ash of our firewood; second, from fine sedimentary matter brought by water and distributed through the coal marsh when the vegetation of the coal was growing. In regard to the first, it is difficult to ascertain the exact amount of inorganic matter properly belonging to the coal vegetation. Different plants and trees yield different amounts of ashes, and different parts of the same plant or tree yield different quantities.

The least ash thus far found in any coal in my district was from a coal in Jackson county, which gave 0.85 per cent. Whether in this we have more than the original vegetation of the coal would supply, it would be difficult to decide. When the Jackson county coals are hereafter studied some light may be thrown on this interesting problem.

In regard to the second source of ash, viz., sediments intermixed with the vegetation, it is unnecessary to state, that we find no two seams of coal alike in the quantity of their earthy matter, and indeed no two portions of the same seam. Sometimes the sediments amounted to a deposit of mud thick enough to make a clay or slate parting in the coal, but more often, a few inches of the coal are principally affected, and we simply find, on analysis, the coal to show an excess of ash or earthy matter. The great Nelsonville seam of coal illustrates both of these statements, for in it we find well-defined and continuous slate partings and also portions of the coal showing far more ash or earthy matter than other portions.

(3.) Again, much of the coal of this great seam contains a small percentage of sulphur. Nothing is so injurious as an excess of sulphur in coal. It unfits the coal for smelting iron, and for gas making. It attacks the iron grate bars when used for the generation of steam, and for all domestic uses a highly sulphurous coal is extremely disagreeable.

By reference to Prof. Wormley's analyses, it will be seen that in the Nelsonville mines and at Haydenville, the most sulphur is found in the top of the seam, and next in the bottom, while that in the middle layer of the seam has comparative little. At Straitsville the most sulphur is found in the upper part of the seam. On the other hand, the most sulphur in the seam, at the Sands bank on Sunday creek, is near the bottom, and next to this, in the third sample from the bottom, as given in No. 18, in the table of analyses. The other five samples, which represented the larger part of this great seam, revealed a comparatively small percentage of sulphur.

On Lost run the analyses revealed more sulphur. As, however, there was very little visible sulphur in the usual form of bi-sulphide of iron in the samples analyzed, I was led to request Prof. Wormley to undertake some additional analyses, to see if there was in the coal as much iron as the revealed sulphur would require to form the bi-sulphide. Prof. Wormley undertook the careful examination of this question, and his results, which are altogether new to science, not only reflect upon him the highest credit, but promise to be of great economic value.

All the authorities on the subject of coal have hitherto supposed the sulphur to be chemically combined with iron in the form of a bi-sulphide of iron ($Fe\ S^2$). Prof. Dana, in his recent great work on Minerology expresses a doubt in regard to this in the following paragraph, page 756:

"Sulphur is present in nearly all coals. It is supposed to be usually combined with iron, and when the coal affords a *red ash* on burning, there is reason for believing this true. But Percy mentions a coal from New Zealand, which gave a peculiarly white ash, although containing from 2 to 3 p. c. of sulphur, a fact showing that it is present not as a sulphide of iron, but as a constituent of an organic compound. The discovery by Church of a resin containing sulphur (see Tasmanite, p. 746), gives reason for inferring that it may exist in this coal in that state, although its presence as a constituent of other organic compounds is quite possible."

By an examination of Prof. Wormley's table of analyses of the Lost run coal, it will be seen that in no case is there iron enough in the coal to take up in combination all the sulphur. In No. 27, the sulpher is 1.01 per cent. Adopting for the combination of the bi-sulphide of iron the proportion given by Prof. Dana, viz., iron 46.7, and sulphur 53.3, in 100 parts, the sulphur in No. 27 would require 0.884 per cent. of iron, whereas Prof. Wormley finds only 0.09 per cent. This 0.09 per cent. of iron would only require 0.102 per cent. of sulphur to make the usual iron pyrites, and there are consequently 0.908 per cent. of sulphur elsewhere in the coal than in combination with iron. This excess of sulphur must be both in the volatile matter and in the coke. The coke retains 0.50 per cent. of sulphur. This shows that part of the sulphur is in permanent combination with the fixed carbon of the coal.

The average loss of sulphur in reducing all the coals from Lost run to coke is 56 per cent.

Another marked illustration of the disproportion of sulphur to the iron in a bituminous coal is found in the analysis of a coal from Washington county. The coal is a white ash coal, and the sample analyzed had been in the cabinet of Marietta college for fourteen years, and showed none of the usual tendency to disintegrate from a change of the bi-sulphide to the sulphate of iron, a salt which, in crystallizing, breaks the coal by its expansion.

The sample was found by Prof. Wormley to contain only 0.390 per cent. of iron, but 3.330 per cent. of sulphur. There should have been but 0.445 per cent. of sulphur, if the sulphur were limited to a bi-sulphide of iron. The coke retained 1.82 per cent. of sulphur.

These analyses are of the highest practical importance. In coals for *gas-*

making it is not enough to know the percentage of sulphur in the coal, but rather how much of sulphur passes into the gas. In the analysis, No. 25, there is in the coal 1.42 per cent. of sulphur, while the coke retains but 0.51 per cent., nearly two-thirds of the sulphur having passed off in the volatile matter. In No. 24, of the 1.07 per cent. of sulphur, 0.79 per cent. remains in the coke, or about three-quarters of the whole.

In coals for *smelting iron*, it is most important that the coke be as free from sulphur as possible. The sulphur in the coke comes in contact with the melting iron in the lower portion of the furnace, and contaminates it, but the sulphur, which passes off while the coal is undergiong the process of coking in the upper part of the stack, does comparatively litle harm. Hence, for the purpose of iron-making, the exact percentage of sulphur remaining in the coke should be carefully ascertained. It is, furthermore, evident that the popular method of determining the quality of a coal by the color of its ash will often prove falacious. A white-ash coal may have an excessive amount of sulphur, and yet contain so little iron that its oxidation in the fire will not redden the ash. This will most certainly be the case where the amount of ash is large and the percentage of iron small.

(4.) Again, the analyses of the great Nelsonville seam of coal, show a large percentage of *fixed carbon*, and *consequent heating power*. The average fixed carbon for all the analyses of the seam at Nelsonville, and at Haydenville, is 56.59 per cent. The average of the seam at Straitsville is 56.96 per cent. The average of seam on Sunday creek is 55.20 per cent. The average of seam on Lost run, excluding the very top coal, which will not be mined on account of its impurities, is 54.43 per cent. The average of all in fixed carbon, is 55.79 per cent.

For the purpose of comparison, I give, from Prof. Wormley's records, the analyses of several of our best iron-making coals:

	No. 29.	No. 30.	No. 31.	No. 32.	No. 33.	No. 34.
Specific gravity	1.282	1.336	1.284	1.247	1.364	1.173
Water	7.75	7.60	3.60	6.95	6 65	5.45
Volatile matter	31.27	30.96	32.58	32 38	34.54	38.76
Fixed carbon.........	58.95	57.65	62.66	57.49	54.28	53.99
Ash..................	2.03	3.79	1.16	3.18	4.53	1.80
Total..........	100.00	100.00	100.00	100.00	100 00	100.00
Sulphur	0.53	0.49	0.85	0.88	1.07	0.75
Color of ash	Reddish.	White.	Red.	Grayish.	Fawn.	Grayish.
Character of coke ...	Pulverulent.	Pulverulent.	Pulverulent.	Very compact.	Quite compact.	Compact

No. 29. Jackson shaft coal................................Jackson, Jackson Co.
" 20. Hill coal .... " "
" 31. "Briar Hill" coal..................................Chestnut Ridge.
" 32. Blue Chippewa coal ....Massillon.
" 33. Coalton or Ashland coal ....Boyd Co., Kentucky.
" 34. Brazil " " ....Clay Co., Indiana.

The average fixed carbon in the above coals, is 57.43 per cent. It will be noticed that the Briar Hill coal, from Chestnut Ridge, contains less than the average quantity of water, and this fact increases the percentage of the fixed carbon and other constituents. The Blue Chippewa coal, from Massillon, contains 6.95 per cent. of water, and the quantity of fixed carbon is 57.49 per cent., which is a little less than that of the two Jackson coals.

The Ashland or Coalton coal † (No. 33) is a very successful furnace coal, from Boyd county, Ky. Its percentage of fixed carbon is 54.28, while the average of the great Nelsonville seam, from all the localities, is 55.79. The proportion of fixed carbon in the Brazil coal, of Indiana, is less than that of the Ashland coal, being 53.99 per cent.

In the light of all these facts, the very great excellence of the Nelsonville seam of coal must be conceded.

For the purpose of additional comparison, I give the results of the analyses of a large number of British coals, used in the manufacture of iron, taken from the Report of the British Association for the Advancement of Science, for the year 1863. They are taken from a very elaborate paper on the "Manufacture of Iron in connexion with the Northumberland and Durham Coal-fields," by Isaac Lowthian Bell, Mayor of Newcastle:

Samples.	Locality.	Sp. gravity.	Carbon.	Hydrogen.	Nitrogen.	Sulphur.	Oxygen.	Ash.	Per centage of coke.	Fixed carbon.*
18	Newcastle......	1.256	82.15	5.31	1.35	1.24	5.69	3.77	60.67	56.90
36	Wales..........	1.315	83.78	4.79	0.98	1.43	4.15	4.91	72.62	67.71
8	Scotland.......	1 259	78.53	5.61	1.00	1.11	9.69	4.03	54.22	50.19
7	Derbyshire.....	1.192	79.68	4.94	1.41	1.01	10.28	2.65	59.32	56.67

In the above analyses we have all the different elements given separately. It will be noticed that the sulphur in the coals runs from 1.01 to 1.43. This is in excess of our better Ohio coals, as will be seen by referring to the analyses of Prof. Wormley. As the English iron manufacturers generally coke the coal, and, in the blast furnaces, they expel, in coking, about one half of the sulphur. In regard to the coke used in the celebrated Cleveland Iron District, England, Mr. Bell, from whom I have first quoted, writes:—"To form an idea of the extent to which ash and sulphur exist in the coke of the South Durham coal-field, the following analyses are extracted from the Clarence Laboratory journal:

* I have given the fixed carbon, as ascertained by subtracting the ash from the coke. The Welsh coals are partly anthracite, hence the large percentage of fixed carbon.

† The sulphur in table doubtless too high for average of the coal.—E. B. A.

Ash, per cent.		Sulphur, per cent.
5.86	....	0.58
5.79	....	0.68
7.54	....	0.77
9.00	....	0.44
8.33	....	0.50

"As a rule," he adds, "6 per cent. of ash and about 0.60 of sulphur may be considered as the average analytical results of the best coke of the district, just quoted."

A more recent authority, Prof. H. Bauerman, of the Royal School of Mines, in a work on Metallurgy, published in London, 1868, says that "the Cleveland district is remarkable for the large size and height of its furnaces (from 70 to 102 feet high), which are entirely worked with hard coke from the south of Durham, containing on an average from 0.60 to 0.80 per cent. of sulphur, and from 4½ to 8 per cent. of ash."

In the examination of the analyses of coals made by Prof. Wormley, and the comparison of his results with most other analyses, it must be remembered that the Professor makes a careful determination of the combined water. The samples analyzed are, of course, dry, in the ordinary sense, to begin with. But if the temperature be kept at 212 deg., the coal continues to lose weight for a considerable time, after which, if the heat is continued, the weight begins to increase, doubtless from the oxidation of one or more of the constituents of the coal. After the loss of weight, if the coal be allowed to cool and remain for a time, it regains from the atmosphere moisture enough to restore its original gravity. The water thus lost is given by Prof. Wormley in the tables. It is not generally given in other analyses of coals, but clearly should be, not only because it is a constant constituent in western coals, generally increasing in quantity the farther west we obtain the coal, but because it is a source of loss to the consumer, who not only buys water, but must use a part of the heating power of his coal to expel it.

One of the most important of the practical questions connected with this coal, is its adaptation to the smelting of iron. It has been already seen that the percentage of sulphur is relatively small, that the ash is small, and that the amount of fixed carbon is large. It is also a dry-burning coal, and could be used in furnaces in the raw state. Where the seam is thickest, six or seven feet of the coal can be obtained which, in all the qualifications named, would be remarkably adapted to iron-making. Can there, then, be any reasonable doubt on this point? I think not, unless it may lurk in the yet undetermined physical properties of the coke. Will the coke be firm and strong enough to resist, without crushing, the great burden which must necessarily come upon it in the furnace? Although a dry coal, and not needing to be coked beforehand, yet it will necessarily be changed to coke in passing from the top of the furnace down to the melting zone in the lower part of the stack. Should the coke, thus formed, be crushed by the imposed burden, the draft of the furnace will be choked, and the working of the furnace seriously hindered.

Some of the analyses show the coke to be firm and compact, while others indicate a pulverulent character. This question can best be solved by actual experiment. Should such a tendency to brittleness be found to exist, the difficulty can be obviated. While in the Cleveland iron district, in England, the coke used is so compact and firm that it supports an enormous pressure in furnaces (sometimes more than one hundred feet in height), yet elsewhere, as in Staffordshire, where the coke is friable, and the ore also, and in South Wales, where the anthracite used decrepitates to such an extent as to produce the same difficulty in the furnace, the furnaces are low, and the superincumbent weight of the "charges" is distributed over a broader base. To sucure combustion in such furnaces, a larger number of twyers is used, and, that the blast may reach the center, the base is often made elliptical instead of round. The difficulty of soft coke being a physical one, it may be overcome by such mechanical arrangements as suggest themselves to intelligent metallurgists.

It might be found desirable to mix with the coal of the great Nelsonville seam a portion of hard coke obtained from some other coal, although such necessity appears to me improbable.

There are in places two seams of coal above the horizon of the Nelsonville seam of workable thickness, the coke of which may answer such a purpose. The coal of one of the seams is reported by Prof. Wormley to make a very compact coke. The coal of the other seam has not yet been analyzed.

That the time is not far distant when the coal of this greatest of Ohio coal seams will be largely used in the manufacture of iron, there can be little doubt.

The coal is already shipped from Nelsonville and vicinity to Chicago, and to other points on the Northern Lakes, from which the rich Lake Superior ores could be brought back as return freight. Limited quantities of lower coal measure ores are to be found in the neighborhood of the coal, especially in the strata lying between the horizon of the Nelsonville coal and the base of the coal measures, which could be used to great advantage as a mixture with the richer northern ores. Should these native ores prove like those used in Jackson, Lawrence and other counties in our furnace district of southern Ohio, the mixture would tend to counteract the red short quality of the Superior ores.

A large blast furnace is now in process of erection at Columbus, by S. Baird, Esq., and others, to use the coal from the great seam. Lake Superior ores are to be mixed with such native ores as can be the most coveniently obtained from our lower coal measures. Limestone for flux can be obtained in ample supply from the great quarries in the immediate neighborhood of Columbus.

Should furnaces be erected in the immediate vicinity of the coal, limestone could be obtained from the "Maxville limestone" stratum at various accessible points. At Maxville, in Perry county, the limestone is well developed. It is also found near Logan. In the Sunday creek valley a white limestone of excellent quality is found on the highest hills, 213 feet above the level of the great coal seam. Another limestone, more earthy in character, but which would doubtless answer for a flux, is found 147 feet above the great seam. For furnaces located at Nelsonville, Haydenville, Logan, Straitsville, and other points on the Columbus & Hocking Valley Railroad and its branches, limestone from the Corniferous beds at Columbus could be used.

STRATA ABOVE THE NELSONVILLE SEAM OF COAL.

Having thus considered the "Nelsonville" seam of coal in its geographical range, its geological relations, its quantity, its quality, and its adaptations, the way is prepared to notice in detail the rocks which lie above it, so far as yet observed.

At Nelsonville, in the hill back of the village, we found the section as follows. (See Fig. 20.)

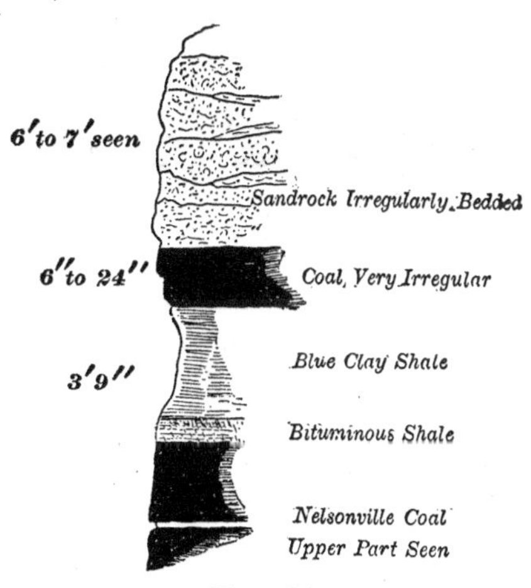

FIG. 20.

As a general rule, there are slates or shales immediately above the coal. Somestimes the sandrock, which is very heavy, lies directly upon the coal, although this, so far as we saw, was uncommon. In many places the sandstone is itself gone, and its place taken by yellow shales, in which we find coal seams. The changes from the sandrock to shales and back again, are so sudden and unexpected, that it is not strange that much confusion has arisen. Generally along the Hocking river we find the heavy sandrock separated from the coal by a few feet of clay shales. This clay sometimes comes down into the coal, filling cavities. The following diagram exhibits two of these "clay veins." (See Fig. 21.)

FIG. 21.

On the west branch of Sunday creek, in Monroe township, I saw two or three places where the coal was entirely gone, and the vacant space filled with a yellow shale. At one point it is cut squarely off where it is 10 or 11 feet thick. The sandy shales appear to have been shoved into the depression, and not to have accumulated by slow sedimentary increments, as there was little appearance of lamination. At another place, the coal seam grows smaller, and ends in a ball of coal, as seen in the accompanying figure. (See fig. 22.)

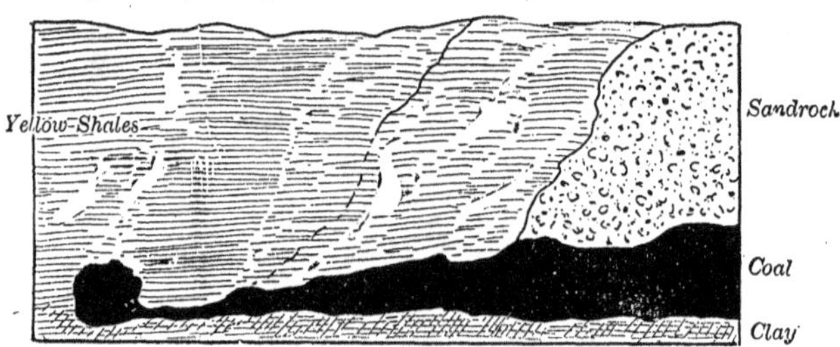

FIG. 22.

It is evident, from the study of the strata immediately over the Nelsonville seam, that there were most remarkable changes in the conditions of deposition in very limited areas. While the strong currents brought in and distributed sands in many places, at the same time there were near by, comparatively still waters, where the finer sediments, which now constitute the yellow shales, were deposited. At times these shales were brought above the surface, and the growth of vegetation afforded seams of coal. At a subsequent time, there were current ways cut down through these yellow shales and coals, removing even the great seam below. This is seen on the farm of Benjamin Saunders, Monroe township, Perry county. Fortunately these breaks in the continuity of the Nelsoville seam are rare and of very limited extent. It should also be remembered as a part of the history, that in some places the currents which brought in the sand of the sandrock removed the top of the coal, sometimes the whole seam, and left sandstone in the place of it. Hence, while below the seam the strata are fine, quiet-water sediments, and distributed with remarkable uniformity and evenness; above it we fi evidence of just the oppo site conditions of deposition. We should expect, therefore, that the seam of coal associated with the shales, above the main seam, would be limited in extent, and the work of grouping them into a system a difficult one.

One of the best exhibitions of the coal seams, above the great seam, is on the farm of Bayliss Glenn, on Snow Fork, Sec. 6, Ward township, Hocking county. (See Section No. 8 on Map of grouped sections.) Most of the section was made on Bear run, where the two upper seams of coal were seen. The lower, 3 ft. thick, is apparently poor in the upper half and good below. Twenty-nine feet above this seam are two or three feet of limestone, the lower part white and good, and the upper 10 inches apparently flinty and covered on the top with a little iron ore. On the limestone rests 5 ft. of shales, upon which is a seam of coal 4 ft. thick, the lower six inches of which is cannel. I had no opportunity to examine the quality of the coal, as no mine is opened. The cannel is rather heavy, with earthy matter. It contains fish remains. There is also in the hills bordering Snow Fork a seam of coal, reported to have been mined, situated a little higher than the seam last mentioned.

Near the head of the East branch, Snow Fork, near Alexander Marshall's, Sec. 35, Salt Lick township, Perry county, there are seen in the shales above the Nelsonville seam, the two coals found on the farm of Mr. Glenn, farther down the run. The coal over the limestone was reported 2½ ft. thick. Near the top of the high hill separating Snow Fork from the West branch of Sunday creek, is the blossom of a coal seam. Its exact height above the Nelsonville seam was not ascertained.

On the farm of Benj. Saunders, on the West branch of Sunday creek, there are two seams of coal above the great seam. These seams are seen in Sec. 22 on Map of grouped sections. The thickness of the first one above the great seam was not ascertained. To the north-west it probably runs out, and its place is taken by heavy sandstone. Near Millerstown, on the land of Mr. Morris, it has an unusual development of 6 feet, and the coal is of very fair quality. On the Grigsby farm it measures 4 feet, and is of good quality. The upper seam is more persistent, as it was found over a considerable area. It measures 4 feet, and, in quality, is highly esteemed in the neighborhood. Mr. Saunders obtains this coal (by stripping) for family use, preferring it to that of the great seam, which is 11 ft. thick on his farm.

Mr. George Stallsmith, in the same neighborhood, has taken out considerable of this coal, for family and neighborhood use. Prof. Wormley has analyzed this coal, with the following results:

Stallsmith's Upper Coal.

Specific gravity	1.254
Combined water	3.80
Ash	4.14
Volatile matter	40.21
Fixed carbon	51.85
Total	100.00
Sulphur	2.62
Permanent gas per lb. coal in cubic feet	4.69
Color of ash	Gray.
Character of coke	Compact.

This coal is rich in gas. It makes also a very compact and durable coke. The amount of sulphur is considerable, and may interfere with the usefulness of the coal for gas and iron making. Should, on coking, a considerable portion of the sulphur be eliminated, the coke might, from its hardness, serve an important purpose for a mixture with the coal of the great seam for iron making.

On the land of James Fowler, Pleasant township, Perry county, there are two seams of coal, as given on the Map of grouped sections, in Sec. No. 28. The lower seam was traced by Hon. Alvah Jones and my assistant, Mr. Ballantine, from Roseville, where it is the upper Lexington seam (the equivalent of the great or Nelsonville seam). The upper, 28½ feet above the lower, measures 4 ft. 10 in. The top 10 inches are not worked in the mine. No partings were seen. Mr. P. Yakey reported having mined the lower seam and found it 4½ feet thick, with a parting. On the land of Ebenezer Pyle, in the same township, there is a seam, 4 ft. 1 in. thick, which is believed to be the same as the upper one on Jas. Fowler's land. Mr. Pyle reports a seam below (probably the upper Lexington seam) and another above.

Doubtless there will be found at other points seams of coal lying above the great Nelsonville seam, and more careful investigations will hereafter be made as we carry our sections upward, above the horizon of the great seam. It is however already evident that, in Hocking and Perry counties, the conditions of deposition were such that we can expect little uniformity in the strata for the 60 or 80 feet above the great Nelsonville coal.

IRON ORES.

It will be almost impossible to make a section of the lower strata of the Productive Coal Measures, at any place, in the field included in this report, without disclosing more or less iron ore. There are a few distinct and well-defined horizons on which the ore is almost always seen. This is rendered evident by an examination of the map of grouped sections.

Beginning at the base of the coal measures, we find ore at a few points below the Maxville limestone. The best development was seen in Section 16, Madison township, Perry county, on the land of Edward Danison. Here upon the top of the Logan sandstone group were seen nodules of siderite ore in clay, measuring from 4 to 8 inches thick, and overlaid by sandy shales. S. Baird, Esq., formerly in charge of the furnace at Logan, reports a layer of ore over a seam of fire-clay resting on the Logan sandstone. This is not far from Logan, and is in the same geological horizon with the last mentioned.

On the top of the Maxville limestone iron ore was seen at several points. On the farm of Mr. Danison, previously alluded to, this ore was found from 4 to 8 inches thick. A sample of this ore was analyzed by Prof. Wormley, and the result given in No. 5 of the appended table of analyses. This ore is interesting, as containing 4.30 per cent. of manganese. No alumina was found, which is remarkable for a coal-measure ore, and one overlaid by a shale containing much clay. Of sulphur and phosphorus it contains only a trace. The percentage of metallic iron, 38.87, added to the unusual purity, would make this a desirable ore for making iron, if it can be obtained in sufficient quantity.

On Section 14, Newton township, Muskingum county, on the farm of Joseph Rambo, nodules of similar ore were found resting upon the great Maxville or Newtonville limestone. No analysis was made of this, but probably it is an excellent ore.

In Section 28, Green township, Hocking county, on James Tannahill's land, is a very thin layer of nodules of iron ore, containing quartz pebbles, resting upon the Maxville limestone. This ore is here the only representative of the true coal-measure conglomerate. The place of the conglomerate is above the Maxville limestone. Dr. Briggs, in the old reports, observes the conglomeratic character of this ore.

On Edward Danison's land, already referred to, there is a thin layer of siderite ore 13½ feet above the limestone ore, and still another layer 3 inches thick, 15 feet higher.

In a section made by Dr. Hildreth, given in the old Geological Reports, and copied as Sec. 35 in my map of grouped sections, on Joseph Baird's land, Sec. 11, Hopewell township, Licking county, a layer of ore 1 foot 4 inches thick, rests upon the Maxville limestone. This is thicker than I found it at any point. Ten feet higher up, Dr. H. reports a seam 8 inches thick. Col. J. W. Foster, in the old geological reports, gives a section (copied as No. 41 in my map of grouped sections) in which are two layers of shale containing nodules of iron ore. These are repectively 15 feet 4 inches and 17 feet 4 inches above the limestone in the bed of the Muskingum, at Zanesville.

At nearly the same geological horizon on the land of Joseph Rambo, Sec. 14, Newton township, Muskingum county, are two small layers of siderite ore, separated by 1 foot 7 inches of light blue clay-shale, the lower 2 inches and the upper 3 to 4 inches thick.

Near John Fluhart's mill, Green township, Hocking county, there were found nodules and thin layers of iron ore, in shales, the upper part black, and the middle white clay, and the lower bluish. There were nodules of ore in all these shales, but probably none were thick enough to work. Some of the ore was flinty.

At Maxville, Perry county, a layer of siderite ore, 3 inches thick, was seen about 20 feet above the top of the Maxville limestone.

These lower ores are found sweeping through the northern half of Perry county, but there was great difficulty in finding such exposures of the rocks as would enable us to determine their exact stratigraphical position. Near Wolfe Station, on the Zanesville and Cincinnati Railroad, one of these layers of ore is somewhat largely mined and sent to a furnace at Zanesville. Mr. Baird, who first used this ore, thinks it is elsewhere represented by the ore resting upon the Maxville limestone. North of this, in the Somerset region, excellent ores are found. Should a railroad be built through that part of the county these ores could be profitably mined and sent to furnaces.

Between 40 and 50 feet above the level of the Maxville limestone is a very well-marked horizon of ore. The ore is seen directly behind the old Hocking furnace at Haydenville, Green township, Hocking county, where the quality is good, but it adheres firmly to the sandstone below it. Where it could be removed from the stone it has been used in the furnace. Below the sandstone, which is 12 inches thick, is a stratum of earthy limestone 1 foot 6 inches thick. Both limestone and sandstone are highly fossiliferous.

On the bank of Monday creek, opposite Henry Hazelton's, Salt Lick township, Perry county, this ore is well seen. Here there are three or four layers. The upper is in nodular masses imbedded in blue shale. The next below is ore of a good quality, and lies in one and sometimes two layers. The lowest is rather a ferriferous flint. In all, there may be 15 inches of ore. Three samples were analyzed by Prof. Wormley, and the results are given in table of analyses of ores. No. 1 was from the top, or nodular layer; No. 2 the next below, and No. 3 the flinty ore. No. 1 is a rich ore, yielding 41.37 per cent. of metallic iron. It is chiefly a carbonate of iron (siderite), but a portion has been changed under atmospheric agencies to limonite or the hydrated sesquioxide. It contains 0.48 per cent. of sulphuric acid and 0.18 of phosphoric acid. No. 2 is also rich in iron, containing 37.59 per cent. The sulphuric acid is 0.75 per cent, but there was no trace of phosphorus. No. 3 is poor, containing only 17.99 per cent. of metallic iron. To what extent these ores could be obtained by "stripping," it is impossible to state without a special investigation. Mining by drifting would be very expensive.

On the land of Samuel Thomson, near Maxville, Monday creek township, Perry county, we find a compact iron ore in thin layers, the whole measuring sixteen inches. It rests on an earthy blue limestone six inches thick, which is separated from another seam of blue limestone, eight inches thick, by five inches of blue clay. Under the limestone are fourteen inches of black sandy bituminous shale, below which are twenty-two inches of coal, this with its under clay resting upon a sandrock. A section of this ore and associated strata is the Sec. No. 11 in the map of grouped sections. No samples of this ore were brought away, but from the unusual thickness of the stratum it is worthy of investigation.

A seam of ore six inches thick was seen near Cusac's mill, on Jonathan's creek, Newton township, Muskingum county. Sec. 30, on the map of grouped sections, represents the position of this ore.

On the land of John Lyle, Sec. 14, Newton township, a layer of nodules of iron ore three inches thick was found, resting upon a stratum of calcareous ferriferous flint, which, in turn, rests upon, or rather, is cemented to a seam, fifteen inches thick, of blue limestone, under which are three inches of coal. The surface of the flint stratum is covered with impressions of the marine plant Spirophyton cauda-galli, or allied species. Fifteen feet above is a thin layer of sandstone, with the same vegetable impressions upon it. A section of this group of strata is on the map of grouped sections No. 33.

Between this horizon of ore and the Putnam Hill limestone above, no other range of ore was observed.

Above the Putnam Hill limestone we find the first ore from five to eight feet over the limestone. It is seen on the map of sections as Sec. 36. Here the nodules of ore are often quite large, and the location is worthy of investigation. I have no doubt the ore is of good quality. In sebtion 40, on the same map, is seen a layer of nodules of ore four inches thick, belonging to the same geological horizon. It is eight feet four inches above the Putnam Hill limestone, resting upon blue calcareous shales which are highly fossiliferous.

At Flint Ridge, a layer of ore is reported resting upon the top of the Putnam Hill limestone, which here includes the calcareous shales seen at the last locality. The shales and limestone have the same fossils.

Higher in the series, ore in considerable quantity was found on the land of Henry Welch, Salt Lick township, Perry county. No measured section was made, but its place, by estimate, is about 30 feet below the great Nelsonville seam of coal. It lies in layers of nodules in blue clay shale. One of the nodules was taken for analysis. Prof. Wormley reports, in No. 6 of the table, the metallic iron to be 27.04. The details of the analysis are not given. Should this ore be found well situated for easy stripping, it would doubtless serve as a good purpose for mixture with other richer ores.

Nowhere have we found so persistent a horizon of ore as that found a few feet below the great coal seam. Attention to this ore was called by Dr. Briggs, in the old Geological Reports. Scarcely anywhere was a section made of this part of the vertical range of strata without the discovery of this ore. It is in nodules, often small, but sometimes very large and heavy. Unfortunately, the nodules are generally too much scattered to make mining profitable, yet there are doubtless many places where this ore might be obtained by stripping, in sufficient quantity to serve a valuable purpose for mixture. A sample obtained on the land of James Hawkins, on Snow Fork of Monday creek, in Ward township, Hocking county, was analyzed by Prof. Wormley. The result is given in No. 4 of the table. The ore is siderite or carbonate of iron, and yields 31.50 per cent. metallic iron. It is often filled with beautiful impressions of coal plants, a collection of which was made for the State cabinet.

On the farm of Benjamin Saunders, on the west branch of Monday creek, the stream has cut its way below the great seam of coal, and revealed the same range of nodular ores, found below the coal on Snow Fork and elsewhere. The ore is rich in iron, but the nodules are too much scattered to make mining profitable. Generally, in the upper Sunday creek valley, this ore would be several feet below the beds of the streams.

IRON ORE ABOVE THE NELSONVILLE COAL.

The strata of rocks lying above the horizon of the great Nelsonville seam of coal are apparently less promising in iron ore than those below it.

On the old Marietta road, one mile north-east from Nelsonville, two ranges of nodular ore were seen, and their places proximately given in No. 1 of the map of grouped sections.

A sandy ore (probably of little value) was seen on the hill near the village of Straitsville, Perry county.

On the headwaters of Sunday creek there was seen at one place, where the shales are not cut away by the heavy sandrock, two lines of small blue kidneys of blue carbonate or siderite, one three and the other four inches thick. The lower line is fifteen feet above the great seam of coal, and the other six feet higher. At one place, near Millerstown, a deposit of five inches of blue carbonate of iron, four feet below the middle or Norris coal, was seen. Whether this will prove a continuous layer or is only a local deposit, I had no means of ascertaining. Fifteen feet above the middle or Norris coal is a quite persistent deposit of ore of the limonite class. This seam can be traced through all the hills to New Lexington, where it is found in its proper place above the upper New Lexington coal, which is the equivalent of the great seam of Sunday creek. It measures in one place thirteen inches in thickness. A few kidneys from three to four inches thick were dug out of this layer, which were rich in iron. One of them was analyzed by Prof. Wormley, and found to contain 43.06 per cent. of metallic iron. If uncontaminated by phosphorus or sulphur—for which, as yet, no examinations have been made—this ore, if found in adequate quantity, will serve an admirable purpose for a mixture with the Lake Superior ores.

Forty feet above this ore, or about fourteen feet above the upper or "Stallsmith" seam of coal, is a deposit, apparently in very large nodules, of an earthy blue carbonate of iron or siderite. On the Latta farm, near Millerstown (Perry county), the thickest nodule measured two feet in thickness. Here there was an evident slip, as the ore was imbedded in earth and not in stratified clays. At this place two or three smaller nodules of siderite, of a different lithological texture, were seen, but their true place could not be ascertained. One was five inches thick. On the Rogers farm, in the same neighborhood, the same earthy blue carbonate of iron was seen, grouped in three layers of nodules, measuring respectively thirteen inches, fourteen inches, and six inches, making in all thirty-three inches. To determine whether these nodules will prove sufficiently contiguous to constitute regular seams, will require additional excavation.

As this was by far the largest development of ore seen above the horizon of the great seam of coal, samples for analysis were taken from both the Latta and Rogers farms. The sample from the Latta farm yielded, according to Prof. Wormley's analysis, 26.12 per cent. of metallic iron, and that from the Rogers farm 23.78 per cent.

A limestone sometimes found in large, scattered nodules, in the yellow clays from fifteen to twenty feet above the great coal seam, on the west branch of Sunday creek, contains a small amount of iron. A sample obtained by Col. James Taylor, of New Lexington, and my assistant, Mr. Gilbert, from near the bridge on the road from Millerstown to tho west branch, was analyzed for iron by Prof. Wormley, and found to contain 2.52 per cent. of iron.

For the purpose of general comparison, I give from Bauerman's Metallurgy of Iron the average richness in iron of the ores used in the famous Cleveland Iron District in England. This average, for four samples from different localities, is 35.79 per cent. of metallic iron, while the average of six samples from our coal-field is 36.57 per cent. In this number I include one sample of ore taken from above the great seam of coal on Sunday creek. In freedom from the deleterious element, phosphoric acid, the Ohio ores are far superior. The Cleveland ores give an average of 1.905 per cent. of phosphoric acid, while of the five samples, thoroughly analyzed, from our coal-field, one yielded 0.18 per cent., two gave a mere chemical trace, and two contained none whatever. The amount of sulphur in our ores is small, not being found at all in some samples, and in others, much of what is found will be removed in roasting the ore. There is therefore little difficulty to be apprehended from the ores of Hocking, Perry and Muskingum counties, in respect to quality; the only question is the one of quantity. This question will be carefully investigated, with respect to any given district, by all intelligent capitalists who propose to erect furnaces in such district and rely upon it for ores. They will not care to repeat the expensive blunders, in ill-judged reliance upon limited ores, which have been made both in the Coal Measures of England and of this country. In regard to the failure of many furnaces in western Pennsylvania, J. P. Lesley, Esq., one of the Geological Corps in the survey of that State, thus writes, in his "Manual of Coal": "In a majority of instances, the furnaces have been built in the neighborhood of very insufficient beds; and a large proportion of those originally erected blew out for the want of ore, and form picturesque ruins in secluded glens among the mountains, and on the banks of the principal affluent waters of the Monogahela and Alleghany. This treachery of the beds of carbonate of iron (the ore is good enough), rather than any want of skill or capital or tariff, has been the secret cause of the periodical and almost universal failure of iron-making in western Pennsylvania, from the beginning until now."

I do not apprehend that the better layers of ore in the counties I have explored will fail in persistency and prove treacherous. The question will be whether, when the more accessible and cheaply-obtained ore has been removed by stripping, it will be found profitable to mine the ore by the process of drifting. This will depend upon the price of labor and the cheapness at which other competing ores can be obtained. One thing is very certain, that considerable ore can be obtained at the northern part of my district, which is excellent in quality, and which will prove valuable for mixing with the richer ores of Lake Superior.

Before closing this subject of ores, it must be remarked that the survey of 1869 did not extend to the iron region of Vinton, Jackson, Scioto and Lawrence counties. In that region the ores are generally richer and better than in the northern part of my district.

I append a table of the analyses of ores from the district already explored.

Analyses of Iron Ores, by Prof. T. G. Wormley, Chemist of the Geological Survey.

	No. 1.	No. 2	No. 3.	No. 4.	No. 5.	No. 6.	No. 7.	No. 8.	No. 9.
Specific gravity	3.540	3,833	2.675	3.200	3.600	3.118	......	......	......
Protoxide of iron......	39.62	40.67	19.48	37.22	37.36	......	......	......	......
Sesquioxide of iron....	15.07	8.54	4.01	3.64	13 30	......	......	......	......
Manganese	......	0 54	......	1.20	4.30	......	......	......	......
Alumina	7.07	......	......	0.60	......	......	......	......	......
Lime	0.60	1.06	......	2.40	2.90	......	......	......	......
Magnesia	0.38	1.33	......	2.16	2.77	......	......	......	......
Foreign matter.........	6.95	21.72	62.60	18.82	5.32	......	......	......	......
Carbonic acid	24.21	20.80	7.15	27.00	28.10	......	......	......	......
Sulphuric acid..........	0.48	0.75	......	......	trace.	......	......	......	......
Phosphoric acid	0.18	......	......	......	trace.	trace.	......	......	......
Combined water........	3.70	0.40	1.55	4.40	5.70	......	......	......	......
Organic matter.........	1.74	} 4.19	......	......	......	......	......	......	......
Loss	......		......	2.56	0.25	......	......	......	......
Total.............	100.00	100.00	......	100.00	100 00	......	......	......	......
Metallic iron	41.37	37.59	17.99	31.50	38.87	27.04	43.06	26.12	23.78

Register of Analyses of Iron Ores.

No. 1. Top on No. 1 layer of ore in front of Henry Hazelton's, Salt Lick Tp., Perry Co.
No. 2. Second layer of ore " " " "
No. 3. Third " " " " "
No. 4. Layer of ore in flat nodular masses, James Hawkins, Sec. 3, Ward township, Hocking county, 9 feet under Nelsonville seam of coal.
No. 5. Iron on top of Maxville Limestone, Edward Danison's, Sec. 16, Madison township, Perry county.
No. 6. Iron ore, 20 or 30 feet below Nelsonville coal, Henry Welch's land, Salt Lick township, Perry county, second from bottom of 4 or 5 layers of nodules.
No. 7. Limonite ore from seam 15 feet above the Middle or Norris coal, Latta farm, Sunday creek, Perry county.
No. 8. Blue carbonate of iron, Latta farm, Sunday creek, Perry county.
No. 9. Same seam as above on Rogers farm, " "

GEOLOGY OF A PART OF WASHINGTON AND NOBLE COUNTIES.

An examination was made of the Duck creek valley for the special determination of the position of the coals. The principal seams of coal in the immediate valley of Duck creek are two—the lower, generally thin, and associated with limestones; and the upper, much thicker, generally found below a heavy sandrock. The two seams are about 70 feet apart, in vertical distance. The general dip of the strata in this valley is to the south and south-east, except where there may be undulations, produced by the same causes which produced the Cow run and Newells run uplifts.

In ascending the valley, we first find the lower coal, with its associated limestone group, in the bed of the creek, near Mr. Flanders', about half a mile above the Cedar Narrows bridge, in the north part of Fearing township. Here the coal was formerly obtained by stripping. Near the bridge, below, an oil well is reported to have passed through the limestone group, about 30 feet below the surface. This would indicate a pretty strong southern dip. Before reaching the mouth of Whipple's run, a mile above Mr. Flanders', the coal and limestones have risen well up in the bank, and from this point the group is everywhere seen, in going north. On Whipple's run the coal has changed into cannel, and, at this point, it was formerly distilled into oil. The cannel is of poor quality, very earthy, and leaves, on combustion, an excessive amount of ashes.

On Pigeon branch of Whipple's run, on the farm of Moses Blake, a part of the limestone group was exposed and the following section made. (See Fig. 23.)

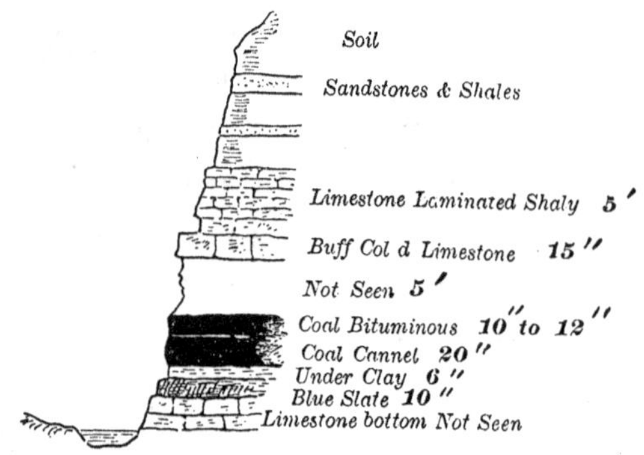

FIG. 23.

Here the lower 15 to 20 inches of the coal are cannel, and the 10 or 12 inches above are bituminous. The buff-colored limestone above the coal is every where persistent. I have traced it from the west side of the Muskingum river, on Wolf creek, through several townships. It is seen, with its associated limestone, in the hills in the vicinity of Beverly; at Coal run, where the associated coal is largely worked; on Bear creek; extensively on Duck creek; on the Little Muskingum; in the uplift on Cow run; and in a similar uplift in the Narrows, above the mouth of Newell's run, below the village of Newport.

The following is an analyses, by Prof. Wormley, of this remarkable limestone, from a sample obtained on Whipple's run:

Matter insoluble in acids	19 10
Carbonate of lime	47.70
Carbonate of magnesia	19.40
Alumina and sesquioxide of iron	2.50
Undetermined	2.65

This analysis shows the stone to be a double carbonate of lime and magnesia. It is worthy of investigation as a water lime. Should it answer for hydraulic purposes, its wide distribution would make it valuable.

This buff limestone is an excellent guide in the study of the geology of Washington county.

The blue slate below the coal at Whipple's run, and at other points, is rich in fossil mollusca.

At Salem village the limestone group is seen, and the coal is reported to be from 20 to 30 inches thick. Here it has lost all cannel structure. The cannel coal on Whipple's run is only a local modification of a bituminous coal seam. This, so far as my observations go, is true of all cannel coals.

At the head of Pigeon branch of Whipple's run, we find, on the farm of Samuel J. Hazen, Salem township, a seam of coal in the hill, estimated to be about 70 feet above the limestone group. This coal is 4 feet thick, with 3 inches black slate under it, below which is the usual under clay. It has 10 inches of black slate over it, above which is a blueish clay, mottled, with red. No heavy sandrock was here seen above the coal. The coal has much resemblance to the Bear creek coal, and in many respects is unlike its geological equivalent, the sandstone coal, found higher up Duck creek. From a careful examination of the coal on Bear creek, made several years since, I was led to believe that that coal was found on the extreme southern edge of the great coal marsh, and was subjected to peculiar tidal inundations, which brought in water-worn or beach-worn sticks, and fragments of wood, which are now found intermingled with the coal. These overflows have doubtless modified the structure of the coal. South of Bear creek, and south of Whipple's run, this seam of coal entirely disappears, or is too thin to work. It is probable that the black, bituminous shales, under a heavy sand rock, seen on the plank road on New-Year's run, about half a mile from its mouth, is the equivalent, in geological position, of the coal seam spoken of. In Salem township, and especially on the East Fork of Duck creek, the upper or sandstone coal is well developed, and mines have been opened on the farms of Vincent Payne, Moses True, Messrs. Hovey, Gould and others. On the farm of Mr. Hill, north of Salem village, the coal is well seen. On the land of Vincent Payne the annexed section of coal was made. (See Fig. 24.)

Direction of vertical planes in this seam, S. 78½° E. The direction of same in the "limestone coal" on Mr. Payne's land, or near it, S. 80° E.

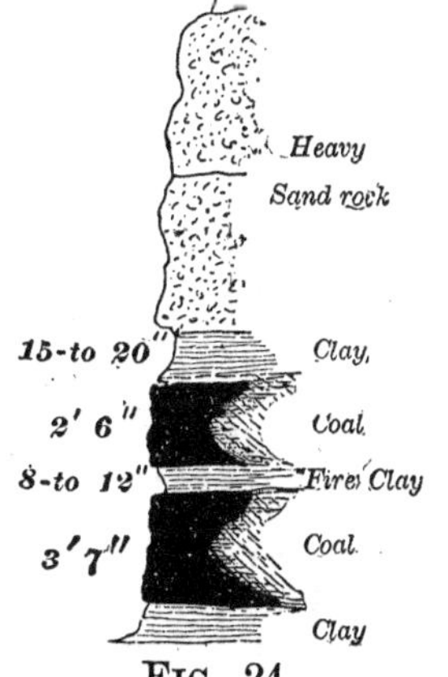

FIG. 24.

On V. Payne's land there is a seam of limestone 144 feet above the sandstone coal, and another 56 feet higher. These limestones are found on all the hills in that region that are high enough to reach them. They are remarkably soluble under atmospheric influences, and have a greater fertilizing power than any limestones I have seen elsewhere in the State. The farmers of Salem have hitherto received far more benefit from these limestones than they have from their abundant coal. There are no richer hill lands in the State.

Explorations up the East Fork of Duck creek will hereafter be made. On the West Fork we found the upper or sandstone coal opened on the farm of Hugh Jackson, in Aurelius township, Washington county. Here the fire clay parting is greatly thickened to 3 feet 4 inches, there being 3 feet 4 inches of coal below it and 1 foot 9 inches above. Here the direction of vertical planes in the coal is N. 80° W. About 70 feet below this coal is the usual limestone group with the layer of buff limestone. No coal was here seen in the limestone group, but it may be present, as no good section of the group could be made. The group is thinner than in Salem. From this point the upper coal is found in all the hills and is mined for neighborhood use. The largest development seen was on the land of David McKee, on Buffalo run, near Newburg, Noble county, where the coal below the clay parting measured 6 feet 8½ inches. The clay above was reported to be about 2 feet thick, above which 2 feet more of coal were reported. This coal appeared to be pretty homogeneous in quality and can be profitably mined when the Marietta and Pittsburg Railroad is completed. One hundred and thirty-five feet above this coal is a limestone seam, probably the same as the one found 144 feet above the sandstone coal on V. Payne's land in Salem. Mr. McKee's coal is 225 feet (by barometer) above the bank of Duck creek, near Newburg. The following is a section of Mr. McKee's coal. The vertical planes run east and west. (See Fig. 25.)

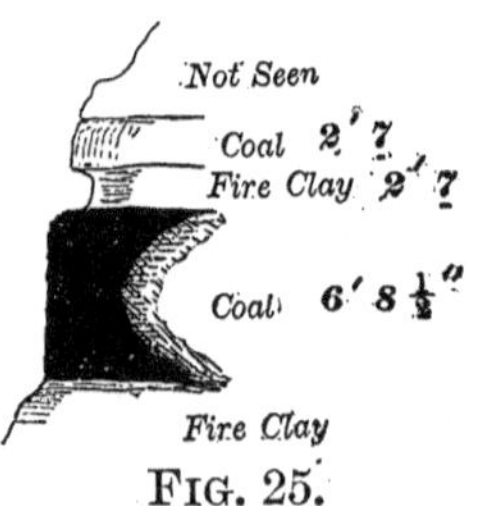

FIG. 25.

On the west side of Duck creek, in the neighborhood of Newburg, the coal seam is thinner. The coal of John McGuire, in Jackson township, Noble county, is 3 feet 6 inches, below the clay parting which is here 2 feet thick. The coal above the parting is only 4 inches in thickness. Mr. McGuire produces about 200 bushels a day for the oil and salt works in the vicinity. Seventy feet below this coal is the limestone group with the usual buff-colored stratum. About 50 feet above McGuire's coal is another group of limestones, perhaps 6 feet thick, with one layer of porous buff-colored limestone.

The height of the summit at the cross-roads, 2 miles west of Newburg, is 375 feet (by barometer), above the Duck creek bridge at Newburg.

On the farm of Mr. Leonard McKee, in Olive township, Noble county, the coal (the same seam as David McKee's), is 5 feet thick below, with 1 to 1½ feet parting of clay and 8 inches of coal above. There are two seams of limestone above the coal, one 43 feet and the other about 60 feet above. The summit of the hill above Leonard McKee's house is 380 feet (by barometer), above the floor of Blake's bridge, over Duck creek, Olive township. The seam of coal is 310 feet above the level of the bridge. On the hills west of Blake's bridge, the same seam of coal is found, but generally thinner. On the land of Aranda Woodford it is reported 3 feet thick. Here the coal is, by barometer, 295 feet above Blake's bridge. As we go north from Olive township, in ascending the Duck creek valley, the coal gets higher and higher in the hills, and at last disappears.

On the farm of Fulton Caldwell, Esq., in Olive townsnip, about a mile below his house, we find 50 feet of sandy shales making cliffs on the immediate bank of Duck creek. Underneath these shales comes up, as we go north, (for the dip is strongly to the south), a limestone 1 foot thick, rich is fossils, below which are 7 feet of blackish shales, also rich is fossils, and under the dark shales is a foot of coal with vertical planes N. 72° W. At "Soak'em" we obtain a section of strata 50 or 60 feet below the coal, composed of clay shales of different colors and one stratum of limestone in nodules. This lower coal under the fossiliferous limestone is, by barometer, 303 feet below the "sandstone coal." The examination did not extend beyond the village of "Soak'em."

SALT IN THE DUCK CREEK VALLEY.

The wells bored for oil in the valley have generally revealed brine. A deep well near Soak'em, Olive township, Noble county, bored by the Ohio Valley Oil Company, struck a light colored sandrock at 763 feet, and continued in it to the depth of 875 feet, when the boring stopped. This well has yielded a copious stream of strong brine which comes up from the bottom sandrock. If, as I have much reason to expect, the "sandstone coal," of the Duck creek valley, is the geological equivalent of the Pomeroy seam, then the light colored sandrock which affords the brine at Soak'em is the equivalent of the saliferous rock reached by the salt wells at Pomeroy and on the Hocking river. The saliferous rock probably belongs to the upper Waverly. The New Jersey Company's deep well on the Dearth farm, Jefferson township, Noble county, passes through the same sandrock as the Soak'em well and found in it abundant brine. While therefore we may infer that the great salt-bearing sandrock which underlies the coal measures in south-eastern Ohio is entirely accessible in the Duck creek valley, it is a matter of good fortune to this district that strong brines can also be found in sandrocks much nearer the surface, as shown by the following interesting facts. Young's salt well, from which salt has been manufactured for several years, situated one mile north of Newburg, Noble county, obtains its brine in a white sandrock, 199 feet below the surface. In the Eastwood and Parker well on the Isaac Davis farm, in Olive township, Noble county, a very large flow of strong brine was obtained in a white sandrock 227 feet below the surface. The same sandrock yields oil.

In the Diamond oil well on David McKee's farm at Newburg, Noble county, brine was struck in a white sandrock 236 feet from the surface. Brine was also found in the same well in a heavy white sandrock 107 feet below the one above mentioned. In David McKee's well, No. 2, brine was found in a white sandrock 347 feet below the surface.

On the flats below Maxburg, Aurelius township, Washington county, abundant brine is found in a sandrock 308 below the surface. It will probably be found that the saliferous rocks of the Upper Duck creek valley will group themselves into three distinct horizons—two upper ones comparatively near the surface, and the other one, underlying the coal measure rocks. The brines, in strength and quality, will hereafter be studied. A little salt for local use has been made in the Upper Duck creek valley for many years, but the difficulty of transportation has prevented its exportation. The difficulty will soon be obviated by the Marietta and Pittsburg Railroad, which passes up the valley. Coal mines affording cheap fuel are found in all the hills bordering Duck creek, from Salem, Washington county, to Soak'em, Noble county. *The Duck creek valley could easily supply the West with salt.*

PRODUCTION OF IRON IN THE SECOND GEOLOGICAL DISTRICT.

Furnaces line the iron ore belt of the lower coal measures, from Logan, Hocking county, on the north, to the Ohio river on the south. This district is universally known as the "Hanging Rock Iron District," and has long been famous for the remarkably fine iron it produces. The ores hitherto used have been chiefly the native ores of the hydrated sesquioxide or limonite group. Of late mixtures of Missouri and Lake Superior ores have been introduced in a few stone coal furnaces. Charcoal is the principal fuel.

The following is a list of the furnaces:

I. Charcoal Furnaces.

Name.	County.	Owners.
Bloom	Scioto	J. Paull & Company.
Buckeye	Jackson	Buckeye Furnace Company.
Buckhorn	Lawrence	Charcoal Iron Company.
Cambria	Jackson	D. Lewis & Company.
Centre	Lawrence	W. D. Kelley & Son.
Clinton	Scioto	Crawford & Bell.
Cincinnati	Vinton	Long & Smith.
Eagle	Vinton	Eagle Furnace Company.
Empire	Scioto	James Forsythe & Company.
Etna	Lawrence	Ellison, Dempsey & Ellison.
Gallia	Gallia	Norton, Campbell & Company.
Hamden	Vinton	Hamden Furnace Company.
Hecla	Lawrence	Hecla Iron and Mining Company.
Harrison	Scioto	Harrison Furnace Company.
Hope	Vinton	Putnam, Welch & Company.
Howard	Scioto	Charcoal Iron Company.
Jackson	Jackson	Jackson Furnace Company.
Jefferson	Jackson	Jefferson Furnace Company.
Keystone	Jackson	E. B. Greene & Company.
Grant	Lawrence	W. D. Kelly & Son.
Lawrence	Lawrence	Peters, Cole & Company.
Latrobe	Jackson	H. S. Bundy.
Limestone	Jackson	Limestone Furnace Company.
Lincoln	Jackson	Wm. McGhee.
Logan	Hocking	Ohio Iron Company.
Monitor	Lawrence	Monitor Furnace Company.
Madison	Lawrence	Peters, Clare & Company.
Monroe	Jackson	Union Iron Company.
Mt. Vernon	Lawrence	Hiram Campbell.
Olive	Lawrence	Campbell, McGugin & Company.
Ohio	Scioto	Means, Kyle & Company.
Pine Grove	Lawrence	Means, Kyle & Company.
Pioneer	Lawrence	Rodgers & Swap.
Scioto	Scioto	L. C. Robinson & Company.
Union	Hocking	Hocking Valley Iron Company.
Vesuvius	Lawrence	Gray, Amos & Company.
Washington	Lawrence	Union Iron Company.
Zaleski	Vinton	Zaleski Furnace Company.

Total number, 38.

II. Furnaces Using Bituminous Coal.

Name.	County.	Owners.
Belfont	Lawrence	Belfont Iron Works Company.
Fulton	Jackson	Fulton Furnace Company.
Orange	Jackson	Orange Furnace Company.
Star	Jackson	Star Furnace Company.
Vinton	Vinton	Vinton Furnace and Coal Company.

Total number, 5.

The following valuable statistics were kindly furnished by Col. Wm. M. Bolles, of Portsmouth:

Amount of charcoal pig-iron made by 38 furnaces during the year 1869, about	90,000 tons.
Amount of iron made with bituminous coal	16,000 "
Total	106,000 "
Amount of native ore used, about	260,000 "
Missouri and Lake Superior ores	15,000 "
Total	275,000 "
Amount of limestone used, about	15,000 "
Number of bushels bituminous coal used in smelting ores for pig-iron	1,400,000

There are extensive rolling mills in the Second Geological District, at Portsmouth, Ironton, Pomeroy, Marietta, Columbus, Zanesville and Newark, but no statistics relative to them have been received.

It is hoped that the work on the Second District will, during the coming season, extend to the great iron belt extending from the Hocking to the Ohio, when not only the stratigraphical position of the various ores, limestones and coals will be obtained and carefully mapped, but also all the ores will be carefully analyzed and studied, with reference to their "cold short" and "red short" and other properties, and the possibilities of combination in various mixtures with each other and with foreign ores, to secure desired results. At the same time all accessible bituminous coals of probable value will be analyzed to determine their fitness for iron making.

There is a furnace at Zanesville in successful operation, using a mixture of foreign ores and native ores chiefly from Perry county. No statistics from it have been received.

A large blast furnace is being erected at Columbus to use the stone coal from the Hocking Valley, and foreign ores chiefly with a small admixture of Ohio ores.

PRODUCTION OF COAL IN THE SECOND GEOLOGICAL DISTRICT.

No full statistics could be obtained of the quantity of coal mined in the Second Geological District. The total annual production at Pomeroy and Syracuse, in Meigs county, is estimated at 9,000,000 bushels. Hon. V. B. Horton, of Pomeroy, gives the total production in the immediate neighborhood of Pomeroy (including the West Virginia side of the Ohio river) at between 11,000,000 and 12,000,000 bushels. In Athens county, coal is largely mined at Nelsonville. The leading producers of coal at Nelsonville are Messrs. Wm. B. Brooks, L. D. Poston, Ashford Poston, T. Longstreth, James Herrold, Mr. Arnold and the Hocking Valley Coal Company, and the Columbus and Hocking Valley Mining Company. The production has been rapidly increasing since the completion of the Columbus and Hocking Valley Railroad to that point.

The extensive mines of Peter Hayden, Esq., are near Haydenville, Hocking county.

Considerable coal is mined at various points on the Marietta and Cincinnati Railroad, in Athens and Vinton counties. At Chauncey and Salina, coal for the salt works is obtained by shaft from the Nelsonville seam. At Jackson and vicinity, on the Portsmouth branch of the M. & C. R. R., coal is largely mined for the blast furnaces. It is also shipped to a considerable extent, especially from the mines of the Petrea Coal Company. The coal used on the locomotives of the M. & C. R. R. is largely from Petrea mines. Coal is also mined largely at Carbondale, Athens county.

Coal is mined for shipment, at the Miami Company's mines, on the line of the Zanesville and Cincinnati Railroad, in Muskingum county, and in that vicinity.

At Zanesville, and at various points on the Muskingum river, coal is extensively mined, but chiefly for consumption in the local manufacturing establishments and for domestic uses. Little is shipped away from the immediate valley.

A considerable quantity of coal is mined near Pine Grove Furnace, and brought by a railway to Hanging Rock, Lawrence county, and shipped by the Ohio river. Extensive mining is done at the Sheridan mines, six miles above Ironton.

On Duck creek and Little Muskingum river, a limited quantity of coal is mined for local use, chiefly for the generation of steam at the oil wells. Coal is pretty largely mined and shipped in Guernsey county, near Cambridge, on the Central Ohio Railroad.

Of the coal mined in Monroe and Belmont counties, I have obtained little definite information. Belmont county has considerable coal.

FIRE CLAYS AND OTHER CLAYS IN THE SECOND GEOLOGICAL DISTRICT.

Fire clays are often found interstratified with our coal measure rocks, and although there has as yet been no time for their special investigation, yet it is believed that the district will prove rich in this important source of wealth. A seam of fire-clay of great purity and excellence is found at the base of the coal measures, in the vicinity of Sciotoville, Scioto county, and two extensive fire-brick and tile establishments are in successful operation at that place. The brick has proved to be of first quality, and is rapidly superseding the Mount Savage and other foreign brick. They are already largely used in our furnaces and rolling-mills.

In Muskingum and Perry counties there are extensive potteries, using the clay found, in geological position, below the New Lexington or Nelsonville coal. Hon. A. A. Guthrie, Collector of Revenue of the 13th District, reports an annual production of stoneware of 1,800,000 gallons, valued at five cents per gallon, or $90,000. There are other pottery establishments in the district, but no statistics have been received in regard to them.

SALT IN THE SECOND GEOLOGICAL DISTRICT.

The principal salt-bearing rocks in my district are the upper Waverly. In railroad cuts, on the Columbus and Hocking Valley and on the Marietta and Cincinnati Railroads, I find, in the dry weather of summer, a saline efflorescence on the rocks. Following these efflorescent rocks in their dip to the south-east, I find that, so far as the facts are yet gathered, the salt wells are bored down to them, and from them obtain their brine. Salt was formerly made near the mouth of Munn's run, on the Ohio river, between Portsmouth and Sciotoville, from wells bored entirely in the Waverly rocks.

The wells of Messrs. Green and Gould, at Salina, Athens county, strike the brine about 570 feet below the surface. It being 110 feet from the surface to the Nelsonville seam of coal, the salt-bearing stratum is reached at 460 feet below the coal. This coincides with the theoretical position of the saliferous rocks of the upper Waverly, as indicated by the efflorescence seen upon the rocks in the railroad cuts above Logan. As we descend the Hocking river the Nelsonville coal dips, and the saliferous strata are found at a correspondingly increased depth. There is an abandoned salt well, where salt was formerly made, on Monday creek, Salt Lick township, Perry county, but the depth of the well was not ascertained.

At Pomeroy, on the Ohio river, the principal sources of brine are found about 1,000 feet below the surface. Here the brine comes from the top of the Waverly.

On the Muskingum river there are many salt wells. They increase in depth with the south-eastern dip of the rocks.

On Duck creek, in Noble county, salt wells are found affording abundant brine, and some salt is made, to supply the local demand. Some of the abandoned oil wells yield a constant outflow of brine.

East of Cambridge, in Guernsey county, salt is made from brine obtained about 800 feet below the surface. These wells are in immediate proximity to a valuable seam of coal from five to six feet thick. There is an ample supply of coal for salt-making on Duck creek.

The wells bored for oil within the last few years have disclosed valuable brines in a large number of the counties in my district. Nor is the brine limited to one group of rocks in the geological series, but we find brine at different geological horizons, from the upper coal measures down to the great Devonian Black Slate. The brines of the district will hereafter be made a subject of special investigation, both in their geological relations and in their chemical constituents. The quantity of salt which can be made in south-eastern Ohio can hardly be computed. We can supply the Republic with salt.

The production of salt in the Muskingum valley, from estimates obtained from Hon. A. A. Guthrie, Collector of Revenue in the 13th District, is from 45,000 to 50,000 barrels per annum. This is all made on the Muskingum river, in Muskingum and Morgan counties.

The production of salt in Athens county, as given by Hon. Jos. L. Kessinger, Collector of Revenue for the 15th District, for the year 1869, is 36,348 barrels. This product is made up as follows:

	Barrels.
M. M. Greene & Co. (two furnaces)	10,528
Hocking Valley Coal and Salt Co. (two furnaces)	13,000
James Herrold (two furnaces)	8,000
Pruden Bros. "	4,820

In Meigs county (as given by Mr. Kessinger) the total production for 1869, from nine furnaces, is 1,866,690 bushels of 50 lbs. each.

The total production for 1869 from the Pomeroy neighborhood, including what is made on the West Virginia bank of the Ohio river, is estimated by Hon. V. B. Horton at about 3,750,000 bushels.

The quantity made in Noble and Guernsey counties has not been definitely obtained, but it is relatively small.

The three essential elements for profitable salt-making are, abundant brine of adequate strength, cheap fuel, and cheap transportation. All these elements are found in combination at a large number of points in the Second Geological District.

GOLD.

Gold has been taken from the drift at several points in Licking county. In the summer of 1868, gold dust of the value of $17.00 was washed out of fine drift material, in a little gully well up the hillside, on the farm of Daniel Drum, Bowling Green township, Licking county, not far from a mile north of the National Road, at Brownsville. The largest grains were reported to be the size of a wheat grain. The above facts were reported by Wm. Anderson, who himself washed out a small part of the gold.

I have no reason to doubt the above statements, as I have myself obtained gold at other points in Licking county. It should be noted, in connection with the gold field near Brownsville, that there are very high lands to the north-east, north, and north-west directions, from which the gold-bearing sands would naturally be brought, if brought by glacial action. The very high range of Flint Ridge, sweeps around the location on the northern side, over which the drift gravel must have been forced, if the gravel had been distributed by glaciers. On the top of Flint Ridge one or two bowlders were seen, but they are very rare. These bowlders I had supposed to be dropped by floating ice, since no other drift material was found upon the top, or clinging to the slopes, of the ridge. At other places in the valley of the Moxahala, are found drift gravel and small bowlders, the locations of which are seemingly inexplicable, by the glacial theory.

Near Newark, and north of the high grounds which divide the waters of the Licking river from those of the Moxahala and its tributaries, are other and larger deposits of gold-bearing sands. The place examined by me was one and a half miles south-east of Newark. Here is a range of drift terraces, about 50 feet above the bed of the Licking river. These terraces are cut through by small streams from the hills, to the south, and in the narrow ravines the gold is obtained, from the sands and clays. The terraces contain also bowlders of granitoid rocks, quartzite, and small pebbles, of white quartz. Bowlders of limestone, containing fossils of the Niagara and Clinton groups, were also found in the terraces. The quantity of gold is small, but, in my own experiments, nearly every panful of dirt showed the "color." Mr. Jacob Schock, jeweler, of Newark, reports finding gold in small fragments of quartz.

EXPLANATION OF THE MAP OF SECTIONS.

The map is intended to show the stratigraphical position and range of the lower strata of the coal measures, extending from the north line of the 2d District to the neighborhood of Nelsonville, on the Hocking river. The distance is abont 40 miles.

The map is divided by horizontal lines into spaces, which represents 10 feet, in vertical distance. The rocks in the hills are presented very much as a hay-stack would be, if cut through vertically by a hay-knife. As the rocks dip to the east and south-east, by going in those directions one is able to obtain the higher strata, and by measuring all the rocks, we are enabled to place them in order, in the vertical series. By bringing the many sections thus obtained, together in a systematic grouping, we obtain the map herewith presented.

It is believed that this new plan of grouping sections, thus presenting at a glance the features of our geology, will be approved. The observer can see, from such maps, what strata are persistent and wide-spread, and what are merely local. He can go back in thought to the time of the deposition of the layers, and see where the stronger currents swept, carrying and distributing coarse sands and gravels, which now form sand rocks, and also where comparatively quiet waters deposited the finer sediments, which now constitute our clays and shales. He can almost see the ancient vegetation of the coal-measures, now growing in small insular patches, and now covering with its luxuriant growth vast savannahs, which stretched for miles and miles along the coast of an ancient ocean. He can see at what times the waters gave up, doubtless, oftentimes to the demands of organic life, its lime, and flint, and iron.

For practical use such a map is invaluable. For example, the intelligent farmer, if he finds upon his farm the so-called Putnam Hill limestone, knows that in his hills, about 80 feet higher, is the place for the Nelsonville or Straitsville seam of coal. In a similar way he obtains the position of other coals, and ores, &c., &c. If such maps can be constructed for my whole district, as they doubtless will be, there could be no greater or more useful contribution to our economic geology. They will be worth a thousand-fold the cost of the very great labor expended in their preparation.

THE SECTIONS OF THE WAVERLY ROCKS.

On the left side of the map are two independent sections, one a section of the Waverly rocks, from the top of the great Ohio Black Slate to the coal measures, taken on the Ohio river; and the other a section, taken in the Hocking valley, from the middle Waverly up to the horizon of the Maxville limestone, now ascertained to be a true lower carboniferous limestone of the age of the Chester group, of Illinois. In this section, directly under the Maxville limestone, and above the Waverly conglomerates, is seen the place of the Logan sandstone group, every where rich in upper Waverly fossils.

PART III.

REPORT ON GEOLOGY OF MONTGOMERY COUNTY,

By EDWARD ORTON,

ASSIST. GEOLOGIST.

GEOLOGY OF MONTGOMERY COUNTY.

Prof. J. S. NEWBERRY, *Chief Geologist:*

SIR:—As Assistant in the Geological Survey of Ohio, I beg leave to make the following report:

My work during 1869 was confined to the Third Geological District of the State, viz., South-western Ohio, having for its boundaries the Scioto River and the National Road.

The instructions that I received from you, bearing date May 7th, 1869, required me to undertake for my first duty, "to trace the line of junction of the Blue Limestone and Cliff Formations—that is, to mark out the Blue Limestone area, and, at the same time, to collect materials for resolving the Cliff into its component elements."

This work I entered upon June 1st, 1869, and continued to be engaged in it, without interruption, until November 20th, 1869.

The report which I herewith transmit treats of the Geological formations that are found along this important line of junction, together with their various economical products and their agricultural relations.

I take great pleasure in acknowledging that I have derived very valuable assistance in my work from the Geological Report of Dr. John Locke, of the former Survey, upon this same portion of the State.

I desire also to acknowledge the very competent and faithful services of Mr. Henry Newton and Mr. H. A. Whiting, volunteer assistants in my district. I am also indebted to Mr. T. J. Browne for important aid in mapping the isolated areas of the Cliff Limestone, in the southern part of Greene county.

I have the honor to remain,
With great respect,
Very truly yours,
EDWARD ORTON.

YELLOW SPRINGS, OHIO,
March 9th, 1870.

The following named counties of South-western Ohio, viz., Preble, Warren, Montgomery, Miami, Clinton, Greene and Clarke, are composed of the same geological formations, and indicate substantially the same geological history. A report upon the geology of any one of the series would, in its general statements, apply to all the rest.

To exhibit the geological features of this portion of the State, and to trace in general terms its history, the county of Montgomery is selected, for the following reasons: It occupies a central position in the series; the various formations are shown within it in very numerous exposures, and with very great distinctness; and its quarries are more widely celebrated than any others in South-western Ohio, for the excellence and value of their products.

Three geological formations are represented in the surface rocks of Montgomery county, viz., the Blue Limestone, the Clinton and the Niagara formations, enumerated in ascending order. Over them all are spread, in beds of varying thickness, the deposits of the Drift period, which include the superficial clays, sands, gravels and bowlders.

By reference to the tabular statement of the rocks of the State, which is given in the report of the Chief Geologist, it will be seen that all the formations which have been mentioned, as constituting the surface rocks of Montgomery county, are embraced in the Palæozoic era—the Blue Limestone belonging to the Hudson River period, of the Lower Silurian age, while the Clinton and Niagara rocks represent epochs of the Niagara period, which is found in the upper division of the Silurian age. The beds of Drift, to which reference has been made, belong to the Human era.

A few statements in regard to the topography of the county are also necessary, inasmuch as its topographical features are intimately connected with its geological formations. A geological map of the county is at the same time, to a good degree, a topographical map.

The bed of the Great Miami river at the southern boundary of the county, may be assumed to be the lowest point within the county limits. This point can not vary far from 250 feet above low water mark at the Ohio river at Cincinnati. The highest land of the county is about 350 feet above the bed of the river at the point named, or about 600 feet above low water mark at Cincinnati, which makes its elevation somewhat more than 1,000 feet above tide water.

As all the strata that are met with in the county are in the main undisturbed, or very nearly horizontal, it is evident that the different levels of the county will be marked by different rock formations, or by different beds of the same formation. It is found accordingly that the Blue Limestone occupies all those portions of the county which are not more than 450 to 475 feet above low water mark at Cincinnati, while the Clinton and Niagara formations are confined to those limited areas which are more than 450 to 475 feet above this level, or in other words, to the hill-tops and highest table lands of the county. In many instances, however, these formations are themselves overlain with heavy beds of drift. Of the 350 feet extreme elevation above mentioned, it will thus be seen that the Blue Limestone series fills 225 feet, while the remaining 125 feet is divided among the Clinton, Niagara and Drift, in the following order: The Clinton holds an average of 20 feet, its thickness diminishing from 30 feet in the northern portions of the county to 9 feet in the southernmost. The Niagara formation of the county has a maximum thickness of 50 feet, which, however, it rarely attains, and it is sometimes found in beds the aggregate of which is not more than 5 feet. A vertical section in the vicinity of Centerville, Washington township, from the surface of the ground to the level of the river, would give approximately the following results: Drift, 15 feet; Niagara, 40 feet; Clinton, 20 feet; Blue Limestone, 225 feet. Total, 300 feet. (See section No. 1, p. 159.)

A section at Webber and Lehman's quarry, east of Dayton 2 miles, gives 8 to 20 feet of Drift sands or clays, 10 feet Niagara, 20 feet Clinton and 150 feet Blue Limestone. Total 200 feet. (See section No. 2, p. 160.)

A section at the Soldiers' Home, 2 miles west of Dayton, gives—Drift, 10 feet; Clinton, 10 feet; Blue Limestone, 160 feet. Total, 180 feet. (See section No. 3, p. 161.)

The last two sections are drawn to the level of the river at Dayton.

The Clinton and Niagara groups are frequently united in popular language under a common designation, viz., "Cliff Limestone." In the accompanying map, the areas occupied by the Blue Limestone and cliff formations respectively are indicated, the latter being designated by the light colored portion of the map, while the blue areas are to be referred to the former. By an examination of this map it will be seen that about three-fourths of the surface of the county are occupied by the Blue Limestones, the remainder being taken up by the Clinton group, which is itself very frequently covered by the Niagara.

We will now proceed to a somewhat more detailed account of these formations:

I. The Blue Limestone formation is confined in its outcrops to Southwestern Ohio, and to the adjacent portions of Indiana, Kentucky and Tennessee, where it attains a thickness of certainly more than 500 feet. It is the geological equivalent of the shales and sandstones that are known as the Hudson River Group in the State of New York. Its name indicates the color and the composition of the rocks that belong to it. The Blue Limestone proper, however, is interstratified with beds of a blue calcareous clay or marl that constitute, in many localities, the larger portion of the system. The solid rock occurs in even layers that sometimes reach a thickness of 10 or 12 inches, but which generally vary from 3 to 6 inches in thickness. Both limestone and marl abound in admirably preserved relics of the living forms that inhabited the ancient seas in which these beds were formed. These fossils belong exclusively to the lower divisions of the animal and vegetable kingdoms. No remains of any vertebrated animal, and no traces of land vegetation have ever yet been discovered in the strata of this group. Sea-weeds and sponges, beautiful star-fishes and stone lilies of exquisite construction, corals in great variety and in infinite number, molluscan shells of all the great classes, so crowded as frequently to constitute the entire substance of the rock, and many species of trilobites, articulated animals of an order long since extinct, are found in all portions of the bedded rock and in its weathered exposures. The general character of these fossils would indicate that the beds were formed at the bottoms of deep seas, and no mark of shore lines or other indications of shallow water ever occur to contradict this inference.

This formation is undoubtedly coextensive with the limits of the county, for it is disclosed in every portion where the channels of the streams have been worn deep enough to reach its proper horizon; and indeed in the valleys of the Great Miami and the Stillwater, it passes northward beyond the county boundary a score of miles. We are warranted, then, in concluding that the whole surface of the county was originally covered with unbroken horizontal beds of the Blue Limestone series, up to a level somewhat more than 450 feet above low water mark at Cincinnati, the level which the upper beds of the formation now hold in all portions of the county in which they occur.

The uppermost layers of the series—from 6 to 20 feet—generally deviate in mineral character from the beds already described in that they consist, for the most part, of red and yellow clays, though occasionally of a yellowish, arenaceous limestone, which is sometimes turned to account as a firestone or as a building rock. It is probable that this portion of the series will be hereafter identified as the representative of a distinct group of rocks, viz., the Medina Sandstone of the New York survey.

II. Clinton.

The Clinton formation is next met with as we ascend in the scale, and is as definitely characterized as the preceding group. It agrees, in stratigraphical position and in its fossil contents, with the formation of the same name in New York. In general terms, it can be described as a crinoidal limestone, of about 20 feet in thickness; the upper layers of which usually break with a crystalline fracture, and the lower beds of which have a distinctly sandy character. The recognition of this latter fact has given the local name of sandstone to the whole formation. The beds above mentioned fully deserve the name, if only it be remembered that they are composed of *lime* sand, and not *silica* sand, a substance which is almost wholly wanting in the Clinton rocks of this portion of the State. In color these rocks have no uniformity, varying not only in different localities, but often, in closely adjacent beds, passing from a marble-like whiteness through various shades of gray, pink, yellow and red. The weathered surfaces have very generally a yellowish, rusty appearance, due to the oxydation of the iron that the rocks contain. The crystalline beds take a good polish, constituting a marble of attractive appearance. The Harrisburgh and Ludlow "marbles" are examples of this quality of the formation.

The rate of growth of this rock would seem to have been exceedingly slow, as no sediments have contributed to the growth of the strata, but they are generally composed, in every particle, of the broken stems and cups of crinoids or stone-lilies. Sometimes, however, there are found associated with these fragments, representatives of the other groups of animals that were named in the Blue Limestone series. Two or more species of chain-corals are quite characteristic fossils of the upper beds.

The Clinton group is known within the county by several local names, in addition to that of "sandstone," already mentioned; such as "Fire-stone,"—"Fire-proof stone,"—"Rotten Limestone,"—"Bastard Limestone." Among the quarry men it is sometimes called "Pink-eye."

Between the Clinton group and the Niagara, which immediately overlies it, there is uniformly interposed a layer of very fine-grained marl, from 2 to 6 inches in thickness, which is to be included with the former group. This marl abounds in the free, perforated, disc-like joints of crinoidal stems of very large species, and certain shells occur here that have not been found elsewhere in the series. As a general rule the Clinton rock is not even-bedded, but, where raised in the quarries, comes out in irregular masses.

III. Niagara.

The Niagara formation has no such uniformity of character as the groups already described. It consists in all cases of even-bedded limestones and marls, it is true, but the limestones have very different degrees of purity, while in hardness, compactness, color, and the presence or absence of fossil contents, they have a very wide range. The celebrated Dayton stone—"Dayton marble" it is sometimes styled—may be assumed as the standard of excellence in this series; but different localities exhibit every degree of gradation, from the admirable qualities of this stone in compactness, durability and color, to the worthless "yellow-back" of the quarrymen, or to the unconsolidated clays that are frequently found as its equivalent. In Montgomery county, the lower layers of the Niagara rocks are always the firmest and most valuable, the 5 to 10 feet immediately overlying the Clinton, constituting in almost every case the sources from which the Dayton stone is derived. The varying thickness of the formation in different localities has already been noted, the limits having been given as from 5 to 50 feet. From the fact that so great variety in composition is found in these rocks, we are warranted in concluding that the Niagara strata were not originally of uniform thickness, as the beds of the previous groups seem to have been. It may be that the higher degrees of excellence in the stone were connected with a slower rate of growth. It is at all events true, that the most valuable deposits of this series in the county are, in every case, shallow.

The lower beds contain but very few fossils, some circular corals, and very rarely a bivalve or chambered shell making out the list, while in higher portions of the group, the strata are frequently crowded with fossils, which differ almost entirely in species from those that are found in the lower groups. One peculiarity of these fossils is that they occur almost always as internal casts, the outer shell or investment having been dissolved and carried away during the past conditions of the rock. One of the most noticeable of all these forms of ancient life is the large, bivalve shell—*Pentamerus oblongus*—known sometimes as the "deer-foot" shell, and quite frequently identified as a petrified hickory-nut. The sections of a large chambered shell, of the genus *Orthoceras*, are also frequently met with, and are sometimes mistaken by the ignorant for the back-bones of fishes or serpents.

The area occupied by the Niagara rocks is not probably more than one-half of that which the Clinton covers. There seems, however, no reason to doubt that both of these members of the Cliff formation were once extended over the whole surface of the county, as their present distribution can be satisfactorily explained by reference to erosive agencies that are known to have been at work upon them—agencies, some of which are still continuing their destructive tasks. By referring to the map on page 158, it will be seen that the Clinton and Niagara, in the eastern portions of the county, occur altogether in insulated masses or islands; on the ridge between the two Miamis, and all the water-courses that flow from these high grounds, have already worn their channels deep into these rocks, not unfrequently completely through them, into the underlying Blue Limestone series. There is, however, a manifest shallowing of the Cliff rocks as we go southward, the Clinton diminishing to 9 feet near the southern line of the county, apparently indicating that the Blue Limestone regions southward were, even at this early time, raised above the surface of the seas, or, in other words, that they were never covered by the limestones of the succeeding Cliff formation.

IV. Drift.

All of the formations above named are covered through almost their entire extent with the deposits of the Drift Period—miles, in some instances, intervening between the exposures of the rocky beds. These deposits vary very much in thickness, in the materials of which they are composed and in the order in which their materials are arranged. No two sections of Drift-beds can be found that will agree in every particular.

Before describing the leading characteristics of these beds, it will be proper to call attention to an interesting fact that must be referred to the same agencies by which the Drift itself is explained. Considerable portions of the rocky surface of the county have been planed, polished, striated and grooved by heavy masses of ice—inclosing sand, gravel and boulders—moving over them. These phenomena can be best observed in the firmer beds of the Niagara limestone, occupying as they do the highest table-lands of the county, but they are by no means confined to them. The great belt of quarries south-east of Dayton, furnish fine exhibitions of this agency. Indeed these naturally planed surfaces are frequently turned to account for door-steps, flagging-stones and other similar uses. It is altogether probable that the whole surface of the county has been exposed to the abrading agencies of the glacial sheet, as we find the marks of these agencies at every point where the rocks are firm enough to retain them. The unconsolidated beds of the Niagara rocks have been in large measure removed by the same force that has planed the harder surfaces, as is evident from an inspection of those higher portions of the system that still remain.

This polished surface of the Niagara rock is generally covered with yellow clays intermingled with gravel and boulders. Sometimes heavy granitic blocks have been left in the clay in almost immediate contact with the bedded rock—their own surfaces having been planed and scored by the service to which they have been put. We see in them the implements of abrasion—the graving-tools—left where the work was done. The thickness of these clay deposits varies from 1 foot to 30 feet, and the upper portions are almost always freer from gravel than the lower portions. Occasionally a limited deposit of blue clay is found on the surface of the rocks, but for the most part these beds of blue clay when they occur, are found overlying yellow clays or beds of gravel, in pockets of small extent. Fragments of drifted coniferous wood are sometimes found buried deep in these deposits.

Next in importance to the yellow clays are the beds of sand and gravel of which the Drift-beds are largely composed. They sometimes overlie the clays—are sometimes interstratified with them, and sometimes they repose directly upon the surface of the rocks. The gravel contains representatives of all the formations that are found to be northward within the limits of the State, viz.: Blue Limestone, Clinton, Niagara, Water Lime, Corniferous and Black Slates, and a considerable part of it is derived from the metamorphic rocks of the Lake Superior region and from the Canadian highlands. To the same source must be referred the sand, as no silicious formation of any considerable extent occurs between these deposits and the line of the great lakes. The sand and gravel have a thickness of at least 100 feet in many instances. The deposits are always distinctly stratified and exhibit many alternations of fine and coarse materials that betoken considerable changes in the conditions of their formation. They often show—especially in the beds that occupy the lower levels of the county—beach-structure or marks of the action of water that could only be impressed upon them while they lay at or near the surface.

The sand and gravel are sometimes cemented into massive blocks by the deposition of carbonate of lime from the spring-water that flows over and through them. Recourse was formerly had to these conglomerates for building-stone, but it was found that they were worthless for such purposes, as they cannot withstand the action of frost.

The lost rocks—boulders, hard-heads, gray-heads, as they are frequently designated—constitute too important a feature of the geology of the county to be omitted in this review. They are irregularly distributed over the face of the country, sometimes thickly sown in belts of several miles in length and breadth, with tolerably definite boundaries, and sometimes scattered singly at wide intervals. They occur through the whole range of the Drift-beds, but are far more abundant in the uppermost portions than in any other. As in the case of the gravel, they are all of northern origin, and by far the largest number have been brought from beyond the great lakes. These boulders weigh not less than 160 pounds to the cubic foot, and the total weight of single blocks sometimes exceeds 10 tons.

The economical values and the agricultural relations of the different formations, will be treated separately. The various products that fall under the head of economical values will be taken up in the following order:

1. Building-Rock.
2. Brick, Draining-Tile and Pottery.
3. Firestone.
4. Lime.
5. Mineral Paint.
6. Gravel.

1. Building Rock.

Each of the formations above enumerated furnishes products in abundance for this important use.

The Blue Limestone affords, in numberless exposures, a building stone that is accessible, easily quarried, even-bedded, of convenient thickness, and very durable. It possesses, however, but little susceptibility of ornamentation. The thinness of its beds, its hardness and brittleness, stand in the way of its improvement by dressing, and its color is too dark to please the eye when it is exposed in large surfaces of masonry.

The Clinton rock, in all of its beds, but especially in its upper ones, affords a building stone that would be highly valued were it not for the close proximity, in most instances, of the quarries of the Niagara group. A similar statement can be made in regard to the products of the Blue Limestone quarries of the county.

When the Clinton stone is first raised from the quarry, it is frequently so soft as to be easily worked; but when the water has escaped from it it becomes a measurably firm and enduring stone. Some of its beds, indeed, are crystalline or semi-crystalline in structure, and leave nothing to be desired as far as durability is concerned. As already remarked, the Clinton group exhibits a great variety of colors, and some of these shades are very pleasing to the eye—a fact which makes this stone susceptible of fine architectural effects, as can be seen to good advantage in the Porter's Lodge at the Soldiers' Home, west of Dayton. This building is constructed of Clinton rock that was quarried upon the grounds. The greatest objection to this series is, that it is not generally even-bedded. The lower strata are very seldom so.

The Niagara group furnishes, however, the best building stone, not only of Montgomery county, but of the whole Miami valley as well. Indeed, for many purposes it is inferior to none. Occurring, as it does, in even-bedded layers of from four to twenty inches in thickness, it is adapted to the purposes of both light and heavy masonry. It is homogeneous in structure, has a beautiful color, takes ornamentation quite kindly, and is durable to any required degree. The value that is attached to it can be judged from the fact that, in some of the quarries nearest to Dayton, the stone sells in the ground at $17.50 per rod, or $2,800 per acre—the title to the land not being alienated. In these quarries there is less than five feet of workable stone, and this can only be reached by removing from five to twenty feet of Drift clays and sands. Five firms in and about Dayton are engaged in quarrying the stone, and the aggregate of their operations is very large. The firm of Webber & Lehman handled more than 9,000 perches during 1869. The same firm is largely engaged in sawing and dressing the stone, and with admirable results.

The supply of the rock, even in this its best estate, is inexhaustible; but the expense of transportation shuts out at present from the general market all the quarries that are more than three or four miles distant from Dayton. The quarries that lie outside of these limits, however, are invaluable for neighborhood supplies.

The quality of the stone, when perfect in every other respect, is sometimes injured by the occurrence of crystals of iron pyrites, which weather into brownish stains when exposed to the air, and disfigure the surface.

In addition to the kind of rock already named, there is in the county a large supply of Niagara rock that falls short of the typical excellence in hardness and color, but which still constitutes a very serviceable and valuable deposit. These beds of inferior quality are sometimes the precise stratigraphical equivalents of the true Dayton stone; that is, they immediately overlie the Clinton formation, but generally they occur at a higher level in the series. The differences in color and hardness alluded to seem connected with differences in chemical composition—the Dayton stone being a nearly pure carbonate of lime, while the inferior grades are composed of the carbonates of lime and magnesia. The color of these last-named beds is not constant, various shades of drab and yellow alternating with shades of blue, sometimes even in the same layer of rock.

The boulders of the Drift are also available for building purposes. They form, in some parts of the county, the main supply for foundations, and when treated with skill give excellent results.

2. Brick, Draining-tile and Pottery Clays.

There is scarcely a section in the county, outside of the alluvial bottom lands, that does not furnish, in its Drift beds, materials from which bricks can be manufactured, but the yellow clays that cover the higher table lands (the Niagara rocks) are decidedly to be preferred for this purpose. In many instances the clay that is removed from a building site can be converted into bricks of the best quality, with which the walls of the dwelling can be constructed.

Beds of blue clay are also abundant, generally at lower levels of the county, from which draining-tile and pottery can be made. For these purposes the blue and yellow clays are generally mixed, the blue clay imparting the necessary strength, and the yellow counteracting the tendency of the former to shrink and crack in the process of baking.

The importance of draining-tile in agriculture begins to be understood. Hundreds of thousands of tiles are now manufactured annually, with a steadily increasing demand.

A third variety of clay is found within the county, in quite limited deposits compared with the preceding. It, also, is called blue clay, but it differs from the ordinary blue clay in containing no iron. It is converted by burning into a cream-colored brick of the same general characters as the Milwaukee brick. It is generally very fine-grained, and has been quite largely used as mineral paint. In composition, it probably consists of little besides alumina, silica and lime.

There is no doubt that these deposits will be regarded with increasing interest as their advantages for architectural purposes come to be recognized.

The heaviest accumulation of this clay now known in Southern Ohio, occurs near Springfield, Clarke county, and it has already been turned to good account in the manufacture of "Milwaukee" brick.

3. Firestone.

A stone that can endure the action of heat admits of many useful applications. Two of the bedded rocks of the county have considerable local reputation as firestones, viz., the sandy limestones that make the uppermost beds of the Blue Limestone series and the Clinton Group. This latter rock certainly answers a tolerable purpose for chimney jambs and kindred uses. It is not easy to see what there is in its composition that enables it to resist unchanged the agency of fire, as the analyses appended to the following section show it to be a true limestone of a good degree of purity. Experience, however, abundantly demonstrates its value in this regard. Chimney-jambs can be shown that have stood for 50 years in service. Farmers are willing to transport it for miles to lay up the arches of their sugar-camps. It must be added that the different beds of the series have very different qualities in this respect, the middle and lower layers furnishing the best firestone, and there is no doubt that the quality in its highest exhibition is local.

4. Lime.

As lime is the great cement employed alike in nature and by human art, the sources of its supply are of more economical value to any community than are the supplies of building-stone and brick-clay even. All the bedded rocks of the Miami Valley, and portions of the Drift as well, furnish materials from which excellent lime can be made. It is needful, however, to remark that the terms *limestone* and *lime* do not convey any precise information as to the chemical composition of the substances to which they are applied. Limestones always contain carbonate of lime, it is true; but besides this, they generally contain various compounds and various proportions of magnesia, alumina (clay), silica (sand) and iron. The limestones of this region that can be burned into valuable lime may be divided into two classes, according to their chemical composition.

The first group comprises those rocks that consist mainly of *carbonate of lime*, or that contain at least 85 per cent. of this substance.

The second group is made up of the *dolomites* or *magnesian limestones*, which have at least 40 per cent. of *carbonate of magnesia* in their composition. Silica, alumina and iron are found in small and varying proportions in each division.

The properties of these limes are very different. Those of the first class require to be submitted to a higher temperature in "burning" than the second. They slake promptly and thoroughly, and in the operation evolve a great degree of heat. From this last fact, they are termed "hot" or "fiery" limes. They "set" or harden so soon that but two or three bricks can be laid with one spreading of mortar, and walls that are made of them have a tendency to "chip-crack." It is quite likely that this last named property can be attributed, in some degree, to the silica and alumina which they contain.

The second group contains those limes that are called "cool." They do not give out as much heat in slaking as the limes of the first class, nor do they "set" as soon. From 5 to 20 bricks can be laid with a single spreading of mortar, and in plastering a corresponding advantage can be obtained.

On purely practical grounds, the builders of southwestern Ohio have come to recognize the greater desirability of the limes of the last-named class, and none others can now find a market in the cities and towns of this portion of the State.

To the first series belong the Blue Limestones, the Clinton Group, and the Dayton beds of the Niagara Group.

The limes of the second series are all obtained from the upper, or Niagara, division of the Cliff limestones, and the kind of rocks from which they are derived constitute almost the entire mass of this formation. It thus appears that the Niagara Group in Ohio is a true magnesian limestone, as all the members of this same great series through its wide western expansion—in Michigan, Wisconsin, Illinois, Iowa and Minnesota—have uniformly been found to be. The only exception to these statements as to the composition of the Niagara series, is found in some of its lowermost beds, where, in limited and isolated areas, the Dayton stone and its equivalents occur. This stone has already been referred to the true limestones, an analysis of it, made by Dr. Locke in 1835, showing that it contains 92 per cent. of carbonate of lime.

While with this exception the whole Niagara series consists of magnesian limestones, it would be wrong to conclude that every portion of this series, taken indifferently, can be burned into valuable lime. The quarries that are worked for lime burning at Cedarville, Yellow Springs, Springfield, Moore's quarries below Springfield, Wilson's quarries north of Dayton, and a few others less widely known, furnish the most valuable limes of the Miami valleys, and largely supply the markets of Cincinnati, Dayton, Hamilton, Springfield, Xenia and the remaining towns and villages of this section. These quarries all lie in the same geological horizon, viz: between 50 and 100 feet above the base of the Niagara rocks. They begin in or above the strata that contain the large shell *Pentamerus oblongus*, and generally include from 10 to 20 feet that overlie the *Pentamerus* beds—a series of thin and irregularly bedded strata—valueless for building stone, largely filled with crinoidal fragments.

The strata that underlie the *Pentamerus* beds consist of blue and drab magnesian limestones which cannot be burned into a good article of common lime, but which there is good reason to believe, possess in greater or less degree the properties of hydraulic cement or water lime. A sample from the quarries of W. Sroufe, Esq., Yellow Springs, when analyzed, was found to agree very closely with a magnesian limestone of France, that is cited by Vicat as an excellent hydraulic cement. The same rock, when treated in laboratory experiments, indicates an eminent degree of hydraulic energy. The analyses are appended:

Magnesian Limestone, Yellow Springs.	
Carbonate of lime	51.10
Carbonate of magnesia	41.12
Sand and silica	5.40
Alumina with trace of iron	1.40
	99.02

Magnesian Limestone, France.	
Carbonate of lime	50.60
Carbonate of magnesia	42.00
Silica	5.00
Alumina	2.00
Iron	40
	100.00

A series of analyses of the various rock formations that have been treated of, is appended, from which these differences in composition can be noted and compared. The analyses are not confined to the rocks of Montgomery county, but various portions of the different series represented there are included. These analyses, with two exceptions, were made by Dr. T. G. Wormley, of Columbus, Chemist of the Survey. The analyses will be grouped under two general classes according to the differences in constitution already noted; the first embracing the true limestones, or those containing at least 85 per cent. of carbonate of lime, and the second class comprising the magnesian limestones.

I. True Limestones Containing at least 85 per cent. of Carbonate of Lime.

A. *Blue Limestones.*

1. From Cincinnati. (Dr. Locke, 1838.)

Carbonate of lime	90.93
Carbonate of magnesia	1.11
Peroxide of iron	3.15
Silica from solution	0.77
Matter insoluble in muriatic acid	1.80
Water expelled by red heat	1.13
	98.89

2. From Waynesville.

Carbonate of lime	91.50
Carbonate of magnesia	5.06
Residue contains iron	96.56

B. *Clinton Limestones.*

1. From Brown's Quarry,* New Carlisle, Clarke county.

Carbonate of lime	95.60
Carbonate of magnesia	3.93
Alumina and iron	0.40
	99.93

2. From Centerville, Montgomery county.

Carbonate of lime	86.30
Carbonate of magnesia	11.34
Silica	0.85
Alumina and iron	0.40
	98.89

3. From Halderman's Quarry,† Eaton, Preble county.

Carbonate of lime	85.21
Carbonate of magnesia	13.56
Silica	0.35
Alumina and iron, chiefly iron	0.80
	99.92

4. From Lick Fork, Adams county, "Flinty Limestone," of Locke.

Carbonate of lime	93.00
Carbonate of magnesia	3.04
Silica and sand	2.00
Alumina and iron	1.60
	99.64

C. *Niagara Group.*

1. From Dayton Quarries. (Dr. Locke, 1835.)

Carbonate of lime	92.40
Carbonate of magnesia	1.10
Matter insoluble in muriatic acid	1.70
Protoxide of iron	0.53
Silex from solution	0.90
Water expelled by red heat	1.08
	97.71

II. Magnesian Limestones—Containing 40 per cent. or more of Carbonate of Magnesia.

1. From Yellow Springs—Sroufe's Quarries.

Carbonate of lime	54.75
Carbonate of magnesia	42.23
Silica	0.40
Alumina and iron	2.00
	99.38

* This is the purest lime found in south-western Ohio.

† This is one of the divisions of the Clinton which has a local reputation as a fire stone.

2. From Hillsboro, Highland county—Col. Trimble's Quarry.*

Carbonate of lime	54.25
Carbonate of magnesia	43.23
Silica	0.40
Alumina and iron (trace)	1.80
	99.68

3. From Thompson's Quarries, Springfield.

Carbonate of lime	50.90
Carbonate of magnesia	39.77
Silicates of lime and magnesia	7.07
Sand	1.19
Alumina	0.70
	99.63

4. From Moore's Quarries, below Springfield.

Carbonate of lime	46.40
Carbonate of magnesia	47.53
Silica, iron and alumina—chiefly the last	4.90
	98.83

5. From Cliff Limestone, West Union, Adams county.†

Carbonate of lime	42.80
Carbonate of magnesia	34.79
Silica and sand	18.80
Alumina and iron	2.20
	98.59

6. From Bierley's Quarries, Greenville, Darke county.‡

Carbonate of lime	44.60
Carbonate of magnesia	50.11
Silica, iron and alumina—chiefly the last	4.60
	99.31

7. From Gard's Quarries, Greenville, Darke county.‡

Carbonate of lime	51.30
Carbonate of magnesia	45.72
Silica, iron and alumina—chiefly the last	2.20
	99.22

8. From Northrup's Quarry, New Madison, Darke county.‡

Carbonate of lime	51.70
Carbonate of magnesia	45.26
Silica, iron and alumina—chiefly iron	2.70
	99.66

---

* NOTE.—This lime has a very excellent reputation in the region where it is produced. It is said to be the "coolest" lime of this portion of the State.

† This analysis would seem to confirm the suggestion of Dr. Locke, that the rock in question would yield hydraulic cement.

‡ Nos. 6 and 7 represent the only quarries in Darke county that have been extensively worked. The stone is of but little value for building purposes, but the lime obtained from it is counted excellent. The geological horizon of the three quarries represented in Nos. 6, 7 and 8 is the same, viz., the upper portion of the Niagara series.

5. Mineral Paints.

The materials from which mineral paints have been manufactured in this portion of the State are all obtained from the beds of Drift. The second variety of blue clay, already described, is principally used for this purpose.

A company has been organized at Miamisburg for two years, for the manufacture of these paints, and their sales last year amounted to over 100,000 lbs. A considerable proportion of lead, however, is included under this aggregate. The bed of clay which is turned to most account is situated on Hole's creek, at no great elevation above the Miami river. The clay seems to be identical in composition with the heavy bank near Springfield, and closely resembles the "Milwaukee brick" clay in composition. As to the durability of these colors, it is too early to decide. It is suggested by painters in Cincinnati, where the coal smoke renders frequent re-painting necessary, that even if they are decidedly inferior to lead in respect to durability, they can still render very useful service because of their greater cheapness.

Many of the gravel beds of the Drift contain accumulations of ochre more or less extensive, and occasionally deposits of the same substance are found unmixed with gravel. The ochre can be separated from the gravel by washing, and proves to be of fair quality.

A large deposit of this ocherous gravel is to be found on the north bank of Twin creek, one mile east of Germantown, Montgomery county. It has been worked for two years, and a considerable quantity of the paint has been brought into market. A bed of brown coal, that occurs in the same gravel bank, has been turned to account for the manufacture of black paint. Mastodon remains, and phosphate of iron, are found also in this locality. Taking all things into the account, no more interesting section of the Drift is to be found in this region than the "Germantown Ochre Bank."

6. Gravel.

It is not easy to set a proper estimate upon the beds of sand and gravel of the county, until a comparison is instituted between a region well supplied with such accumulations and another, which is destitute of them.

The gravel knolls and ridges with which, in the southern and eastern portions of the county, almost every farm abounds, affords very desirable building-sites, and are generally selected for such purposes.

Sand of the best quality, for mortar cement and brick making, is everywhere within easy access.

An inexhaustible supply of excellent materials for road-making—what is frequently designated "clean limestone gravel," though in reality largely composed of granitic pebbles—is found in the Drift deposits, from which hundreds of miles of turnpikes have been already constructed in the county, thus affording free communication between farm and market, at all seasons of the year. The smaller bowlders, of Canadian origin, are selected from the gravel banks for paving-stones, and transported to the neighboring cities.

In regions where stone suitable for macadamized pikes can be obtained, good roads can be had, even though gravel is wanting, but at largely increased expense above that of gravel turnpikes. The districts which are supplied with neither, can certainly never compete in desirability with these gravel-strewn regions.

The Agricultural Relations of the different formations of Montgomery county, remain to be briefly discussed. Only those points will be touched upon which are especially noticeable.

From what has been already said of the distribution of the Drift, it may be inferred that this formation will conceal or obscure all the rest, and, to a considerable extent, this will be found to be the case. There are large areas in which the underlying rock seems to have no direct effect upon the superficial beds, further than to control the general features of their arrangement. In such cases, the soil depends directly upon the composition of the drift beds, and will be found light, warm and dry, or heavy, cold and wet, according as sand or clay predominates in these beds.

There are, however, several varieties of soil that receive their leading characteristics directly from the rock with which they are associated. The high table-lands of the Niagara limestone, which are mostly confined to the northern portions of the county, furnish the first example. These limestones are often covered with but a shallow deposit of clay, yellow originally, but blackened by organic matter for a foot or two from the surface. These table-lands hold so nearly a horizontal position, that the streams that have their sources in them have but a sluggish flow. Indeed these districts, until they are cleared and ditched, are almost always marshy in their conditions, and though occupying the highest levels of the county, are universally spoken of as low-lying lands. They contain abundant elements of agricultural wealth, but demand a more painstaking and scientific kind of treatment than our farmers are generally willing to bestow. In default of this, they are largely dependent on the seasons—favorable seasons bringing a large reward, and unfavorable ones being marked by failures, more or less complete. The water-supply in these locations is generally derived from drilled wells, which it is sometimes necessary to carry to a depth of 60 feet, though one-third of this depth usually suffices.

In their present condition, they constitute the lowest-priced lands of the county, unless, as in a few instances, their contiguity to markets has led to their thorough improvement. In these cases, they show themselves to be possessed of admirable qualities for farming lands, and also give examples of what may be hoped for from the remainder of this formation.

A belt of still more pronounced character, in which the agricultural relations are still more closely connected with the geological structure, is furnished in the line of junction of the Blue Limestone and Clinton formations, or, what is the same thing, in the line of junction of the Lower and Upper Silurian.

It will be remembered that the uppermost beds of the Blue Limestone series consist, for the most part, of unconsolidated clays, while the lower portion of the overlying Cliff formation, viz., the Clinton rock, is largely composed of beds of a porous sandstone (lime-sand). The result of this order of sequence is, that the clays of the Blue Limestone series are the water-bearers of the region which they occupy, as was long ago pointed out by Dr. Locke. The strongest springs of South-western Ohio mark quite accurately this line of junction. The clays constitute a gradual slope—sometimes one-fourth of a mile in breadth—from the foot of the cliff. The springs that flow out along the line, gave, before the country was cleared, a marshy character to this belt, as is shown in the black and fertile loam by which it is still marked. They also serve to distribute, to some degree, the waste of the cliff to the slope below. The early settlers located their homes in the vicinity of these perennial springs, and the prosperity which has attended the labors of husbandry upon these fruitful tracts, is well attested in the comfortable and tasteful homes which mark the lowermost outcrop of the Cliff limestones. Perhaps no other geological horizon of the State is so definitely connected with human interests.

The Blue Limestones give rise, in limited areas, to soils of great fertility. The rocks of this age, for the most part, are covered deep by beds of modified drift, lying, as they do, at a lower level than the other rocks of the county; but occasionally a slope is found that is derived directly from the weathering of the Blue Limestone beds. The rocks of this series are rich in phosphates, a fact which accounts for their value in agriculture. An analysis by Dr. Wormley, Chemist of the Survey, give 16-hundredths of one per cent. of phosphoric acid in the bedded clays. This proportion shows that a soil one foot in depth, formed from the weathering of these clays, would contain to the acre very nearly 7,500 lbs. of phosphoric acid, a substance indispensable to the growth of the higher forms of vegetation.

The celebrated Blue Grass country of Kentucky is derived directly from the rocks of this formation, without the addition of our Drift clays and sands.

A discussion of the Drift in these connections, would be, under another name, a treatise upon the general agriculture of the county, and cannot here be entered upon. Suffice it to say that the character of the Drift deposits, largely determines for each locality, the market value of its lands, the kinds of crops that can be cultivated with profit, the nature and amount of its water-supply, the quality of its highways, its degree of healthfulness, and in short, its general desirability for human occupancy.

Attention will be called to but one more point in this connection.

The river-valleys of South-western Ohio are known to have been deeper than they are at present. In other words, they are now partly filled with drift and the streams no longer flow upon rocky beds. Not only is the absolute depth of the valleys diminished by these deposits, but the abruptness of the declivity is greatly modified by them. Instead of a precipitous descent over the naked edges of the rocks, a well-graded slope, consisting frequently of the best road-gravel, leads from the high lands to the river-bottoms. The nature and order of succession of the formations previously described renders it certain that were it not for the interposition of the Drift, the line of junction of the Blue Limestone and Cliff formation would be an impassable belt of miry clay for one-third of the year, unless relieved by expensive, artificial roads. A similar state of things would be found throughout much of the Blue Limestone regions.

The leading points in the geology of the line of junction of the Lower and Upper Silurian formations of South-western Ohio, have now been briefly noticed. The attempt has been made to treat the subjects in such a way that they can be understood by any intelligent reader, even though he is entirely unacquainted with the technicalities of geological science. At the same time, many facts of interest to the geologist are here published for the first time. Among these facts may be named the probable identification of the Medina Sandstone in Southern Ohio, the first, clear identification of the Clinton group within the same limits, the division of the Niagara formation into two well-marked varieties, viz. the Magnesian and Limestone varieties, and the connection of these differences in composition with equally marked differences in use, for lime and building-stone.

Among the points of economical interest may be mentioned the establishment of the limits within which the Dayton stone is to be found, lying as it does at the very base of the Niagara series; the recognition of the fact that the best lime of this part of the State comes from an horizon about 100 feet higher in the series than that which the Dayton stone occupies, with the consequent knowledge of the areas within which it occurs; and the discovery that certain beds of the same series afford hydraulic lime of excellent quality.

The great value of the Dayton stone naturally leads to considerable interest in the discovery of new deposits of it. A safe guide for all future investigations will be found in the order of sequence of the great formations, which these pages have clearly stated, an order which practical men, engaged for years in quarrying the stone, have generally failed to recognize.

It remains but to add, in conclusion, that nothing more than a geological reconnoisance of South-western·Ohio has been possible in the time that has passed since the survey was ordered. Many topics are left for future investigation—such as the accurate measurements of the formations; the determination of their dip; the enumeration and description of fossils; the details of stratification generally; and all of these subjects possess a good degree of economical or educational importance.

SECTION No. 1.

Centreville, Montgomery County.

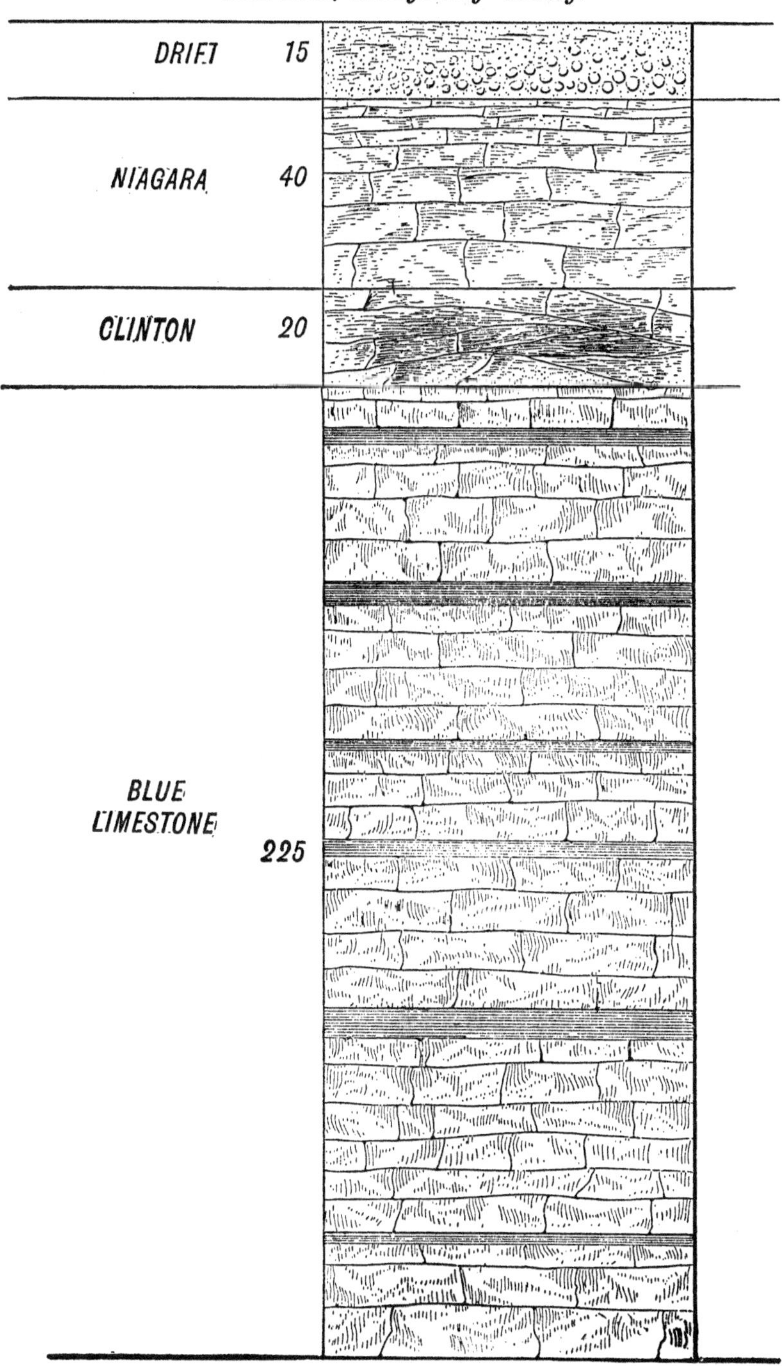

SECTION No. 2.

Webber & Lehman's Quarry, east of Dayton, two miles.

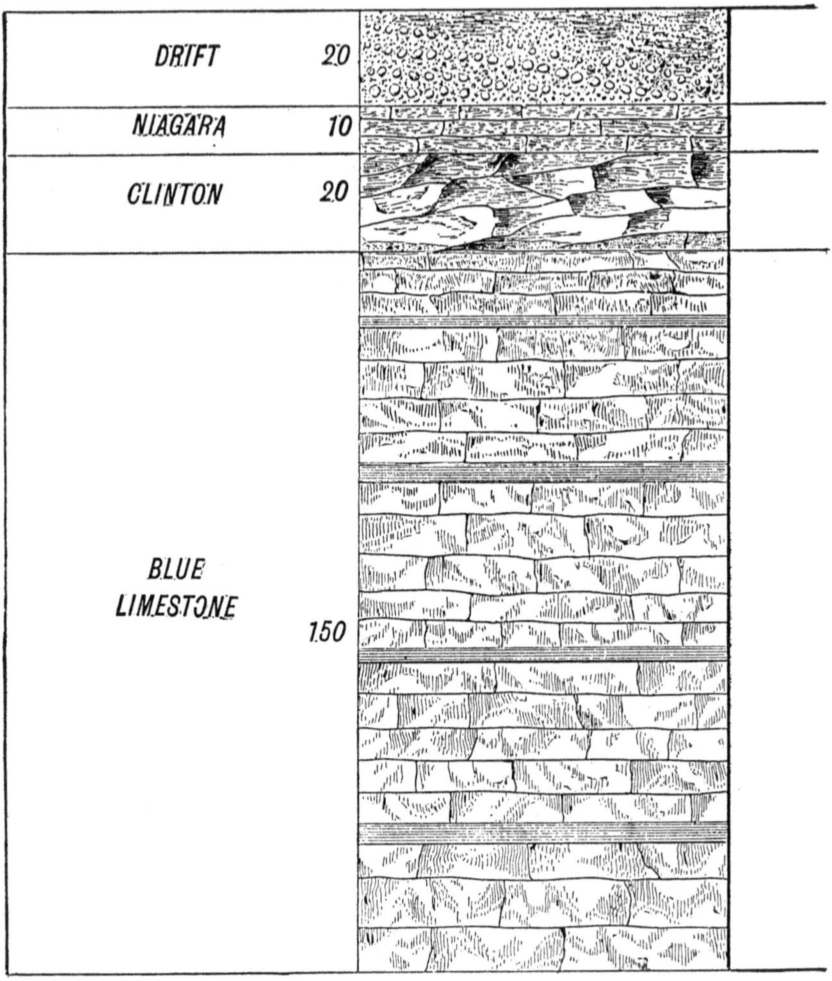

Formation	Thickness
DRIFT	20
NIAGARA	10
CLINTON	20
BLUE LIMESTONE	150

SECTION No. 3.

Soldiers' Home, west of Dayton two miles.

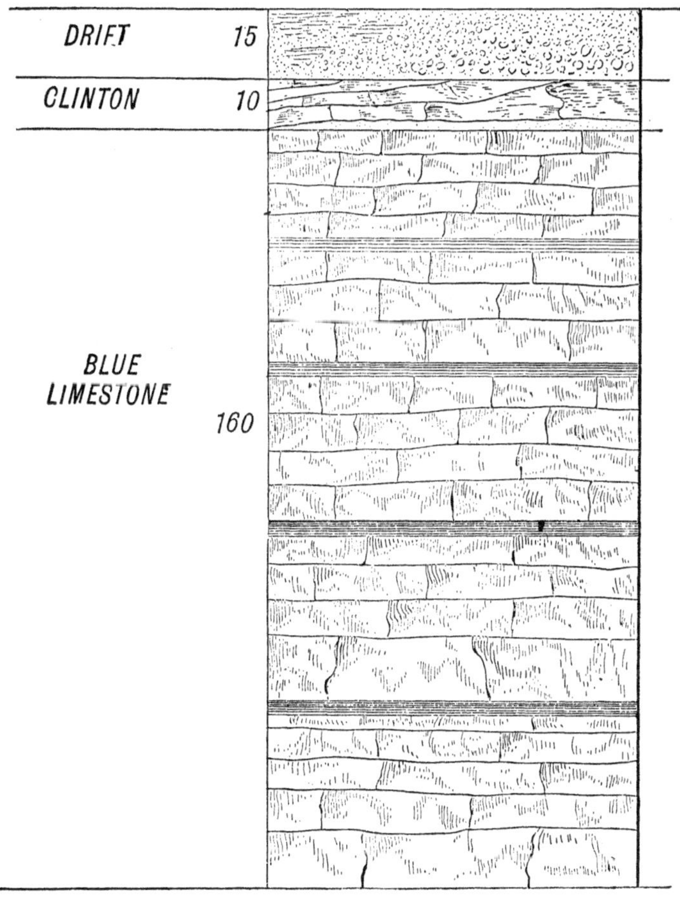

EXPLANATION OF MAP OF GROUPED SECTIONS.

The horizontal lines indicate spaces 10 feet apart.

No.

1. Sec. near Nelsonville, on old Marietta road, on hill between the Hocking River and Monday Creek, Athens county.
2. Sec. in hill back of old Hocking furnace, Haydenville, Hocking county.
3. Sec. John Tannihill's, Sec. 28, Green township, Hocking county.
4. Sec. of coal, Nelsonville seam, hill back of Nelsonville, Athens county.
5. Sec. (composition) near Nelsonville, York township, Athens county. This includes a section of W. B. Brooks' coal.
6. Sec. Peter Hayden's coal, Green township, Hocking county.
7. Sec. James Hawkins, Snow Fork, Sec. 3, Ward township, Hocking county.
8. Sec. Bayliss Glenn's, Sec. 6, Ward township, Hocking county, partly on Snow Fork and partly on Bear run.
9. Sec. Position of coal blossom, James Hawkins, Snow Fork, Sec. 3, Ward towhship, Hocking county.
10. Sec. showing position of fire-clay and ore, near Logan, as given by S. Baird, Esq.
11. Sec. Samuel Thompson's, Monday Creek township, Perry county, near Maxville.
12. Sec. Maxville Limestone, David Hardy's, Maxville, Perry county. Showing the position of limestone over Logan Sandstone group (Waverly).
13. Sec. Maxville, Monday Creek township, Perry county. Showing strata above the limestone.
14. Sec. (composition) near John Fluhart's mill, Green township, Hocking county.
15. Sec. Horace Hazelton's, Salt Lick township, Perry county.
16. Sec. John La Rue's, Salt Lick township, Perry county.
17. Sec. on Mr. Harbaugh's land, on Monday Creek, 3 m. north Straitsville, Perry county.
18. Sec. (composition.) Henry Hazelton's, on Monday Creek, Salt Lick township, Perry county.
19. Sec. Thomas Barnes', Lost run, Salt Lick township, Perry county
20. Sec. Thomas McGinness', Straitsville, Perry county.

21. Sec. L. D. McDonald's Alderman farm, W. Br. Sunday Creek, Sec. 13, Salt Lick township, Perry county.
22. Sec. (composition.) Benjamin Saunders', W. Br. Sunday Creek, Monroe township, Perry county.
23. Sec. Gaver's Mill, Coaldale P. O., Salt Lick township, Perry county.
24. Sec. William Bennett's, Sunday Creek, Pleasant township, Perry county.
25. Sec. Joshua Sands', Sunday Creek, Pleasant township, Perry county.
26. Sec. John Clarke's, near Bristol, Pike township, Perry county.
27. Sec. Eli Bell's, Sec. 34, Jackson township, Perry county.
28. Sec. James Fowler's, Pleasant township, Perry county.
29. Sec. Levi Rarick's, near Bristol, Pike Township, Perry county.
30. Sec. near Cusac's mill, Jonathan Creek, Newton township, Muskingum county.
31. Sec. G. W. Rankin's, Newton township, Muskingum county.
32. Sec. at Newtonville, Newton township, Muskingum county.
33. Sec. John Lyle's, Newton township, Muskingum county.
34. Sec. Henry Jones', McLuney Station, Harrison township, Perry county.
35. Sec. by Dr. Hildreth in old Geol. Report, on land of Joseph Baird, Sec, 11, Hopewell township, Licking county.
36. Sec. ½ mile from Miami Company's mines, Newton township, Muskingum county.
37. Sec. Edward Danison's, Sec. 16, Madison township, Perry county.
38. General section, Roseville, Clay township, Muskingum county.
39. Sec. at Roseville, Clay township, Muskingum county.
40. Sec. John Roberts', Newton township, Muskingum county.
41. Sec. at Zanesville, by Col. J. W. Foster, taken from old Geol. Report.
42. Sec. Joseph Rambeau's, Sec. 14, Newton township, Muskingum county, near Perry county line.
43. Sec. Miami Company's mines, Newton township, Muskingum county.
44. Sec. Tunnel Hill, 3 miles east of New Lexington, Perry county.
45. Sec. W. H. Wheeler's, Sec. 14, Clay township, Muskingum county.
46. Sec. Joseph Porters', 100 acre lot, No. 16, Hopewell township, Muskingum county.
47. Sec. Bradford & Pollock's mine, Flint Ridge, Hopewell township, Licking country.
48. Sec. (composition) near McLuney's Station, Harrison township, Perry county.

www.ingramcontent.com/pod-product-compliance
Lightning Source LLC
LaVergne TN
LVHW021401110826
845150LV00007B/1741
9781425514167